POLITICIANS MANIPULATI

Highly original and insightful, Michael Billig and Cristina Marinho's book investigates how politicians misuse official statistics. Setting this problem in its historical context – and offering vivid case studies of Donald Trump, Boris Johnson and Gérald Darmanin – the authors demonstrate that the manipulation of statistics involves the misuse of words as well as the misuse of numbers. Most importantly, the authors show that politicians will manipulate official statisticians to produce politically convenient, but statistically inappropriate, numbers. Another unique part of the book is that the authors are not content with analysing how statistics are manipulated; they also rigorously analyse the efforts of statistical agencies in France and Britain to combat such manipulation. These chapters herald unsung heroes who operate largely 'behind the scenes' to expose and oppose the corruption of statistics. An indispensable read for anyone concerned with the intersection of power and data.

MICHAEL BILLIG is Emeritus Professor at Loughborough University. He is a Fellow of the British Academy and received the British Psychological Society's 2023 award for Lifetime Achievement.

CRISTINA MARINHO is Lecturer in the Department of Psychology, University of Edinburgh. Together with Michael Billig, she is the author of *The Politics and Rhetoric of Commemoration*.

POLITICIANS MANIPULATING STATISTICS

How They Do It and How to Oppose Them

MICHAEL BILLIG

Loughborough University

CRISTINA MARINHO

University of Edinburgh

CAMBRIDGE
UNIVERSITY PRESS

CAMBRIDGE
UNIVERSITY PRESS

Shaftesbury Road, Cambridge CB2 8EA, United Kingdom

One Liberty Plaza, 20th Floor, New York, NY 10006, USA

477 Williamstown Road, Port Melbourne, VIC 3207, Australia

314–321, 3rd Floor, Plot 3, Splendor Forum, Jasola District Centre, New Delhi – 110025, India

103 Penang Road, #05-06/07, Visioncrest Commercial, Singapore 238467

Cambridge University Press is part of Cambridge University Press & Assessment, a department of the University of Cambridge.

We share the University's mission to contribute to society through the pursuit of education, learning and research at the highest international levels of excellence.

www.cambridge.org
Information on this title: www.cambridge.org/9781009488136

DOI: 10.1017/9781009488143

First published 2025

A catalogue record for this publication is available from the British Library.

Library of Congress Cataloging-in-Publication Data
NAMES: Billig, Michael, author. | Marinho, Cristina, author.
TITLE: Politicians manipulating statistics : how they do it and how to oppose them / Michael Billig, Loughborough University, Cristina Marinho, University of Edinburgh.
DESCRIPTION: Cambridge, United Kingdom ; New York, NY : Cambridge University Press, [2024] | Includes bibliographical references and index. | Summary: "Explore Billig and Marinho's highly original study of politicians misusing statistics, misleading the public, and manipulating statisticians. This book also highlights how the British and French statistical agencies aim to combat this increasingly serious problem. Tailored for all audiences, it is a clearly written, insightful, and witty work"– Provided by publisher.
IDENTIFIERS: LCCN 2024023202 (print) | LCCN 2024023203 (ebook) | ISBN 9781009488136 (hardback) | ISBN 9781009488167 (paperback) | ISBN 9781009488143 (epub)
SUBJECTS: LCSH: Political statistics. | Statistics–Political aspects. | Political corruption.
CLASSIFICATION: LCC JA71.7 .B68 2024 (print) | LCC JA71.7 (ebook) |
DDC 320.072/7–DC23/eng/20240708
LC record available at https://lccn.loc.gov/2024023202
LC ebook record available at https://lccn.loc.gov/2024023203

ISBN 978-1-009-48813-6 Hardback
ISBN 978-1-009-48816-7 Paperback

Contents

Acknowledgements   *page* vi
List of Abbreviations   viii

1	Introduction	1
2	The Rise of Statistics	10
3	Different Ways of Manipulating	39
4	Donald Trump: Master Manipulator	63
5	Manipulating Statistics and Statisticians	91
6	Establishing a Statistical Authority in Britain	122
7	Establishing a Statistical Authority in France	145
8	Gérald Darmanin: Populism against Statistics	169
9	Boris Johnson: Untruthful Words and Numbers	189
10	How a Manipulated Covid Target Was Exposed	216
11	Final Comments	241

Index   253

Acknowledgements

There are a number of people whom we would like to thank for their help with this book and also more generally for their help and friendship over a long period.

Michael would like to thank Charles Antaki for his great friendship and collegiality over many years. It was a huge pleasure to work alongside Charles at Loughborough. Michael would also like to thank Simon Goodman for doing so much in recent years – his efforts have been much appreciated.

Cristina would like to acknowledge her debt to Jorge Vala, who set her on the path to an academic career and who has always represented a fine academic example for her. Cristina would also like to thank Sue Widdicombe, Anne Templeton, Emma Waterston, Rahul Sambaraju and Umberto Noe for being such friendly and helpful colleagues at Edinburgh. Also thank you Paul Jenner for your continual presence and good humour.

Both Michael and Cristina have greatly benefitted from the kindness, encouragement and intellectual commitment of John Richardson. We would also like to record our admiration of Ruth Wodak for her creativity, courage and willingness to help others; and also our admiration of the enormous work that Teun van Dijk has done to foster the critical study of language. To all these and many others, we say 'thank you'.

Regarding this book, we would particularly like to thank Joel Best for his help. Both of us admire his work on statistics, and he has been generous with his encouragement of our book.

Then there is the editorial team at Cambridge University Press. Emily Watton has been an ideal editor – always enthusiastic, helpful and prompt to reply. Neema, Emily's assistant, has also been a great help. We are grateful that she has inherited Emily's promptness and consideration. Thank you, Emily and Neema. We are indebted to the friendly, talented and understanding team that Cambridge University Press assembled to see our book safely through to publication: Sari Wastell and Jasintha Srinivasan and Dhanujha Harikrishna. Also we would like to thank Andrew Chapman, our superb copy editor. It has been a great pleasure to work with you all.

And, of course, there are our respective families.

Michael has so much to thank Sheila for. Not just you, Sheila, but also our children – Daniel, Becky, Rachel and Benjamin. And not just them, but also their children – Ari, Monica, Hannah, Elsie, Artie, Jacob, Felix, Juno and Coco. It is wonderful to be surrounded by you all.

Cristina thanks her family: my father and my mother; my brother Benjamim, his wife Inês, and their children, Diana and Duarte. Thank you for being such a wonderful family.

List of Abbreviations

Statistical organisations and constructs

ASA	American Statistical Association
ASP	Authority for Public Statistics (France)
BLS	Bureau of Labor Statistics (USA)
BPP	Billion Prices Project (a way of calculating CPI)
CPI	consumer price index
ELSTAT	Hellenic Statistical Authority (Greece)
GDP	gross domestic product
GRO	General Register Office (England and Wales)
GROS	General Register Office for Scotland
INDEC	National Institute of Statistics and Censuses (Argentina)
INSEE	National Institute of Statistics and Economic Studies (France)
NBS	National Bureau of Statistics (China)
NSSG	National Statistical Service of Greece
ONS	Office for National Statistics (United Kingdom)
SSM	Ministerial Statistical Services (France)
SSMSI	Ministry of Internal Security's Statistical Services (France)
TsUNKhU	Central Statistical Office (USSR)
UKSA	United Kingdom Statistics Authority

CHAPTER I

Introduction

Sometimes what people do not say is just as revealing as what they do say. We have experienced this over the past few years. Friends, family and fellow academics have asked us what our book will be about and we have answered 'How politicians manipulate statistics'. What never came next is revealing. No one expressed amazement, saying words to the effect: 'What an odd topic – surely you don't suppose that politicians manipulate statistics? You're not going to find anything to write about.' Everyone seemed to assume that we would find plenty of stuff to occupy our attention. They all presumed that politicians do not invariably tell the truth, the whole truth and nothing but the truth. Public opinion polls back up this belief. For the past forty years in Britain, where most of these conversations took place, Ipsos has been conducting annual surveys into trustworthiness. The 2023 survey revealed that the two least trusted professions were 'politicians generally' and 'government ministers'. Less than 10 per cent of the population trusted politicians – a new record low.[1] Surveys conducted across the world also report that people are becoming increasingly distrustful of politicians and governments.[2]

If people tend to generally distrust what politicians say, then it is likely that they will distrust what they say about statistics. There has been long-term distrust of statistics, as expressed by the well-known saying that dates

---

[1] IPSOS (2023), 'Trust in politicians reaches its lowest score in 40 years', www.ipsos.com/en-uk/ipsos-trust-in-professions-veracity-index-2023. The survey uses the Ipsos Veracity Index.
[2] The Edelman Trust Barometer for 2024 surveyed twenty-eight countries and reported that in seventeen of those, more people distrusted their governments than trusted them. The most trusted governments tended to be non-democratic: Edelman Barometer (2024), '2024 Edelman Trust Barometer: Global Report', www.edelman.com/sites/g/files/aatuss191/files/2024-01/2024%20Edelman%20Trust%20Barometer%20Global%20Report_0.pdf, p. 42. Two years previously the Edelman Barometer had reported that 76 per cent of all the respondents surveyed in twenty-seven countries indicated that they worried about fake news: Edelman Barometer (2022), '2022 Edelman Trust Barometer: Global Report', www.edelman.com/sites/g/files/aatuss191/files/2022-01/2022%20Edelman%20Trust%20Barometer%20FINAL_Jan25.pdf, p. 8. See also: Esteban Ortiz-Ospina and Max Roser (2016), *Trust*, Our World in Data, https://ourworldindata.org/trust.

from the latter part of the late nineteenth century: 'There are lies, damned lies and statistics'. In his excellent book *Damned Lies and Statistics*, Joel Best writes that some people have attributed the saying to Mark Twain and others to Benjamin Disraeli.[3] Convincing evidence about the saying's originator does not exist.[4] However, its fame and easily understood humour taps into a widespread suspicion that statisticians and the politicians who quote them can make numbers mean whatever they want them to mean. This suspicion of statistics is certainly not confined to the nineteenth century. Following its publication in 1954, Darrell Huff's book *How to Lie with Statistics* was for a good number of years the best-selling work on statistics. In his introductory chapter, Huff described his book as 'a sort of primer in ways of using statistics to deceive'.[5]

Consequently, there are reasons to think that people might become extra suspicious when they hear a politician spouting numbers, especially if those numbers do not match their own experiences or their long-held beliefs. To mention again the conversations about our book's topic, no one said to us: 'No, no, no! Think what you like about politicians, but when it comes to numbers, politicians are pretty straightforward.' Once more, the absence of words spoke loudly. And we should say here, in the opening part of our introduction, that we have not struggled to find examples of politicians manipulating statistics. In fact, we have had to be selective, choosing which examples to analyse in detail and excluding, for reasons of space, a far greater number of possibilities.

Rhetoric of Numbers

There is one thing to emphasise right at the start. This may be a book about numbers and statistics, but it is not a mathematical book. There are no complicated formulae or pages full of numbers and technical symbols that only those with mathematical training can understand. Our medium is words, and words constitute much of our topic. That might seem strange given that we are writing about statistics, but statistics are much more than numbers: they need words.

The sort of statistics that we are dealing with are official statistics, and it is not possible to have official statistics that are purely numerical. To be

---

[3] Joel Best (2001), *Damned Lies and Statistics*, Berkeley: University of California Press.
[4] Anyone interested should definitely look at the website established by Peter M. Lee. More than twenty possible sources for the saying are listed: Peter M. Lee (2012), 'Lies, damned lies, and statistics', www.york.ac.uk/depts/maths/histstat/lies.htm.
[5] Darrell Huff (1982/1954), *How to Lie with Statistics*, New York: W.W. Norton, p. 11.

both meaningfully official and meaningfully statistical, the numbers must be linked to words. The official statistician will attempt to calculate social phenomena such as the level of unemployment, the rate of crime and the gross national product. These social phenomena – the things to be measured – are identified by words. Statisticians must always label the numbers that they calculate.

There may be different ways of making the calculations and these different calculations may produce different numbers, often with the same label attached. There again, statisticians, economists and politicians may dispute what is the most appropriate number for each label. Does unemployment currently stand at 5.5 per cent or at 9.0 per cent? If we measure it this way it is 5.5, but if we measure it that way it is 9.0. So, which is the better way of calculating the rate of unemployment? Although this type of dispute is a numerical one, it cannot be conducted entirely in numbers for the disputants will phrase their arguments in words: 'Your measure does not count those people who have stopped looking for work' to be countered by 'But yours includes those who do not want to look for work'. Such disputes are often about the links between numbers and their verbal labels. In Chapter 4, we examine how Donald Trump, not the most sophisticated mathematician in the world, entered into such a debate about the rate of unemployment in the United States.

Modern life is saturated in numbers. In the United Kingdom, we can expect to encounter them when we watch the news, read a newspaper or surf current affairs on the internet. According to one survey, almost three-quarters of respondents reported seeing statistics on the news several times a week.[6] One study, which for a month examined broadcast and online news platforms in the UK, calculated that 22 per cent of all news items contained at least one statistical reference.[7] Often journalists use statistics to give their stories 'colour'; in consequence, they tend not to present their statistics in any detail or depth.[8] There are some topics that are rarely presented with statistics – such as stories about celebrities. Stories about terrorist attacks are unlikely to be accompanied by comparative statistics, especially those which might indicate that the risk of being killed in a

---

[6] Sarah Butt, Benjamin Swannell and Alisa Pathania (2022), *Public Confidence in Official Statistics 2021*, National Centre for Social Research, https://natcen.ac.uk/our-research/research/public-confidence-in-official-statistics/.

[7] Stephen Cushion, Justin Lewis and Robert Callaghan (2017), 'Data journalism, impartiality and statistical claims', *Journalism Practice*, 11, 1198–215.

[8] Brendan T. Lawson (2022), 'Re-imagining the quantitative–qualitative relationship through "colouring" and "anchoring"', *Journalism*, 23, 1736–50.

terrorist attack is likely to be considerably lower than the risk of being killed in a road accident.[9] Had such comparative figures been presented, the dramatic 'colour' of the terror story would have become that bit drabber.

When journalists and politicians use numbers, they generally give those numbers rhetorical meaning. We will be examining Trump and his views on US unemployment figures. When he quoted the official figures before he became president, he left no doubt that he thought the figures far, far too low to be trusted; and he suggested that the 'real' figures were far, far higher (much higher than our imaginary 9.0 per cent illustration). By his choice of words, he gave political and emotional meaning to the numbers.

Giving rhetorical meaning to numbers is certainly not peculiar to Trump or to his particular view of the world. When the news breaks about a new treatment for a disease such as cancer, the reporters may cite the success rate for the new treatment. The statistic on its own would not convey much because the audience will not know the rates for other treatments. So, the reporters will indicate whether this new number should be understood as being a low or high success rate. Some researchers call these verbal guides to cited numbers 'quantification rhetoric'.[10] David Spiegelhalter, the distinguished British statistician, emphasises that we have to speak on behalf of our numbers, for the numbers cannot speak for themselves.[11]

Some numbers are used as if they are words that contain their own rhetorical signals. Campaigners for a cause which they believe has been ignored by the public will frequently cite numbers to indicate that the problem is widespread. Again, the number on its own is not sufficient to accomplish their purpose; they must indicate that the number represents a figure that is far too high for comfort.[12] Often precise numbers or statistics are not available because the problem has been ignored. Then campaigners might use intentionally imprecise numbers, expressed in words not

---

[9] Cushion et al. (2017).
[10] The concept of 'quantification rhetoric' describes how numbers are presented with verbal indicators suggesting whether the numbers should be understood as high or low, good or bad, worrying or comforting, etc.: Jonathan Potter, Margaret Wetherell and Andrew Chitty (1991), 'Quantification rhetoric – cancer on television', *Discourse & Society*, 2, 333–65. For announcements of miracle medical cures and why their exaggerated statistics should be distrusted, see: Tim Harford (2021), *How to Make the World Add Up*, London: Bridge Street Press. See also: Daniel Libertz (2018), 'Framed for lying: statistics as in/artistic proof', *Res Rhetorica*, 5(4), www.resrhetorica.com/index .php/RR/article/view/289/177.
[11] David Spiegelhalter (2020), *The Art of Statistics*, Harmondsworth: Penguin.
[12] Joel Best (2001), 'Promoting bad statistics', *Society*, 38(3), 10–15.

numerals, that rhetorically convey hugeness – i.e. 'thousands and thousands' or 'millions' or 'billions'.[13] These sorts of semi-magical, round
numbers are often used by those who wish to play what Teun van Dijk
calls the 'numbers game' in relation to immigration: 'thousands upon
thousands are pouring in every day'.[14]

We will be looking at examples of politicians using numbers rhetorically
throughout the book, but using numbers rhetorically does not necessarily
mean that the numbers are being manipulated. In Chapter 10 we examine
in detail a British government minister of health who used rhetoric to
suggest that he had successfully organised a large number of tests for
Covid-19. It is not the minister's use of rhetoric that makes the example
so suitable for being discussed here, but that the numbers, which he was
claiming to be so large, had been manipulated to appear larger than they
were. This illustrates a general point. If you want to understand how
politicians manipulate numbers for their own purposes, then you have to
look at what they are doing with their numbers rhetorically; and what they
are doing may lead you towards recognising some of the ways and means
of manipulating numbers and audiences.

Yet, to understand how and when manipulation occurs, you must go a
bit further than noting the rhetorical uses of numbers. That is why we start
our book with two historical chapters, which chart the rise of our two key
words: 'statistics' and 'manipulation'. Both words emerged in the late
eighteenth and early nineteenth centuries. And both have had more than
a single meaning. By following the words through time, we can compare
statistical manipulation today with the past. We will be seeing how the
early originators of numerical statistics were social campaigners. They used
their numbers rhetorically, even creating entirely new ways to depict
numbers graphically to achieve maximum effect. This does not mean that
they manipulated their numbers, certainly not in the ways that have
developed in recent years. The history of the very phrase 'statistical
manipulation' contains a story in itself.

---

[13] Michael Billig (2021), 'Uses of precise numbers and semi-magical round numbers in political
discourse about Covid-19: examples from the government of the United Kingdom', *Discourse &
Society*, 32, 542–58.
[14] Teun A. van Dijk (2018), 'Discourse and migration', in Ricard Zapata-Barrero and Evren Yalaz
(eds.), *Qualitative Research in European Migration Studies*, OAPEN https://library.oapen.org/
handle/20.500.12657/29754?show=full. For analyses of the use of numbers in immigration
rhetoric, see: Charlotte Taylor (2021), 'Metaphors of migration over time', *Discourse & Society*,
32, 463–81; Simon Goodman and Steve Kirkwood, (2019), 'Political and media discourses about
integrating refugees in the UK', *European Journal of Social Psychology*, 49, 1456–70.

Manipulating Public Statistics and Public Statisticians

Recently, there have been a number of well-written, insightful books about public statistics, written by authors such as Joel Best, Tim Harford, Brendan Lawson, Reimund Mink, Georgina Sturge and David Spiegelhalter.[15] These fine books are addressed to general readers as well as specialists. They are public-spirited works, because their authors aim to correct misconceptions about statistics and to educate their readers to spot poor, misleading data. We shall be drawing on these works in the course of our book.

One might wonder whether there is a need for yet another book about the uses and misuses of public statistics. However, the topic is broad: it covers different countries, different policies, different types of government and different ways of misusing data. The authors whom we have just mentioned have their own slants and special interests. Although they might sometimes use similar examples and draw insights from each other, none of their books is redundant – each makes an original contribution. If you want to understand the sociology of statistics, turn to Best; if your interest is in the imprecision of statistics, then Spiegelhalter is your statistician; should you want to know how particular numbers can become publicly important for a time before fading away, then you must read Lawson on the lives of numbers; Mink will tell you about the organisation of public statistics around the world; and Sturge will give you insightful anecdotes about British politicians and the poor data that they sometimes use, whether by choice or necessity. Joel Best demonstrates how seemingly inexhaustible the topic is. Having published his *Damned Lies and Statistics*, he found he had a whole new range of stories to tell and examples to offer: hence *More Damned Lies and Statistics*.[16] And still the politicians of the world provide new material for the analysts to write about and the public to distrust.

Our book has its own particular emphases. Our primary emphasis is on manipulation, and that is why we have an early chapter on the history of the word. Generally, we are interested in language and this lies at the root of our interest in the rhetorical usage of numbers. In the past, we have studied how politicians perform actions with words. If their actions are not

---

[15] Best, *Damned Lies and Statistics*, 2001; Harford (2021); Brendan T. Lawson (2023), *The Life of a Number*, Bristol: Bristol University Press; Reimund Mink (2023), *Official Statistics – a Plaything of Politics?* Cham: Springer; Spiegelhalter (2020); Georgina Sturge (2022), *Bad Data*, London: Bridge Street Press.

[16] Joel Best (2012), *More Damned Lies and Statistics*, Berkeley: University of California Press.

straightforward, as is often the case, then you must look very closely at what they are saying in order to spot the gaps between their words and apparent actions.[17] As a result, when we analyse how politicians manipulate statistics, we will be paying attention to some very small aspects of language. To manipulate numbers deviously, politicians and others need to use language subtly.[18]

In addition, we will be stressing that statistical manipulation is not a simple action, something that many theorists of manipulation have tended to overlook. Government ministers are not typically skilled statisticians, so if they want particular numbers for political reasons, they will have to get their statisticians to produce those numbers for them. There can be a double-barrelled process of manipulation, as politicians manipulate statisticians to manipulate the statistics. This is a recurring theme throughout our analytic chapters.

We have different sorts of analytic chapters. There are three biographical chapters, each of which looks at the way a single politician has manipulated statistics over the course of their career. Each of our chosen three has held, still holds or dreams of holding senior office in the future, and each comes from a different country: Donald Trump from the United States, Gérald Darmanin from France and Boris Johnson from the United Kingdom. There are similarities and differences between the three in their ways of misusing and degrading statistics.

We also have a chapter which looks at incidents of statistical manipulation in four very different countries: the autocracies of Stalin's Russia and contemporary China; and democracies in Argentina and Greece. We relate these specific incidents to what we offer as a schematic guide to how politicians manipulate statistics. This guide points to three stages, two of which typically occur away from public sight. We stress that incidents of statistical manipulation do not necessarily go through all the three stages, nor necessarily in the 'right' order – not even the incidents that we discuss

---

[17] Our previous work on political language includes: Michael Billig and Cristina Marinho (2017), *The Politics and Rhetoric of Commemoration*, London: Bloomsbury; Michael Billig and Cristina Marinho (2019), 'Literal and metaphorical silences in rhetoric: examples from the celebration of the 1974 Revolution in the Portuguese parliament', in Amy Jo Murray and Kevin Durrheim (eds.), *Qualitative Studies of Silence*, Cambridge: Cambridge University Press, pp. 21–37.

[18] We will be offering examples throughout the book. We have written about the importance of social scientists using examples: Michael Billig (2019), *More Examples, Less Theory*, Cambridge: Cambridge University Press; Michael Billig and Cristina Marinho (2022), 'Using examples to misrepresent the world', in Jeanne Fahnestock and Randy A. Harris (eds.), *Routledge Handbook of Persuasive Language*, New York: Routledge, pp. 113–28.

in the chapter. That is why the schema is offered only as a guide, not as a theory.

Then there are chapters that reflect the second distinctive concern of our book. We are not just interested in examining how the politicians might manipulate statistics and statisticians, but also how such manipulation might be exposed and opposed, at least in democracies. Our interest is not primarily theoretical. We are not saying 'If only society could be organised in a better way, then we would be able to trust what our politicians tell us about numbers'. Our interest in combatting manipulation is empirical. We look at the regulatory authorities which have been legally established in Britain and France to oversee the standards of official statistics. We devote a chapter to each authority, examining how it was established and how it operates. Most importantly, we examine the strategies that each authority uses in its mission to counter bad official statistics. We note something surprising – at least it was something that surprised us. Both authorities combat statistical manipulation by virtually never using the word 'manipulation' (whether the French or English word) in their official documents.

In the biographical chapters on Darmanin and Johnson, we concentrate on both politicians' clashes with their respective national statistical agencies. We closely observe how these politicians used their official powers to ignore the recommendations of their agencies and how they both tried to devalue statistics. When the agencies confront powerful politicians they are hampered by a lack of power. They can only recommend, not enforce, good statistical practice. Yet, the agencies tended to come out on top in their confrontations with Darmanin and Johnson, and we examine how and why this happened.

The final analytic chapter digs down deeply into a single incident that occurred in Britain during Johnson's time as prime minister. The incident did not directly involve Johnson. We see in detail how the authority's strategy was initially to be diplomatic, but when the minister ignored its advice, it switched to using more direct language. This brought immediate results, but without a total victory. A manipulative politician can indeed be a slippery customer.

As far as we are aware, the actions of the British and French statistical regulators have not previously been examined, certainly not in the depth that we have studied them. Just as the biographical chapters tend to reveal villains, so the later chapters on the authorities throw up some rather surprising, bureaucratic heroes. We discuss the implications of this in the final chapter, and we briefly say why it is so difficult, perhaps virtually impossible, to establish similar authorities in the United States.

Lastly a word about our writing. We have tried to avoid using technical language, whether that of statistics or of linguistics. Nor do we use the technical language of social psychology, the academic discipline in which we both trained. Social psychology is probably the discipline that has most studied the topic of persuasion; and it has produced shelf-loads of specialist words. Instead of reaching out for technical terms, many of which would be unsuitable for our purposes, we have tried to explain the processes of statistical manipulation and counter-manipulation as simply as we can. Although psychologists might look for, and fail to find, their own terminology in our writing, we consider this to be a psychological work. Each time we examine an example of political manipulation, we come back to the motives of the political manipulator and what they are seeking to gain by their manipulations. We try to look at their actions, words and motives as directly as we can, rather than through the intervening lens of a favourite theory.[19]

We believe that statistical manipulation is a worrying feature of the modern world and one that potentially corrupts democracy. In this book, we occasionally use irony. This is not because we want to get a cheap laugh or because we think our topic is full of fun. Quite the reverse. In our view, political leaders who are so confident of themselves that they have few scruples about inventing their own numbers pose a dangerous problem. It is because such leaders take themselves and their invented untruths seriously that they deserve to be mocked.

---

[19] Marie Jahoda, the great social psychologist of a previous era, advocated that psychologists should try to look at the world directly, even naively. See: Marie Jahoda (1989), 'Why a non-reductionist social psychology is almost too difficult to be tackled, but too fascinating to be left alone', *British Journal of Social Psychology*, 28, 71–8. See: Billig (2020), chapter 8, for an appreciation of Jahoda. See also: Alexandra Rutherford, Rhoda Unger and Frances Cherry (2011), 'Reclaiming SPSSI's sociological past: Marie Jahoda and the immersion tradition in social psychology', *Journal of Social Issues*, 67, 42–58.

CHAPTER 2

The Rise of Statistics

Our main topic – politicians manipulating statistics – is very much part of present times. Official statistics have grown in importance during the past fifty years, especially in political life. Today politicians are constantly ready to quote statistics as rhetorical weapons to boost their own case and to weaken the arguments of their opponents. Opinion polls show that the public's trust in politics has declined significantly and that politicians are now widely suspected of manipulating the statistics that they cite. Thus, our problem seems to be very much a modern one.

In later chapters we will be showing some high-profile politicians manipulating statistics to their own advantage. But before this, a bit of history might give some perspective. In this chapter we look back to the early days when statistics, as we understand them today, were not yet called 'statistics'. We look backwards for two basic reasons. The first is a general point: most explorations in the social sciences benefit from having a historical dimension. If our thinking remains locked within our own times, then we run the risk of imagining that the world has always been the same; or conversely that our own times are absolutely without precedent.

A historical perspective will help us to pinpoint why the political manipulation of statistics has developed as it has. We will be making a point that might seem obvious once it has been made: namely, when governments acquire the power to control statistics, they will try to use that power. In this chapter we look backwards to the first half of the nineteenth century, when public statistics grew dramatically but politicians had little power over their day-to-day production, analysis and dissemination.

There is a second reason for looking backwards. It is to meet some fascinating individuals. We will encounter the Belgian polymath Adolphe Quetelet, a key figure in the early social sciences, and William Farr, the notable but often forgotten founder of medical statistics in the United Kingdom. It is easy to assume that statistics provides a very masculine way of perceiving the social world. However, the most famous woman in

Victorian Britain, after the Queen herself, was a pioneering statistician. She was a friend of Farr and hailed Quetelet as 'the creator of statistics'. She was also socially well situated. She knew some of the leading political figures of her day and appreciated that social statistics needed to be political if they were to change the world for the better. Her story points towards the fact that in her day the main conditions for politicians to manipulate statistics had not yet been set in place.

Pure and Applied Origins

Innovative scientists are often, by force of necessity, linguistic innovators. If you discover a new species of insect, a new virus or a new chemical reaction, your finding will need to be named in order for it to be properly welcomed into the world of science, where it can be written about, discussed and disputed. In consequence, discoverers will not only add new phenomena to the sciences but will also contribute to the words and phrases of their fellow scientists.[1] Occasionally the new word or phrase will seep out of the narrow language of scientists and into the general language of non-specialists. The philosopher Ian Hacking has discussed how those creative mathematicians who devised probability theory in the nineteenth century needed to build new vocabularies to express their original ideas about chance. Words and phrases such as 'probabilities', 'intervals' and 'random variables' took on new meanings, and some entirely new words, like 'correlation', had to be created.[2]

All this is normal in the development of science. In the case of probability theory, there was something else. Beyond the technical terminology for denoting arcane mathematical procedures, there stood a word which did not just seep into public discourse, but gushed into it. Today the word seems to have always been there, circulating round our talk with just the meaning that it has today. That word is 'statistics'. But as words go, this one is a comparative newcomer, which was born in a strange house.

The word 'statistics' incorporates the technicalities of probability theory, as well as the numbers on which the theory depends. If you want to assess the chance that a five-year-old child living in a particular place at a particular time will live long enough to become an adult, you need to

[1] M. A. K. Halliday (2004), *The Language of Science*, London: Continuum; M. A. K. Halliday and J. R. Martin (1993), *Writing Science*, London: Falmer.
[2] Ian Hacking (1965/2016), *Logic of Statistical Inference*, Cambridge: Cambridge University Press; Ian Hacking (2006), *The Emergence of Probability*, Cambridge: Cambridge University Press.

have lots of numbers, of the sort that we would now call 'statistics'. You cannot make a scientific estimate of the probability without having the numbers. In the case of estimating a five-year-old's chance of becoming an adult, we would need to have data on the deaths of children as a proportion of the total population of children. Just finding a number that indicates that proportion does not tell you much. You will want to know whether the deaths of children at this time in this place are high or low. For this you need more data to make comparisons and give meaning to the single probability that you have found. Then if the proportion seems to be high, then you will want even more data to discover what is the reason for this enhanced chance of childhood death. In this place at this time, is there a high proportion of deaths from contagious illnesses, accidents, warfare, famine and so on?

Once you start using your data to calculate important probabilities there seems to be an inexhaustible need for even more data – or, as we might say today, for more statistics. So, 'statistics' as a word came to represent both the calculation of probabilities and the data on which the calculations were based. In the early history of statistics, this data was almost entirely based on numbers that had been collected by states about their citizens, such as records of marriages, births and death – and above all, official censuses. It is no coincidence that there were giant steps taken in the mathematics of probability just at the time when large banks of data were being founded, courtesy of nation states.

Within the general area of statistics there have been, and continue to be, 'pure' and 'applied' aspects. The pure side is represented by the mathematics of probability theory – for instance, how to devise ever more complex formulae for calculating probabilities, such as those that might be applied to calculating the probability that a child might live to become an adult. The 'applied' areas have dealt with problems relating to the collection and analysis of public data – such as how to improve the accuracy of censuses or how to obtain reliable records of health. Some of the early pioneers of statistics, like Quetelet, were deeply involved in both aspects: he was not only fascinated by the mathematics of probability, but he wanted to apply that knowledge to measure social phenomena and, thereby, to improve society scientifically. 'Statistics' came to be used as the overall term to denote both the pure and the applied areas, and this continues in the present.[3]

---

[3] The history of the *Journal of the Royal Statistical Society* illustrates the divergence of these branches of statistics. The *Journal* has been published continuously since 1838, originally under the title of *Journal of the Statistical Society of London*. For the first 110 years of its existence, the journal published contributions on social statistics and probability theory. In 1948, realising that the journal had two very different readerships, the Royal Statistical Society split its journal into *Series A (General)* and *Series B (Methodological)*. In 1988, *Series A* was renamed as *Statistics in Society*.

There is something else that emerges from our brief history of the word 'statistics'. The word developed its modern meaning with the censuses that in the early 1800s governments were keenly interested in conducting. Where you have governments and their interests, you are unlikely to have pure knowledge: impurities will abound. So it was with statistics. The new science was closely connected historically, semantically and pragmatically to the old practices of politics and power.

Statistics without Numbers

The British statistician George Yule began his statistical textbook, which was first published in 1911, by recounting how the word 'statistics' came into the English language.[4] According to Yule, 'statistics' was derived from *status*, which in mediaeval Latin meant a political state. German authors had introduced the term during the eighteenth century, meaning 'simply the exposition of the noteworthy characteristics of a state'. Their mode of analysis was 'preponderantly verbal', not mathematical.[5]

Yule identified a German professor, Eberhard Zimmermann, as being probably the first author to use the word 'statistics' when writing in English (although the *Oxford English Dictionary* cites earlier uses of the word). Zimmermann did this in the preface to his English-language book about politics in Europe. Zimmermann wrote that in Germany this sort of political survey was now being 'distinguished by the new-coined name of *Statistics*'.[6] Apart from this one sentence, he did not use the word again in this book. Two years later in 1791, the first volume of Sir John Sinclair's *Statistical Account of Scotland* appeared.[7] This was the book that really brought 'statistics' into the English language, for Sinclair was a public figure – a member of parliament with a keen interest in agriculture, the church and self-promotion.[8]

---

[4] George U. Yule (1911), *An Introduction to the Theory of Statistics*, London: Charles Griffin.
[5] Ibid., p. 2.
[6] Eberhard A. W. Zimmermann (1787), *A Political Survey of the Present State of Europe*. London: C. Dilly, p. ii.
[7] John Sinclair (1791–1799), *The Statistical Account of Scotland: Drawn up from the Communications of the Ministers of the Different Parishes*, Edinburgh: William Creech. Certainly George Yule (1911, pp. 2ff.) thought that Sinclair did more than Zimmermann to establish the word 'statistics' in English.
[8] For a barbed obituary, see: David R. Fisher (1986), 'Sinclair, Sir John, 1st Bt. (1754–1835), of Ulbster and Thurso Castle, Caithness', in R. Thorne (ed.), *The History of Parliament: The House of Commons, 1790–1820*, London: Boydell and Brewer, www.historyofparliamentonline.org/volume/1790-1820/member/sinclair-sir-john-1754-1835.

Sinclair's book is notable not only because the title contains the word 'statistical'. It was also a massive examination of Scotland, with its twenty-one volumes appearing over a period of eight years. As a leading member of the Church of Scotland, Sinclair wrote to the ministers of all the Church's 938 Scottish parishes, asking them to answer a standard list of questions about their parish and its parishioners. Some questions invited discursive answers, such as those about the parish's history, antiquities and 'eminent men'. Other questions invited numerical answers, such as the parish's population and the number of marriages, births and deaths.[9] Most of the ministers found it easier to write about the antiquities in their parish than to count the number of sheep, houses or dovecotes, as Sinclair requested them to do. Sometimes they ignored these numerical questions.

In the introduction to the opening volume, Sinclair wrote that he had planned to combine the ministers' individual responses into a 'general Statistical view of North Britain'. That would have required considerable extra work on his part. Besides, the clergymen had provided 'so many useful facts and important observations' that he could not deprive them of the credit they were entitled 'from such laborious exertions'.[10] The result was that the book lacked a common style or standardised method. The minister of Lochcarron even wrote part of his response in verse, humorously explaining his numerical omissions:

> Now good Sir John, it was for you
> I gather'd all my news,
> But you will say that I forgot
> To count the sheep and cows.[11]

Only speakers of English raised in Scotland or northern England are likely to pronounce 'cows' to rhyme with 'news'.

More seriously, the clergymen also made their religious preferences plain when answering questions about the number of marriages in their parish. Instead of trying to estimate an accurate number, using the records from their church and from other churches, they sometimes concentrated on criticising 'irregular' marriages, conducted by dissenting sects or by magistrates.[12] According to the minister of Graitney, it was disgraceful for a 'civilized country to permit such irregularities to be practised with

---

[9] For a discussion of Sinclair's general method, see: Chris Pritchard (1992), 'The contributions of four Scots to the early development of statistics', *The Mathematical Gazette*, 76(475), 61–8.
[10] Sinclair (1791–9), vol. I, pp. xiii–x.   [11] Ibid., vol. XIII, p. 600.
[12] See, for example: ibid., vol. I, p.9; vol. IX. p. 173.

impunity'.[13] In consequence, the ministers often excluded 'irregular' marriages from the total number of parish marriages, on the grounds that these were not proper marriages.

In his final volume Sinclair wrote about his use of the unusual words 'statistics' and 'statistical'. When touring Germany in 1786, he found people gave the name of 'statistics' to studies of 'the political strength of a country'. He annexed their word, using it to describe 'an inquiry into the state of a country'. He added, almost guilelessly, that he used the unfamiliar word because he thought that it might attract 'more public attention'.[14]

Sinclair's non-statistical use of 'statistics' did anticipate some future, statistical trends. First, his example showed that the work of producing a view of a country – especially if it was a numerical view – was far too great for a single person. Sinclair recruited more than 900 clergymen to gather his data. He also paid for secretarial assistance to deal with the hundreds of letters that he wrote and received. Modern censuses that produced numerical data would require a vast bureaucracy.

Second, we can see that the beliefs of the data collectors influenced how they gathered their data. The religious ministers distinguished between what they counted as a marriage and what they did not count as one. This general problem was not just a leftover from pre-census times that would soon be swept away by the coming trend for numbers. Those who were to formulate censuses would have to decide what categories should be used and how these categories should be interpreted. The move to numerical data would not, and indeed could not, make semantic problems disappear.

Sinclair's statistics anticipate another feature of numerical statistics: the national context. There is no mistaking Sinclair's feeling for Scotland. He hoped that his data would help the social improvement of his homeland, increasing 'its quantum of happiness'.[15] The future generation of numerical statisticians would have similar hopes. They would have clear ideas about using their data to improve the conditions of life in their state. They would realise that to reduce the quantum of national misery, they would first need to improve the quality of national data.

'Statistics' Becoming Numerical

The semantic movement towards linking 'statistics' with numbers was becoming inevitable. Between 1820 and 1840, there was what Ian

---

[13] Ibid., vol. IX. p. 352.   [14] Ibid., vol. I, pp. xiii–xiv.   [15] Ibid., pp. xiii–xiv.

Hacking has described as 'the avalanche of printed numbers'.[16] This is partly matched by a rise in the use of the word 'statistics'. According to Google's corpus of British books, during this period the word's use rose roughly fourfold in proportion to the total number of books published. Whether or not this represents a semantic avalanche, it certainly is a notable increase, one which would be maintained throughout the rest of the nineteenth century and into the early years of the twentieth, by which time the old sense of 'statistics' had disappeared.[17]

The driving force behind the meaning of 'statistics' was that national states were increasingly collecting numerical information about their populations, particularly by instituting national censuses and the compulsory registration of births, marriages and death. Large bureaucracies were established to collect and calculate this information. For example, the British Parliament passed the Births and Deaths Registration Act of 1836, which made the civic registration of all births, marriages and deaths compulsory in England and Wales.

To carry out this work, the General Register Office (GRO) was established in London. Thomas Lister was appointed to be the first registrar general. One of his duties was to write an annual report that would be delivered to the home secretary and then published publicly.[18] As a novelist Lister may have lacked mathematical training and expertise, but his aristocratic family connections included Lord John Russell, the Whig home secretary to whom the new registrar general would submit his first annual report.

Lister was responsible for recruiting and administering the large staff required for registrations and national censuses. In his first annual report, he recounted that over 2,500 registrars had been appointed, as well as more than 600 superintendent registrars.[19] GRO's central office at Somerset House in London required more than a hundred clerks and other

---

[16] Ian Hacking (1982), 'Biopower and the avalanche of printed numbers', *Humanities in Society*, 5, 279–95, p. 280.

[17] For the Google evidence on the use of 'statistics', calculated as a proportion of the total use of words published in English books, see: https://books.google.com/ngrams/graph?content=statistics&year_start=1800&year_end=2000&corpus=26&smoothing=3.

[18] Edward Higgs has contributed greatly to our knowledge of the history of GRO. See, for instance: Edward Higgs (2004), *Life, Death and Statistics*, Hatfield: Local Population Studies. See also: Edward Higgs (2003), 'The General Register Office and the tabulation of data 1837–1939', in Martin Campbell-Kelly, Mary Croarken and Raymond Flood (eds.), *From Sumer to Spreadsheets*, Oxford: Oxford University Press, pp. 209–34.

[19] Registrar-General [T. H. Lister] (1839), *First Annual Report of the Registrar General of Births, Deaths and Marriages in England*, London: W. Clowes, pp. 4ff.

administrators.[20] This was no small bureaucracy that could share a couple of desks in a back-street office.

Similar organisations were being established in other European countries. The French equivalent, Statistique générale de la France, had been set up in 1833.[21] In Belgium, the statistical movement was driven by the great statistician, astronomer and all-round polymath Adolphe Quetelet. He ensured the establishment of the Commission centrale de statistique in 1841 to coordinate the various statistical activities of the nation. He used the data to advance his own statistical inquiries into the 'average person' as a social and moral ideal.[22]

The British GRO might have resembled those two francophone organisations in many of its practices and responsibilities, but regarding its name it differed from them. 'Statistics' found no place in the GRO's official title. When Lister set up the administrative structure of the GRO, he created no Statistical Department to sit alongside Correspondence, Accounts and the department dedicated to 'Arrangements and indexing of certified copies of all registers'. However, the rise of 'statistics' in name and practice was unstoppable. Lister's successor, George Graham, was to establish a specific Statistical Department in the GRO.[23]

The passing of the Registration Act of 1836 had been politically sensitive. Parliament had rejected earlier versions with the strongest opposition coming from the Church of England. The Act would ensure that the Church would lose its powers to determine who was legally living, dying and marrying in the country. Before the Act the Church could and did exert its powers, especially in relation to marriage. In England and Wales, just like Scotland, the Church could exclude 'irregular' marriages from being registered as marriages.

The Act put a stop to that. All legal marriages, whether the ceremony was religious or civil, or whether conducted by mainstream churchmen, by nonconformists or by recognised leaders of other faiths, were officially

---

[20] Noel A. Humphreys (1885), 'Biographical sketch of William Farr, M.D., D.C.L., C.B., F.R.S', in Noel A. Humphreys (ed.), *Vital Statistics: a Memorial Volume of Selection from the Reports and Writings of William Farr, M.D., D.C.L., C.B., F.R.S.*, London: Offices of the Sanitary Institute, pp. vii–xxiii.

[21] Higgs (2004), p. 17.

[22] Quetelet believed it would be possible to discover the underlying workings of society by using statistics; and he also sought to discover the laws of psychology by investigating *l'homme moyen* or average man. See, for example: M. A. Quetelet (1842), *A Treatise on Man and the Development of his Faculties*, Edinburgh: William and Robert Chambers, https://archive.org/details/treatiseonmandevooquet/page/6/mode/2up.

[23] Higgs (2004), pp. 29ff.

counted as marriages. Thus the Act marked an important step towards religious freedom for dissenters and other non-Anglican Christians. The dissenters were politically split among themselves. Some thought that they should cooperate with the official church to prevent the whole business of registration slipping out of the hands of religious authorities into the hands of atheists and non-Christians. Others thought that cooperation was a betrayal of their principles. These divisions were decisive in enabling the civic authorities to gain ultimate victory.[24]

The 1836 Act only applied to England and Wales, with the Church of Scotland holding on to its powerful position. The title of John Sinclair's book might at first sight appear to be a sign of things to come, with Scotland ahead of England in using the word 'statistical'. However, Sinclair's clergymen – his 'statisticians' – were, a generation later, the sort of clergy who were successfully resisting ceding control of registration in their parishes to civic authorities. They wanted to continue controlling what counted as a proper marriage and to link births with official baptisms. When Scotland finally abandoned its old religious-based system of registration, most west European countries had already moved to civic registration. The passing of the Registration of Births, Deaths and Marriages (Scotland) Act in 1854 did not mean that control of Scotland's civic registration slipped southwards to London, but it remained north of the border with the creation of the General Register Office for Scotland (GROS). The new office reserved the right to deviate from the GRO and to do things in a Scottish way.[25]

Thomas Lister's tenure as registrar general for England and Wales only lasted until 1842, when he died of tuberculosis. He was a lax administrator who failed to detect some corrupt practices which were developing within the GRO.[26] Nevertheless, he took one decision that was to have a notable effect on the GRO and its standing in the world. Lister realised that he needed to appoint someone to organise and present the data which the registrars were gathering: in short, he needed to appoint a proficient 'statistician'. Lister did not advertise for a statistician, but for a 'Compiler

---

[24] For the complex politics of the 1836 Act, see the classic study: Michael J. Cullen (1974), 'The making of the Civil Registration Act of 1836', *Journal of Ecclesiastical History*, 25, 39–59.

[25] A. Cameron (2007), 'Medicine, meteorology and vital statistics: the influence of the Royal College of Physicians of Edinburgh upon Scottish civil registration, c.1840–1855', *Journal of Royal College of Physicians Edinburgh*, 37, 173–80. For details of Scottish civic registration, see: Cecil Sinclair (2000), *Jock Tamson's Bairns: A History of the Records of the General Register Office for Scotland*, Edinburgh: General Register Office for Scotland.

[26] For details, see: Higgs (2004).

of Abstracts'. In this context, 'abstracts' meant tables of numbers. A young man of thirty-one, William Farr, applied and in 1839 was appointed at the comparatively modest salary of £350 a year.[27] During his short time as registrar general, Lister never made a better decision.

Farr and His Statistical Nosology

William Farr's great scientific and statistical achievements need to be set against his inauspicious start to life. Nineteenth-century England was a rigidly structured society, and few coming from his background would make much a mark. Farr was born in 1807 to impoverished parents in a small village in rural Shropshire. His parents could scarcely afford to look after him and, when still an infant, he passed into the care of a well-off, elderly couple who lived nearby. This move enabled the young William to have a comfortable childhood and, most importantly, an education. His foster father left him a sufficiently large bequest so that he could study medicine. He became a surgeon's dresser – the person who dressed the wounds of a patient following surgery. Rather than returning to Shropshire as a doctor, the young man's interests turned to the study of illness, particularly to the question of how numerical information might advance our knowledge of disease.[28]

After publishing several short articles in the new medical journal *The Lancet*, Farr was invited to contribute to John McCulloch's *Descriptive and Statistical Account of the British Empire*.[29] The book's title indicates how by 1830s the word 'statistical' was changing its meaning. Unlike Sinclair, McCulloch was not using 'statistical' to describe his topic, but to indicate a means of studying it. The phrase 'descriptive and statistical' suggests a contrast between two sorts of analysis. Some chapters were traditionally 'descriptive', such as the chapter on the history of the English language. Others were built around numbers. Farr's chapter, entitled 'Vital statistics', was of the latter type.

Of course, Farr's chapter was not just numbers, because statistics are always more than numbers. Ian Hacking put this well in his memorable

---

[27] Humphreys (1885).
[28] Ibid., For more recent biographical tributes to Farr, see: Peter M. Dunn (2002), 'Dr William Farr of Shropshire (1807–1883): obstetric mortality and training', *Archives of Diseases of Childhood: Fetal & Neonatal*, 86, F67–F69; Stephen Halliday (2000), 'William Farr: campaigning statistician', *Journal of Medical Biography*, 8, 220–27.
[29] J. M. McCulloch, (1837/1854). *A Descriptive and Statistical Account of the British Empire*, London: Longman, Brown, Green and Longman.

maxim: 'counting is hungry for categories'.[30] Measures have to be measures of something, whether the number of citizens, the number of legal
marriages or the number of those afflicted with smallpox. So, the official
statistical numbers are always accompanied by verbal labels. In his chapter
for McCulloch's book, Farr did much more than label his vital statistics,
for he was making an argument about numbers. Information about rates of
living and dying – 'vital statistics' – would enable investigators to understand how deadly diseases spread and how they might be controlled. For
this, it was necessary to have the sort of numbers that could be compared.
This was a point that he would make time and again throughout his long
statistical career.[31]

It was on the basis of this article that Farr obtained his post at the GRO.
When in 1839 the registrar general published his first annual report, it
contained a contribution from Farr, tucked away as Appendix P, but
taking the form of an eighty-page 'letter' from Farr to the registrar general.
Its positioning in the report belies how scientifically important this letter
would become.[32] To be fair, Lister drew attention to Farr's work in the
main body of his report. It would be important, Lister wrote, to use the
correct name for diseases if 'the science of Vital Statistics' is to advance.[33]
Lister went on to say that Farr's letter contained 'abstracts' presenting the
various causes of death, and that it also explained 'the classification [of
diseases] which has been adopted'.[34]

Farr's 'letter' contained a section which was entitled 'Statistical
Nosology' and which contained no numbers. In this section Farr explained
the importance of having a systematic classification of diseases, or nosology. He was writing about the need for doctors and registrars to use
accurate and, above all, consistent terminology when registering causes of
death. Farr's statistical nosology was not a nosology produced *by* statistics
but it was a nosology fit *for* statistical practice.

---

[30] Hacking (1982), p. 280.
[31] Farr's chapter, 'Vital statistics', was Chapter VII of Part V in the second volume of McCulloch's
      Descriptive and Statistical Account, pp. 541–624. In the book Farr is not named as the author of this
      substantial chapter.
[32] 'Appendix P: Letter to Registrar-General from William Farr 6 May 1839, respecting abstracts of the
      recorded causes of deaths registered during the half-year ending December 31 1837 with numerous
      tables', in Registrar-General (1839), *First Annual Report of the Registrar General of Births, Deaths and
      Marriages in England*, London: W. Clowes, pp. 86–166.
[33] Higgs (2004) points out that Farr made medical issues central to the GRO's work. The
      1836 Registration Act made no mention of registering the cause of death. Farr's influence can be
      seen in the very first Registrar-General's Report, in which Farr's letter in Appendix P was by far the
      longest and most substantial section of the whole report.
[34] Registrar-General (1839), p. 12.

Farr's 'statistical nosology' illustrates an important feature about the new statistics. The apparent opposition between descriptions and statistics, implied in the title of McCulloch's book, was much too simple, because an investigator who used statistics would also be using words to describe what the numbers indicated. If Farr was to fulfil his contract to compile tables, then he could not merely produce columns and rows of numbers: the columns and rows needed to be labelled with descriptions. Farr appreciated that good counting requires good describing and unreliable descriptions will produce unreliable numbers.

Farr had recognised that not all medical practitioners used the same names for diseases; nor did they agree about the essential characteristics of many diseases. The result was that some doctors might describe different diseases with the same name, and others might use different names to describe the same disease. If experts in vital statistics merely counted the number of times such descriptions were registered as causes of death, then they would run the risk of obtaining misleading totals about the number of fatalities caused by specific diseases.

Farr was convinced that knowledge about the spread of diseases would only become possible once there were medically agreed terms for potentially fatal diseases. Accordingly, Farr proposed a unified classificatory system for medical practitioners and registrars filling out the official forms for cause of death. Farr aimed to distinguish between each condition that would be liable to cause death and proposed a single name for each condition. For example, 'diarrhoea' was presented as the recommended term to be used on official forms, and equivalent to such synonyms as 'looseness', 'purging' and 'bowel complaint'. As a potentially fatal disease 'diarrhoea' was included under the general category of 'Epidemic, Endemic and Contagious Diseases'.[35]

Farr wrote that a shared nosology was of equal importance in medical statistics 'as weights and measures in the physical sciences'.[36] He recognised, however, that every nosology must necessarily be imperfect, including his own. Diseases, he wrote, are not 'always easily distinguished'. This was not the fault of medical practitioners, but arose because the symptoms of different diseases 'appear simultaneously and confounded'. There was no way of preventing this because obstacles to 'the accurate determination of disease' were 'inherent in the subject'.[37]

Medical statisticians should strive to make things as clear as possible but they should not expect perfection. Over the years, Farr continued to revise

---

[35] Farr (1839), p. 95.   [36] Ibid., p. 99.   [37] Ibid., p. 93.

his nosology, taking into account changes in diagnoses following advances in medical knowledge. His 1839 nosology classified typhus and typhoid together, but by 1869 they were distinguished as separate conditions.[38] As Farr recognised, there would always be difficult cases that would tax even the most experienced practitioners. Because knowledge of disease would never be complete, no nosology could be presumed perfect.

Farr was touching on something that is endemic to all major forms of official statistics. No system for counting important phenomena can ever be perfect. Statisticians should not expect to produce figures that are absolute truths. Nevertheless, some figures are more accurate than others and some may be too inaccurate to be trusted at all. In practical terms, statistics itself is a probabilistic science: of some measures we can say that they are probably more accurate than other measures.

In the nineteenth century the registrar general's registration forms had no category for stillbirths. Farr wanted to include stillbirths on the register of births but George Graham, Lister's successor, overrode him. These were not purely medical decisions. The registrar general was following legal, rather than medical, advice about the start of a person's life. In nineteenth-century Britain, the first breath was not the legal marker of independent life: life started when the baby was completely extruded from the mother's body.[39] There would be difficult, contestable cases – for instance, there were legal disputes about what constituted *complete* extrusion from the body. In consequence, registrars had to make awkward decisions, deciding for example whether or not a baby legally had a moment of life. If a registrar decided that the baby had lived for a moment, then they would need to issue a death certificate. The problem is that statistics require sharp-edged decisions to be made with fuzzy-edged categories.

We might suppose that nineteenth-century debates about stillbirths and the start of life reflect defects in nineteenth-century medicine. However, not all the difficulties have now been resolved, nor are they all medical. Tim Harford in *How to Make the World Add Up* discusses the comparatively recent case of two groupings of hospitals in the United Kingdom with different rates of stillbirth.[40] The obvious explanation for the difference would be that the hospital grouping with the higher rate of death was providing a worse standard of care.

However, the reason for the difference lay in decisions about how to describe tragedies. When a baby is born prematurely at twenty-four weeks

---

[38] See: Higgs (2004) for more details and further examples.   [39] Ibid.
[40] Tim Harford (2021), *How to Make the World Add Up*, London: Bridge Street Press, pp. 55ff.

in the UK, it should be registered as a birth – either a stillbirth if it is born dead or a living birth if it survives awhile. When a pregnancy ends at twenty-two or twenty-three weeks and results in the death of the foetus, there is legal and medical ambiguity, especially because the length of the gestation period cannot be calculated with certainty. Some doctors will classify such a loss as 'a late miscarriage', even if the infant took a few breaths. Other doctors, possibly to soften the parents' immense grief, will describe it as a birth, although the baby might have been born without obvious signs of life. It appears that the numerical differences between the two hospital groupings in their recorded rates of stillbirth was due to their different ways of recording these tragic cases. The grouping which may have been showing greater sympathy with the grieving parents was appearing, according to the public numbers, as if it were offering a lower quality of medical care.

Having discretion in how a particular instance is to be categorised can lead to a specific set of problems that did not exist in Farr's day. Modern societies are metric societies in which people and institutions are widely evaluated according to statistical criteria.[41] It is expected that institutions such as hospitals, schools and large businesses, as well as individual employees within those institutions, will be regularly evaluated statistically and that much will hang on these evaluations. Funding, salaries, promotions and so on will be determined by numbers of infant deaths, examinations passed, sales obtained and so on. When hospitals are financially punished for the number of infant deaths recorded, then one can predict that there will be pressure to record ambiguous deaths as miscarriages.

This will lead to something that the social psychologist Donald Campbell recognised in the 1970s about the way that measurements can become corrupted and fail to measure what they are intended to measure. He proposed as a law: '*The more any quantitative social indicator is used for social decision-making, the more subject it will be to corruption pressures and the more apt it will be to distort and corrupt the social processes it is intended to monitor*'.[42] In other words, whenever organisations and employees are set targets and statistically evaluated to see whether they have met their targets, then the measures for evaluating performance will become corrupted.

---

[41] On the danger of metric societies, see: Steffen Mau (2019), *The Metric Society*, Cambridge: Polity.
[42] Donald T. Campbell, D. T. (1979), 'Assessing the impact of planned social change', *Evaluation and Program Planning*, 2, 67–90. Quotation on p. 85, italics in original.

Campbell gave a number of examples to show this corruption of measures. One concerned plea bargaining which was common in the US. The police are set statistically evaluated targets for solving recorded crimes. So, it is in the interests of each police force to have as high a figure as possible for solved crimes. The police will then attempt to induce arrested criminals to confess to crimes, even crimes that they did not commit. According to Campbell: 'A burglar who is caught in the act can end up getting a lighter sentence the more prior unsolved burglaries he is willing to confess to'.[43]

Both burglar and police gain from this arrangement: the burglar with a lighter sentence and the police with higher rates of solved crimes. What suffers is the measure for evaluating how many crimes are solved: the numbers will be too high because of the deals with the police and the attitude of the judiciary. As one sociologist has written, Campbell's law and his examples show 'how people will adapt to a particular valuation and reward system and try to extract the most they can from it'.[44]

Joel Best has written acutely about Campbell's law – how it remains relevant today and how it relates to politics.[45] We live in highly evaluated times and this causes problems unknown in the nineteenth century. Our interest here is not in targets that commercial organisations set for their employees. We are concerned with politicians, especially those in government, who set targets for themselves and then superintend statistical ways to measure whether they have met their own targets. Governments will be motivated to produce ways of evaluating their targets to maximise the possibility of obtaining positive results, 'proving' that they have succeeded in meeting their self-set, self-measured targets.

This problem did not occur in the days of Farr, not least because governing politicians tended not to set themselves numerically defined targets. Early statistics were not corrupted in Campbell's sense, at least in the period after they were taken out of the hands of those religious ministers who might exclude 'irregular' births, marriages and deaths, and before they were put in the hands of political ministers. Farr did not construct his nosology to meet a statistically defined interest. He had nothing to gain professionally, economically or politically by raising some numbers and lowering others, as if he might personally gain by grouping

---

[43] Campbell (1979), p. 85.   [44] Mau (2019), p. 130.
[45] Joel Best (2021), 'How to lie with Coronavirus statistics: Campbell's law and measuring the effects of Covid-19', *Numeracy*, 14 (1: Article 6), https://digitalcommons.usf.edu/numeracy/vol14/iss1/art6/.

typhoid with typhus rather than separating them. He was not trying to mislead but he was seeking to produce the best statistical nosology that he could, while being aware that perfection was not a possibility. Even so, politics was not entirely absent from Farr's understanding of disease or from his methods of collecting data – but not all politics is manipulation.

Farr and the Passionate Statistician

A nation's statistical bureaucracy must be established by political action. The decision can be politically controversial, as was the decision to establish the GRO. Even after it was established some Christians thought that it was wrong for someone like Farr, lacking social standing and obvious religious affiliations, to have control over decisions concerning life, death and marriage. Farr, as a compiler of abstracts from a humble background, possessed little direct political influence, especially in the early years of his career. Nevertheless, within fifteen years of his appointment, he was to gain a friend and ally who had mixed socially with some of the highest aristocrats and politicians in the land.

Florence Nightingale was known throughout Britain as the 'Lady with the Lamp' for her nursing work during the Crimean War. The military campaign had been disastrous for the British army with large losses of life. Nightingale ran the military hospital at Scutari, while being closely involved in tending to the sick, wounded and dying. As the public turned on the politicians who had badly equipped the British troops, and on the military leaders whose decisions ensured death and defeat, so they came to idolise Nightingale – the ministering angel and the shining light of dark times.

Nightingale had arrived at Scutari in late 1854 and had been immediately appalled by the filthy, insanitary conditions of the hospital. More soldiers were dying from diseases caught in the hospital than were dying from wounds inflicted on the battlefield. Nightingale informed the army authorities of this shocking fact, but they dithered before responding to her appeals. She returned to Britain in 1856 after peace had been signed. She brought back a sickness that would affect her for many years, debilitating her with pain, weakness and depression. Because of her lack of energy, Nightingale seldom went out to take part in social or political activities. Nevertheless, she stayed at home, furiously writing books, pamphlets and letters. Her collected works amount to sixteen substantial volumes.[46]

---

[46] Florence Nightingale (2001–2012), *The Collected Works*, vols. 1–16, ed. Lynn Macdonald, Ontario: Wilfred Laurier University Press.

Today, it can be seen that Nightingale's symptoms match those of chronic brucellosis, a severe bacterial disease which she could well have caught in Crimea. The disease was not on Farr's nosology for a good reason: it was unknown and would only be identified thirty years later. During Nightingale's lifetime, many suspected, wrongly as it turned out, that she was malingering or was suffering from a mental illness.[47]

Despite her physical condition, the ministering angel never became a meek soul. On her return from Crimea, Nightingale was determined to expose the conditions that she had witnessed. She wanted the leading politicians of the land to be aware what the injured troops had to suffer. She pinned the blame on poor sanitation and sought to persuade politicians to improve the sanitary conditions of the nation in general and the army in particular. She knew that it would be insufficient just to complain loudly. She needed facts, scientifically based facts. And she knew who to approach to help her find the scientific evidence: William Farr.

Some may be surprised to learn that Nightingale was a committed statistician, for mathematical statistics does not seem to fit with the female stereotype underlying her great reputation as the nursing angel. Sir Edward Cook, whose massive biography of Nightingale was published three years after her death, called her 'the passionate statistician'. He wrote: 'Few books made a greater impression on Miss Florence Nightingale than those of Adolphe Quetelet ... and she had few friends she valued more highly than Dr William Farr'.[48] In 1858 she became the first woman to be elected a Fellow of the London Statistical Society, which later would receive a Royal Charter to become the Royal Statistical Society. Farr headed the signatories on her nomination form.

The friendship between Farr and Nightingale was based on more than a common interest in statistics: it was rooted in a shared understanding that statistics would demonstrate the need for social reform. They believed that statistics could reveal how the appalling living conditions caused unnecessary death and suffering. Farr had been comparing the mortality rates of different districts in England. In his view, the high mortality rates of what he called the 'unhealthy' districts would fall, if their insanitary conditions could be improved to match the living conditions of the 'healthy districts'.

[47] D. A. B. Young (1995), 'Florence Nightingale's fever', *British Medical Journal*, 311, 1697–700.
[48] Edward Cook (1913), *The Life of Florence Nightingale*, vol. I (1820–1861), London: Macmillan, p. 428. For more recent, briefer biographies see: Hugh Small (2017), *A Brief History of Florence Nightingale*, London: Robinson; Hugh Small (2013), *Florence Nightingale: Avenging Angel*, London: Knowledge Leak; Lynn McDonald (2017), *Florence Nightingale: a Very Brief History*, London: SPCK.

Nightingale's experiences in the Crimean war had convinced her of much the same: the diseases that ravaged her hospital would have been largely preventable had there been cleanliness, fresh water and working sewage systems. Two years after her return she published a large book of careful statistical analyses which called the bulk of deaths in her hospital 'preventable' because they would not have occurred had the sanitation been adequate.[49] She described the conditions in an anonymous, hard-hitting work: 'the Hospitals were most defectively drained; they had no water closets, and consequently the effluvia from the sewers pervaded all the buildings'.[50]

In writing of preventable diseases, and bringing these matters to the attention of the public, Nightingale and Farr were not confining themselves to medical or statistical matters. They were providing numerical evidence which underlined the need for political action to provide the necessary funds for improved sanitation and thereby to prevent socially preventable diseases. The registrar general added his voice in his Annual Report for 1862. He used Farr's figures and the terminology of 'unnatural' deaths, as he too urged that the living conditions of the poor should be improved.[51]

Statisticians Influencing and Not Influencing Politicians

Florence Nightingale had few inhibitions about contacting high-ranking politicians, especially those she had known before she went to Crimea. On her return she was convinced that a Royal Commission should investigate the insanitary conditions endured by the troops. Farr supported her, but he lacked the social confidence to approach the great and the good. Nightingale's pressure was successful. A Royal Commission sat between May and July of 1857, and its lengthy report appeared early in the following year.[52]

---

[49] Florence Nightingale (1858), *Notes on Matters Affecting the Health, Efficiency, and Hospital Administration of the British Army: Founded Chiefly on the Experience of the Late War*, London: Harrison & Sons.

[50] Anonymous [Florence Nightingale] (1859), *A Contribution to The Sanitary History of the British Army During the Late War with Russia*, London: John W. Parker and Son, p. 10.

[51] Registrar-General (1862), *Twenty-third Annual Report of the Registrar-General of the Births, Deaths, and Marriages in England*, London: Eyre and Spottiswoode, p. xxx.

[52] *Report of the Commissioners Appointed to Inquire into The Regulations Affecting the Sanitary Condition of the Army, the Organization of Military Hospitals, and the Treatment of the Sick and Wounded: with evidence and appendix* (1858), Presented to both Houses of Parliament by Command of Her Majesty, London: Eyre and Spottiswood.

Sir Herbert Sidney, the minister of war during the Crimean war and one of Nightingale's friends, chaired the Commission. Nightingale's influence is reflected in some of the Commission's aims. The Report's preface states that the Commission aimed to examine the state of the military hospitals, and it would inquire into the sorts of records army medical officers should keep 'with a view to the preparation of well digested and accurate medical statistics'.[53]

Owing to her illness, Nightingale was unable to attend the Commission in person. Instead, she sent the Commission a written submission which included her answers to questions that she expected she would have been asked if she had attended. These were included in the final report.[54] Her answer to the question 'To what do you mainly ascribe the deaths in the hospitals?' was terse: 'To sanitary defects'.[55]

Farr submitted a detailed report, entitled 'Comparison of mortality of the troops serving at home with that of different classes of civil population'. This was also included as an appendix in the published report.[56] Farr's careful, numbers-filled report dealt with a potentially explosive issue on which he and Nightingale had been collaborating. They were comparing the morbidity rates of troops stationed in Britain with those of the rest of the population. The evidence showed that the troops were dying in far greater numbers than would be expected for men of their age. Living in army barracks in the middle of peaceful England was dangerous.

Attached to Farr's Appendix was an addition containing several diagrams. Here Nightingale demonstrated her unique contribution to statistics. She devised diagrams to catch the attention and draw out the meaning of Farr's tables. Her famous 'rose petal' or 'coxcomb' diagram (a super-extended pie chart) illustrated the rate of deaths in the Scutari hospital before and after the army acted on Nightingale's call to clean up the place. The difference is immediately visible. Also included were her coloured line diagrams showing that, for each age group, deaths in the English army based in England substantially exceeded those for Englishmen in the

[53] *Report of the Commissioners* (1858), p. v.
[54] Nightingale's answers appeared in the Report as 'Answers to written questions addressed to Miss Nightingale', pp. 361–94.
[55] *Report of the Commissioners* (1858), p. 364.
[56] William Farr (1858), 'Appendix LXX, Comparisons of the mortality of the troops serving at home with that of different classes of the civil population', in *Report of the Commissioners* (1858): see p. 506; 'Appendix LXXII, Description of tables and diagrams prepared by Dr Farr, illustrative of the numerical results in the report showing the mortality in the British army', pp. 516–26.

population at large. The Report did not credit the diagrams to Nightingale.[57]

Although Nightingale may have benefitted much from Farr's statistical expertise, she certainly did not owe her dramatic diagrams to his influence.[58] Victorian readers were not accustomed to seeing bar charts or line diagrams, but anyone seeing her line diagram about army deaths in England would have immediately grasped its shocking facts. Here numbers and words were perfectly combined in a striking visual design. As Farr wrote in his Appendix, diagrams of vital statistics can convey ideas 'through the eye which cannot be so easily contained' in numbers.[59]

Florence Nightingale was not the first statistician to portray numbers graphically. Hugh Small, who has written extensively about Nightingale, suggests that she was, however, the first person to devise ways of presenting data visually with the aim of persuading people of the need for social change.[60] Nightingale may have used diagrams persuasively but this does not mean she did so manipulatively. In later chapters, we shall encounter those who manipulate diagrams to transmit information misleadingly. By contrast, Nightingale was careful that her illustrations presented the statistics accurately and dramatically.[61]

Nightingale understood that statistics needed art as much as they needed numbers and categories. In his influential book, *The Signal and the Noise*, Nate Silver wrote that numbers 'have no way of speaking for themselves', but 'we speak for them', imbuing them with meaning.[62] Whatever mathematical and medical skills Farr might have possessed, he was not a talented rhetorician. He needed Florence Nightingale to speak for the numbers that

---

[57] In the Report the diagrams follow Farr's Appendix LXXII. The diagrams are identified by letters A–H; the pages on which they appear are unnumbered because they are folded inserts. Nightingale reproduced these diagrams elsewhere. The rose petal and line diagrams appear in Florence Nightingale (1858), page facing p. 311; the rose petal diagram also appears in Anonymous [Florence Nightingale] (1859).

[58] On Farr's statistical influence on Nightingale, see: C. G. Cook and A. J. Webb (2001), 'William Farr's influence on Florence Nightingale', *Journal of Medical Biography*, May 9, 122. For a corrective account emphasising Nightingale's influence on Farr, see: Tim Harford (2021), pp. 162f.

[59] Farr (1858), Appendix LXXII, p. 516.

[60] Hugh Small (1998), 'Florence Nightingale's statistical diagrams', paper delivered at Stats & Lamps Research Conference, Florence Nightingale Museum, 18 March, www.york.ac.uk/depts/maths/histstat/small.htm; see also: Small (2017).

[61] Alberto Cairo, a leading visual statistician, makes this point: Alberto Cairo (2020), *How Charts Lie*, New York: W. W. Norton. In his final chapter Cairo compares Nightingale's ethical use of visual statistics with those who have misused charts and diagrams for political advantage.

[62] Nate Silver (2012), *The Signal and the Noise*, London: Penguin, p. 9. Spiegelhalter (2020) uses Silver's quotation as an epigram in his own book, which is entitled significantly *The Art of Statistics*, not the *science* or the *mathematics* of statistics.

they computed. Farr knew that those in power listened when she spoke. If her chronic illness prevented her from speaking directly to the powerful, then she possessed the skill to let her diagrams speak on her and Farr's behalf – and on behalf of those who were dying unnecessarily.

So far we have seen statisticians influencing politicians. Nightingale and Farr had wanted a Royal Commission and they obtained one. Better still, the Commission took their statistical evidence seriously and its conclusions were in line with this evidence. But there were limits to the influence that statisticians – even Florence Nightingale – could exert over the politicians.

Nightingale and Farr wanted the national census to include questions about the habitation in which people were living and the illnesses that they might be suffering from. In their opinion, this information would be important for furthering knowledge about the connection between sanitation and disease. In 1860 an amendment to the Census Bill for England was introduced to Parliament. It contained a proposal to add to the census form the questions that Farr and Nightingale wanted. The Bill, however, was rejected. Hansard, the record of British parliamentary proceedings, shows that members of Parliament were bothered by considerations that still bother politicians today: cost, trouble and a reluctance to introduce change.[63]

It is too simple to imagine that all the fervour for statistics came from statisticians and little from politicians. Right from the early days, some politicians associated themselves with the new science. Sinclair had been an early supporter of numerical statistics, as well as non-numerical statistics.[64] The Marquis of Lansdowne, who had a long and distinguished political career, was first president of the London Statistical Society. When William Gladstone became prime minister in 1868, he was the Society's current president.

Nevertheless, most members of the British parliament were neither interested in, nor particularly knowledgeable about statistics. This became apparent in 1879 when the second registrar general retired, and the government needed to appoint his successor. Farr, who was clearly the most eminent professional statistician in Britain, applied for the position. He was rejected and someone from the British upper classes was appointed: Sir Brydges Henniker. Farr immediately resigned from the GRO, as the evidence was telling him that social class counted more than expertise.

[63] See: Hansard (1860, 24 April), hansard.parliament.uk/Commons/1860-04-24/debates/ 38fd5810–4211-4b93–829b-c540ebd60dfb/Census(England)Bill.
[64] John Pullinger (2013), 'Statistics making an impact', *Journal of the Royal Statistical Society, A*, 176, 819–39.

Certainly statisticians around the world held Farr in great regard. The assistant registrar commented that Farr's work 'has indeed been more fully appreciated on the continent and in America than has been the case in England'.[65] Many of Britain's doctors felt personally slighted by Farr's rejection. In January 1880 the *British Medical Journal* published reports of doctors complaining that a 'great injustice had been done to Dr Farr', and that his rejection was an 'insult' to the medical profession as a whole.[66]

This was another example of British politicians exerting control over British statistics. Not only had they influenced which questions should, and should not be, in the national census, but now they were appointing to the top post someone who would be socially congenial rather than professionally qualified. As the volume of statistical information grew, so this power would become increasingly important; and with it would come the possibility of using political power to manipulate the statistical information itself. In Farr's day that was still a long way off.

International Statistical Congresses

The major producers of statistical data were nationally based, and they mostly worked in institutions like GRO and the Statistique générale de la France, producing official numbers for and about their own nations. Nevertheless, statistics was also developing internationally. Quetelet believed that the new discipline was revealing scientific facts that transcended national boundaries.[67] He was keen that statisticians from around the world should meet regularly in order to develop a common, international science.

Today, international conferences for academics are commonplace, but in the nineteenth century they were rare. Following Quetelet's prompting, the International Congress of Statistics was established, and it held regular meetings between 1853 and 1876. Leading statisticians from America and Europe attended; so did a number of politicians and bureaucrats responsible for national censuses. Nico Randeraad's histories are invaluable for understanding the importance of these congresses and the difficulties that they faced.[68]

---

[65] Humphreys (1885), p. xviii.
[66] Anon (1880), 'Dr. William Farr and the office of Registrar-General', *The British Medical Journal*, 31 January, 996 (1), pp. 181–3. The quotation appears on p. 182.
[67] Quetelet (1842).
[68] Nico Randeraad (2010), *States and Statistics in the Nineteenth Century*, Manchester: Manchester University Press; see also: Nico Randeraad (2011), 'The International Statistical Congress (1853–1876): knowledge transfers and their limits', *European History Quarterly*, 41(1), 50–65.

Farr regularly participated, mostly as 'the official delegate of the English [sic] government'.[69] He was much more than a representative of the government, for his nosology was well known to statisticians around the world. In fact, Farr's nosology proved to be the major success of these meetings. The Congress of 1864 accepted his nosology and, according to one health expert, Farr's system remains 'the bedrock for the International Classification of Diseases, now in its tenth revision'.[70]

The 1860 Congress was held in London with Farr and Nightingale closely involved in its organisation. Because of her health Nightingale did not feel that she could attend in person. Instead, she invited delegates to visit her and, thus, she was able to meet Quetelet. The meeting meant a great deal to Nightingale and the two remained in correspondence until Quetelet's death in 1874.[71] When both volumes of Quetelet's *Physique sociale* were republished in 1869, he sent her copies. In her letter of thanks, she addressed her hero as 'Monsieur Quetelet, creator of statistics'.[72]

The Congresses often disappointed Quetelet, because there was little international accord. There were constant arguments about the choice of language for conducting the business, with the major nations championing their own languages. As Randeraad shows, there were national arguments about the suitable methods for acquiring census data and calculating a nation's population. Some nations only counted legal citizens, some counted all those who were present within the state on a particular day, and some used a combination of these two methods. Some only counted those having fixed addresses, while others sought out seasonal farm workers sleeping in barns and fields.

In theory, the politicians, bureaucrats and statistical scientists supported adopting a universal method for measuring populations, not least because that would enable data from different nations to be easily combined and easily compared. In practice, politicians and bureaucrats only supported an international method so long as it was their country's chosen method of measurement. As well as national *amour propre*, there were political gains and losses at stake. French politicians, for instance, were sensitive about the declining population of France, and they wanted censuses that would appear to minimise this decline. In the words of Randeraad, the international gatherings, far from creating universal methods, 'became the battleground for national interests'.[73]

---

[69] Humphreys (1885), p. xvii. [70] Dunn (2002), p. F67. [71] Randeraad (2010), p. 94.
[72] Gustav Jahoda (2015), 'Quetelet and the emergence of the behavioural sciences', *SpringerPlus*, 4, 473.
[73] Randeraad (2010), p. 6.

Nevertheless, there were some delegates to the Congresses who saw them as a welcome relief from the politics back home. Joseph Kennedy, who was in charge of organising American censuses for sixteen years, enjoyed meeting international statistical stars like Quetelet. However much wrangling there was at the Congresses, it could not match the bitter disputes around the American census: between those who saw further national censuses as a move to strengthen central government over the states, and those who took the reverse position. Increasingly fraught were the differences between the slave-owning and abolitionist states about how the census should be conducted, especially in relation to the enslaved.[74]

Overall, however, Quetelet became disillusioned with the Congresses and their failure to resolve national differences in statistics. As chairman of the 1869 Congress, he inquired about the progress towards establishing an international statistical system. He was disappointed to discover that the relevant committee had never met. The Congress of 1876 was to be the final one. To quote Randeraad again, the Congresses had shown that 'the migration of knowledge is no less conflict-ridden than the migration of people'.[75]

Inclusive and Exclusive Statistics

The story of early statistics seems to be about the victorious rise of inclusive, secular politics. The control of registering birth, marriages and deaths was wrested from the hands of religious authorities. In the United Kingdom, no longer could the marriages of Catholics or Protestant dissenters be categorised as 'irregular' and thereby excluded from the official category of 'marriage'. Similarly, those who wanted a civil, non-religious wedding could have one. There is a general lesson for the age of statistics. Those who are responsible for counting types of social phenomena may find that the categories which they are expected to count may be widened or contracted for reasons which are not purely statistical.

This means that we should take care not to equate statistical thinking with inclusive politics and the widening of important social categories. Those who wish to promote a narrowing of citizenship can have their own statisticians and conduct their own statistical inquiries in their own ways. As we saw, the International Congresses were beset with arguments about official censuses; these were arguments about who should be counted.

---

[74] Margo J. Anderson (2015), *The American Census*, New Haven: Yale University Press, especially chapter two.
[75] Randeraad (2011), p. 52.

In the second half of the nineteenth century, one of Britain's most creative statisticians was responsible for formulating a non-inclusive social vision, which he explicitly rooted in statistical thinking. There is no disputing that Francis Galton, a cousin of Darwin, was a statistical innovator, formulating the notions of correlation and regression towards the mean.[76] In 1865 he published in two parts what is often considered to be the first psychology paper published in Britain.[77] It was about the inheritance of mental characteristics. Making a distinction between distinguished and non-distinguished men, Galton argued that high mental ability ran in families and therefore that mental ability, whether high or low, was inherited. He chose this explanation, although the family differences that he presented could just as easily be explained by saying that family environments and living conditions caused the co-occurrence of abilities within families. Galton presented the same data and ideas in greater detail in his book *Hereditary Genius*.[78]

Galton claimed to be basing his work on Quetelet's central statistical idea about human and animal characteristics. Quetelet had claimed that most human and animal data sets share a common pattern: the average scores – whether of height, chest measurements, weight – tend to be the most frequently occurring, and the more that scores diverge from the central point, the rarer they become. In an age in which the visual representation of data has become common, Quetelet's discovery today is often understood as 'the normal curve', although professional statisticians will often prefer to describe it as the 'normal distribution'. Galton said that he was applying Quetelet's findings to mental abilities.[79]

Nevertheless, there was a huge philosophical difference between the ideas of the two statisticians. Quetelet valued the 'average person', while Galton constantly looked for differences – whether it was differences between so-called races, or differences between the 'higher' and 'lower' quality individuals within those 'races'. Using Quetelet's statistics, Galton said that the pattern of mental abilities was similar among the 'Anglo-Saxon race' as the 'negro race': each had their common average types and

---

[76] Among psychologists, Galton is now a deeply controversial figure, more likely to be criticised than venerated. For a critical biographical study of Galton, see: Martin Brookes (2004), *Extreme Measures: The Dark Visions and Bright Ideas of Francis Galton*, London: Bloomsbury.

[77] Francis Galton (1865a), 'Hereditary character and talent: Part I', *Macmillan's Magazine*, 12, 157–66. Francis Galton (1865b), 'Hereditary character and talent: Part II', *Macmillan's Magazine*, 12, 318–27.

[78] Francis Galton (1869), *Hereditary Genius*, London: Macmillan.

[79] See particularly the Appendix of Galton (1869); and his preface for the second edition: Francis Galton (1892), *Hereditary Genius*, second edition, London: Macmillan, especially pp. xiff.

rarer high and low types. However, Galton stressed that overall the distribution of 'Anglo-Saxon' mental ability was statistically two 'grades' higher than it was for 'negros'. Thus, the average 'negro' was of lower mental quality than the average 'Anglo-Saxon'; and 'negros' of higher mental quality far rarer than 'Anglo-Saxons' of high mental quality.[80]

It did not stop there. Even in that early work, Galton was to link his statistical themes to political proposals that were very different from those of Quetelet, Farr and Nightingale. Galton was obsessed with the notion that the 'superior races', like the Anglo-Saxons, would decline fatally if their highest-quality members did not breed at a greater rate than the lower-quality members who packed the slums and reproduced in huge numbers. If the 'Anglo-Saxons' declined, then they would be overtaken by the 'primitive' races in the uncompromising battle for survival. So it was necessary to take steps to encourage the better quality 'Anglo-Saxons' to breed. As for breeding with 'negros' or with other 'primitives', that would be fatal.[81]

Galton would become obsessed with his racist politics, for which he was to invent the name of 'eugenics', and which he claimed to be founded on the scientific theory of probability.[82] With the rise of eugenic thinking in the latter part of the nineteenth century and first part of the twentieth, statistical science was no longer the preserve of reforming liberals. This was a significant development. The far right would have their own statisticians to produce numbers that would support their policies of racial exclusion. The category of citizenship would be contracted in countries governed by eugenicist parties. Who counted as a citizen and who was not to be counted as a citizen would, in extreme cases, become a matter of life and death.

Preconditions for Statistical Manipulation

One of the reasons for this chapter's journey back to the early days of statistics is that some of the basic preconditions for politically manipulating statistics might have been there right from the start, but the circumstances that favoured manipulation were not. In those days politicians were not regularly distorting the statisticians' numbers to their own advantage or commissioning the statisticians to produce more convenient figures.

---

[80] Francis Galton (1869), pp. 338f.
[81] In *Hereditary Talent* and especially in the earlier two-part *Macmillan's Magazine* article, Galton used deeply racist language which was extreme even for the times. See: Michael Billig (1982), 'The origins of race psychology – I', *Patterns of Prejudice*, 16, 3–16; Graham Richards (2003), *"Race", Racism and psychology: Towards a Reflexive History*, London: Routledge.
[82] Francis Galton (1907), *Probability, the Foundation of Eugenics*, Oxford: Clarendon Press.

By comparison with today, those earlier times might appear more innocent. Statisticians like Farr and Nightingale might be using numbers for
political purposes, but they treated their numbers almost as sacred entities.
Nor were the politicians in the habit of putting pressure on the statisticians
to change the numbers for political reasons. There were, however, some
worrying instances. One way of manipulating statistics is by manipulating
the language that is used to describe what is being counted. As we will see in
later chapters this has become common in politics today. There are 'new
hospitals' that are anything but new; 'administered Covid tests' can include
tests that were never administered. In this way, numbers which the government finds politically desirable are boosted. Or categories can be narrowed
to lower the numbers; so, some crimes are removed from the list of crimes
being counted and the government can boast that it is reducing crime.[83]

The potential for this sort of manipulation was always present. As has
been mentioned, French political leaders encouraged their statisticians to
use methods for collecting French census data that would not emphasise
the decline of France's population. In the 1830s and 1840s the work of
prominent Russian statisticians was censored and some even lost their
positions because they were publishing figures that the authorities claimed
were presenting unfavourable views of rural Russia.[84] In Britain and
elsewhere, the censuses asked about employment, but some forms of
employment seemed to slip through the official categories.

One of the most troubling disappearing tricks was the disappearance of
prostitution. It was known at the time that many poor women resorted to
prostitution as the only means of feeding and clothing their children.
Judith Walkowitz, in her classic book on prostitution in Victorian
England, asks why no prostitutes, living in London, were recorded on
the 1881 census.[85] She chose the year and place with good reason. For a
short time, prostitution was legal in London so long as the prostitutes were
registered. Walkowitz calculated from the registration figures that about
24,000 prostitutes were working in London during that period, but none
appeared in the census.

We can see how the disappearing act was accomplished. First, there is a
general problem: census respondents might describe their occupation in
many different ways when filling out their census forms. The wide variety
of jobs that existed and the variety of descriptions that census fillers used

[83] See below, Chapters 9 and 10.   [84] Randeraad (2011), pp. 170f.
[85] Judith R. Walkowitz (1983), *Prostitution and Victorian Society*, Cambridge: Cambridge University
     Press.

for the same job had to be reduced by the census enumerators so that standardised categories could be counted. The result was that some specific ways of earning a living became invisible when the counts were made, because they were included as an instance of a wider category.[86]

Then there were specific problems associated with the term 'prostitute'.[87] Generally, the census enumerators avoided the term except when describing the occupation of prisoners who had been specifically convicted of 'prostitution'. Even if census enumerators suspected that a woman (or man) was earning their living through prostitution, the enumerator would hide them away under categories such as 'milliner', 'seamstress' or 'unfortunate'.[88] In this way, what many Victorians considered to be a moral stain on the nation's reputation was excluded from the official records and from the nation's official view of itself.

That may not have been the only, or even dominant, consideration of the census takers. As we have seen, many were social reformers, and many social reformers understood how poverty was driving desperate women to prostitution. A census is not an anonymous document. By law, everyone has to give their name and address. Those deriving money from prostitution would have been unlikely to want to be publicly identified as such; nor would they want their home address to be identified as a prostitute's address, even if they worked the streets. So, it is likely those census organisers and enumerators who were sympathetic to social reform went along with the fiction. Indeed, they could have justified their actions on methodological grounds as well as moral ones. Censuses require cooperation from their respondents. How could the census organisers expect such cooperation if the respondents feared they would be publicly shamed and liable to prosecution for answering truthfully? The rate of response could be adversely affected.

Throughout the history of official statistics, the information gatherers have needed to put questions of morality and respect for their respondents alongside issues of methodology. Of course, the work of the early census directors belongs to its time, but it is also surprisingly modern. As for

---

[86] Edward Higgs (2004b), 'The linguistic construction of social and medical categories in the work of the English General Register Office, 1837–1950', in Simon Szreter, Hania Sholkamy and A. Dharmalingam (eds.), *Categories and Contexts: Anthropological and Historical Studies in Critical Demography*, Oxford: Oxford University Press, pp. 86–106.

[87] Matthew Woollard (1999), 'The classification of occupations in the 1881 census of England and Wales', Historical Censuses and Social Surveys Research Group, Occasional Paper No. 1, www .henleycensus.info/articles/Woollard_1881_Classifications.pdf.

[88] Woollard (1999), p. 7.

politicians manipulating the work of the statisticians, we can see that some of the preconditions existed in the era of Quetelet, Farr and Nightingale. There were always different ways of categorising and counting phenomena such as deaths, populations and professions. There has never been a single, perfect way of measuring these phenomena. And there will always be politicians who will believe they, their party and their nation will benefit from using one way of measuring over another.

In the early days of statistics, the routes of influence tended to flow from statisticians to political leaders rather than vice versa. However, the spread of statistics across society has created a condition that did not really exist in those early days. Today, in democracies and autocracies the need for official statistical information is too great to be left to a single organisation, such as the GRO and its equivalents in other countries. Different government departments will employ their own statisticians to collect and analyse the information that the particular department requires.

This means that small groups of statisticians can find themselves coming into regular contact with the member of the government who is heading the department. By comparison the large statistical bureaucracies, in which statisticians like Farr and Quetelet worked, were more independent both physically and politically. The GRO, for example, occupied a large building that was not close to the offices of senior figures of the government. Accordingly, someone like Farr could control his statistical work for it was safely removed from the constant demands of politicians.

Later we will be seeing that the modern government can offer a very different environment for its statisticians. Some work in conditions where there are pressures to do the bidding of powerful politicians. We might say that these conditions maximise the chances that politicians will try to manipulate statistics.

Before we discuss the conditions that encourage political manipulations, we will need to say something about what 'manipulation' is. Only after that will it become clearer how nineteenth-century statistical achievements, such as Farr's great nosology or Nightingale's strikingly persuasive diagrams, differ from the frequently petty, but ultimately dangerous, manipulation of statistics that we can see and suspect today.

CHAPTER 3

Different Ways of Manipulating

To begin with, a deceptively simple and seemingly necessary question: what do we mean by 'manipulate' and 'manipulation'? Answering should be straightforward, for these are not technical terms. The *Oxford English Dictionary* (OED) divides English words into eight broad categories on the basis of their usage. The eighth category contains words with the highest frequency, and the first category contains those of the lowest frequency.[1] 'Manipulation' and 'manipulate' both come in the sixth category. This band contains nouns such as 'dog', 'horse' and 'ship' – words that any competent speaker of English can be expected to understand. Consequently, the average English speaker should have a good idea what the words 'manipulation' and 'manipulate' mean.

Nevertheless, this does not imply that all competent English speakers will use these words in the same way. Many common words have several meanings and sometimes people dispute which meaning should be used in which context, or even which is the 'real' meaning. People might understand the meaning of common words like 'good' and 'bad', but they can vigorously dispute what conduct should be described by former term and what by the latter. In the case of 'manipulation' and 'manipulate', things are not straightforward because both terms have two distinct meanings, one which expresses something positive and the other something negative.

We should emphasise that in this book we will be principally using 'manipulation' and 'manipulate' in their negative senses – to denote actions which we disapprove of. Nevertheless, we will not be saying that those who use manipulation words in the positive sense are using the words wrongly or even necessarily expressing values which we do not hold.

---

[1] OED frequencies for contemporary use are derived from a corpus of 20 billion words compiled by Oxford Languages. The measures of historical usage come from Google Books Ngrams, which is taken from a corpus of English language books published between 1500 and 2010. For more details, see: www.oed.com/information/understanding-entries/frequency/.

As we will see in this chapter, one historically important scientist can be credited with using both words in their positive senses. Also some of today's most distinguished statistical experts praise 'statistical manipulation'. In fact, their positive usage is part of the topic that we are investigating. It's just that we will not be using the words in this way.

Many, if not most, social scientists begin the reports of their investigations with carefully crafted definitions of key terms. We might be expected to do likewise, regarding 'manipulation' and 'statistical manipulation'. We will not, however, be following this familiar practice for reasons which should become clearer during the course of this chapter. Let us just say for now that there have been many researchers who have examined manipulation. They have come from a variety of academic backgrounds: there have been social psychologists, philosophers, political scientists, sociologists and, increasingly in recent years, linguists. And they cannot agree among themselves how to define 'manipulation'.

Many of the investigators have either proposed their own definitions of 'manipulation' or have adapted, sometimes with added tweaks, definitions formulated by prominent academics. Some have claimed that 'manipulation' involves conscious deceit, even lying;[2] others have denied this, and asserted that all forms of persuasion involve some degree of 'manipulation';[3] then there are those who claim that manipulation involves using fallacious arguments, with or without an intention to deceive;[4] some

---

[2] For linguistic analyses of ways to manipulate truth, see: Viviana Masia (2021), *The Manipulative Disguise of Truth*, Amsterdam: John Benjamins; Regina Blass (2005), 'Manipulation in the speeches of Hitler and the NSDAP from a relevance theoretic point of view', in L. de Saussure and P. Schulz (eds.), *Manipulation and Ideologies in the Twentieth Century*, Amsterdam: John Benjamins, pp. 169–90; Rom Harré (1985), 'Persuasion and manipulation', in Teun A. van Dijk (ed.), *Discourse and Communication*, Berlin: de Gruyter, pp. 126–42.

[3] This is the approach of the social psychologist David Buss, who has studied manipulation widely and sees the ability to manipulate as an evolutionary adaptive trait. He defines manipulation in terms of the ways that 'individuals intentionally or purposefully (although not necessarily consciously) alter, change, influence, or exploit others'. He specifically states that 'no evil, malicious or pernicious intent' need be involved: David M. Buss (1987), 'Selection, evocation and manipulation', *Journal of Personality and Social Psychology*, 53, 1214–21. See also: David M. Buss, Mary Gomes, Dolly S. Higgins and Karen Lauterbach (1987), 'Tactics of manipulation', *Journal of Personality and Social Psychology*, 52, 1219–29; David M. Buss (1992), 'Manipulation in close relationships: five personality factors in interactional context', *Journal of Personality*, 60, 477–99.

[4] Paul Danler (2005), 'Morpho-syntactic and textual realizations as deliberative pragmatic argumentative tools?' in L. de Saussure and P. Schulz (eds.), *Manipulation and Ideologies in the Twentieth Century*, Amsterdam: John Benjamins, pp. 45–60; Manfred Kienpointner (2005), 'Racist manipulation within Austrian, German, Dutch, French and Italian right-wing populism', in L. de Saussure and P. Schulz (eds.), *Manipulation and Ideologies in the Twentieth century*, Amsterdam: John Benjamins, pp. 213–36; Eddo Rigotti (2005), 'Towards a typology of manipulative processes', in L. de Saussure and P. Schulz (eds.), *Manipulation and Ideologies in the Twentieth Century*, Amsterdam: John Benjamins, pp. 61–84.

linguists claim that 'manipulation' is primarily an attempt to change the opinions of others;[5] and, of course, there will be other linguists who dispute this.[6] The situation resembles something that Gerd Gigerenzer noted about his fellow psychologists. He said that psychologists tend to treat theories rather like toothbrushes: no one likes to use someone else's.[7] It is the same with social scientists and their definitions of manipulation: each would prefer to use their own.

We have no intention of adding to this chaos of definitions. Regarding 'statistical manipulation', we stand in line with the distinguished statistician David Spiegelhalter, who declares: 'I feel that we should try to avoid giving yet more technical definitions to words in routine use'.[8] One problem with offering definitions of a phenomenon such as 'manipulation' is that the definition can be used to narrow the range of actions that are being examined. If we say that manipulation involves conscious lying, then we will be excluding someone whose skill rests in their ability to mislead without actually uttering a downright lie. Or if we say that statistical manipulation involves producing misleading numbers, then what of politicians who commission statisticians to produce the numbers, but do not produce the numbers themselves? If we define statistical manipulation too tightly, then practically all politicians will escape the charge of manipulating numbers, for they personally tend not to know enough statistics to be able to manipulate their own numbers.

Sometimes it is better to avoid oversimplifying a phenomenon with a strict definition, but, instead, to examine how that phenomenon might actually occur in all its complexity.[9] David Runciman takes this line in his excellent book on hypocrisy. He argues that 'hypocrisy comes in a variety of different forms which is why it is important to keep them separate rather

---

[5] Masia (2021); Didier Maillat (2013), 'Constraining context selection: on the pragmatic inevitability of manipulation', *Journal of Pragmatics*, 59, 190–99; Didier Maillat and Steve Oswald (2009), 'Defining manipulative discourse: the pragmatics of cognitive illusions', *International Review of Pragmatics*, 1, 348–70; Louis de Saussure (2013), 'Background relevance', *Journal of Pragmatics*, 59, 178–89.

[6] Sandrine Sorlin (2017), 'The pragmatics of manipulation: exploiting im/politeness theories', *Journal of Pragmatics*, 121, 132–46. See also: Paul Chilton (1990), 'Politeness, politics and diplomacy', *Discourse & Society*, 1, 201–24.

[7] Gerd Gigerenzer (2010), 'Personal reflections on theory and psychology', *Theory & Psychology*, 20, 733–43.

[8] David Spiegelhalter (2017), 'Trust in numbers', *Journal of Royal Statistical Society A*, 180 (Part 4), 949–65, p. 950.

[9] David Buss took a similar approach in relation to his studies of manipulation in close personal relationships. Rather working out from a definition of what really is interpersonal manipulation, he asked respondents what tactics they use to try to get their partners to do something. Then he listed the five most reported. See: Buss (1992); Buss et al (1987).

than lumping them all together'. Accordingly, he avoids providing 'a catch-all definition of what hypocrisy is, nor how it must relate to sincerity on the one hand or to lying on the other'.[10] Our tactic is to do something similar with regard to manipulation in general, and to the manipulation of statistics in particular.

One particular type of political manipulation that political scientists have studied is the manipulation of elections by political leaders. Because there are different ways to manipulate elections, Gregory Whitfield has argued that we should try to understand the varieties of political manipulation, rather than expecting all varieties to fit a common form.[11] Rather like statistical manipulation, political leaders cannot manipulate elections on their own but they will need to recruit willing helpers to do most of the dirty work, such as stuffing the ballot boxes, threatening potential opponents, making it dangerous for opposition parties to campaign, making it difficult for voters to vote for other parties and so on.[12] This means that those investigating electoral manipulation should be prepared to examine complex, interrelated and infinitely variable forms of behaviour.

We will try to bear this in mind when looking at politicians manipulating statistics. We do not begin with a definition and then decree what is a 'real' act of statistical manipulation and what is not. We start with a general, non-technical idea of what can be called 'statistical manipulation', and then we seek out examples to examine in detail. Hence, we proceed with a belief that examples may teach us more about the complex and infinitely variable world of the political manipulator than definitions will.[13]

Above all, we hope to be guided by Hannah Arendt's wise words. She suggested that if scholars want to increase their understanding of the world, they will not succeed by devising new, technical terminology, but they 'must become very humble again and listen closely to the popular language'.[14]

[10] David Runciman (2008), *Political Hypocrisy*, Princeton: Princeton University Press, p. 7.
[11] Gregory Whitfield (2022), 'On the concept of political manipulation', *European Journal of Political Theory*, 21, 783–807, p. 784.
[12] See, for example: Alberto Simpser (2014), *Why Governments and Parties Manipulate Elections*, Cambridge: Cambridge University Press; Waldemar Wojtasik (2019), 'Electoral manipulation via media: theory and evidence', *Communication Today*, 10(2), 28–40; Carlo M. Horz (2021), 'Electoral manipulation in polarized societies', *Journal of Politics*, 83, 483–97.
[13] Michael Billig (2019), *More Examples, Less Theory*, Cambridge: Cambridge University Press.
[14] Hannah Arendt (1994/1954), 'Understanding and politics', in Hannah Arendt (ed.), *Essays in Understanding, 1930–1954*, New York: Schocken Books, p. 311.

Three Brief Examples of 'Manipulating Statistics'

We will start with three brief examples to illustrate what might be meant by 'manipulating statistics'. In two of the examples the word 'manipulate' is used but in different senses. In the first example, which is taken from a newspaper report, the word is used to criticise the person doing the manipulating. In the third example, the word is used to praise. In the middle example, we are the ones who are using the word, and not in a complimentary way.

The British Politician Measuring the Nostalgia for
Non-metric Measurements

Our first illustrative example comes from recent British politics. It involves the Conservative government minister Jacob Rees-Mogg, who has a penchant for dressing and speaking in an outdated style, as if he were an actor playing the part of a bygone member of the English upper class. The example occurred in 2022 during the last year of Boris Johnson's premiership. Later, we will be discussing Boris Johnson's overly flexible approach to truth-telling and his use, or rather his misuse, of statistics.[15]

This episode only involves Johnson indirectly. Johnson and Rees-Mogg had closely cooperated during the successful referendum campaign of 2016 for Britain to leave the European Union. This success led to Johnson becoming the country's premier in 2019. Rees-Mogg received his reward for good service in February 2022 when Johnson promoted him to the cabinet to fill the newly created position of Minister of State for Brexit Opportunities and Government Efficiency – a position whose title sounds more like a campaign slogan than a traditional high office of state.

A major part of Rees-Mogg's ministerial role was to discover and to promote publicly the advantages of Britain leaving the European Union. One advantage of Brexit, according to Rees-Mogg, was that the country could free itself from the so-called tyranny of the European metric system and return to the old, supposedly much-loved imperial system of weights and measures – a return to pints, tons, feet, inches and so on. A survey was announced to 'test' attitudes about this 'Brexit bonus'. *The Observer*, a Sunday newspaper with a pro-European editorial stance, reported on the survey.[16]

---

[15] See below, Chapter 6.
[16] Jon Ungoed-Thomas (2022), 'Jacob Rees-Mogg's imperial measurements consultation "biased" after no option given to say no', *Observer*, 18 September, www.theguardian.com/politics/2022/sep/18/metric-system-imperial-measures-consultation-brexit.

According to the newspaper, one of the questions that respondents were to be asked was 'If you had a choice, would you want to purchase items: i) in imperial units ii) in imperial units alongside a metric equivalent.' Respondents were not offered a third answer: 'iii) in metric units'. Restricting answers to the first two alternatives would ensure that the results would be biased, because pro-metric respondents were excluded from using the formal possible answers. In response to questions put by the *Observer* journalist, officials from the government said that 'respondents who wanted to keep the current metric system could send in an email to the department or give their views in one of the text boxes in the survey'. The journalist declared the survey to be 'a nonsense' and asserted that the government was 'facing claims of manipulating questions to get [the] desired result from survey on "Brexit bonus"'.

Here was a particularly bad example of statistical practice, but, for our purposes, it was an excellent, illustrative example of statistical manipulation. The survey had been crudely designed to obtain the politically desired responses, and, when the individual answers were totted up, to obtain the politically desired statistics. Thus, the percentage of respondents supporting a return to the imperial systems of weights and measures was being methodologically boosted. Even the name of the survey, 'Brexit bonus', was politically biased. Any first-year undergraduate in the social sciences who was beginning a course on constructing questionnaires should be able to see what was wrong with this survey. They would probably fail their module if they couldn't. There again the survey's purpose was not scientific investigation; it was to create politically useful propaganda.

Little wonder, then, that the *Observer* described the government as 'manipulating' the survey. Any numerical results coming from the survey – such as the percentage of respondents wanting a return to the imperial system – would be the result of 'statistical manipulation'. If we had defined 'statistical manipulation' in terms of working on or calculating statistics in a devious manner, there would be no problem with describing the survey as an example.

But there would be a problem with describing Rees-Mogg as a statistical manipulator. He is unlikely to have personally formulated the Brexit survey's questions. He was the minister, not the minister's statistician. In fact, he did not physically have his own ministerial office, equipped with its own statisticians, because his office was situated in the prime minister's official residence in Downing Street. Many of the data analysts based in

Downing Street were not civil servants but were employed by the same private company, Data Science, that had been hired by the Brexit team during the referendum campaign.[17]

It is likely that these employees, who were experienced in using statistical skills for campaigning, did the business of framing the questions and devising the answer boxes, and then totting up the answers to show the proportion of respondents favouring a return to imperial measurements. If things happened in this way (and we do not know how they actually happened, because they occurred behind closed doors), then Rees-Mogg, or any politician in his position, would be able to disclaim, without directly telling a lie, that they had anything to do with any of the statistical manipulations that the *Observer* had rightly exposed as constituting such bad methodological practice. Probably Rees-Mogg did not need to manipulate his data analysts into devising such a flawed survey. Just half an ounce of a suggestion, and certainly not a kilogram of pressure, should have been sufficient to have set them working enthusiastically on their task.

The example highlights the difference between good and bad methodological practice. In the previous chapter we discussed William Farr's 'nosological' categories of disease. He was seeking to standardise the categories that medical doctors would use when officially giving causes of death on death certificates. Farr was not seeking to boost the numbers of one disease over another disease for political purposes. He was working to obtain as accurate a picture as possible and he knew that lives could depend on the accuracy of his work. Most importantly, Farr openly reported his reasons for constructing the categories as he did. He was not trying to hide his methodology behind closed doors.

Unlike the Brexit survey, Farr's nosology does not fit the late nineteenth-century adage that 'there are lies, damned lies and statistics'.[18] Significantly, the government never published the results of its Brexit bonus survey. Perhaps the *Observer* report showed how easy it was to point out the survey's faults, including its damned lies.

The President and His Favourite Map

It is probably no surprise that one of our three examples features the American president, Donald Trump, who has become known in some

---

[17] See below, Chapter 6.

[18] See: Joel Best (2001), *Damned Lies and Statistics*, University of California Press. Best shows why, in dismissing all statistics, the adage fails to identify actual statistical manipulation.

quarters of the press as 'the master manipulator'.[19] The example occurred about a year after Trump's presidential victory of 2016. Alberto Cairo describes it in the introductory chapter of his perceptive book about the ways that charts and diagrams can lie about the statistical information that they purport to depict.[20]

Although Trump had won the presidential election, he had obtained almost three million fewer votes in total than his opponent Hillary Clinton. Her percentage of the overall vote was two per cent higher than Trump's. This was possible because the American presidential election is not decided by the overall numbers of votes cast for each candidate. It is decided on the complicated electoral college system, based on the voting patterns within each state, with some states having more electoral college votes per head of population than others. Most states allot all the electoral college votes to the candidate who obtains the most votes within the state. A few divide up the college votes in proportion to the votes cast for each candidate. This means that it is possible for a candidate who wins the states with the greater number of college votes per head of population to win the overall presidential election despite receiving fewer votes across the whole country than their opponent.

Trump was irked by the fact that his opponent had received more votes than him.[21] He clearly wanted to believe that more Americans had voted for him than had voted for Clinton. A right-wing supporter had produced a map of America which appeared to show graphically that the country had voted for him. Most of America was coloured red (indicating areas of Republican/Trump support) with only small patches coloured grey (indicating areas of Democrat/Clinton support).[22] Trump began distributing copies of this map to journalists, and Cairo reports that Trump had a large framed copy of the map hanging in the West Wing of the White House.

The map was entitled 'Shares of vote in 2016 Presidential Election'. It was intentionally misleading, so much so that Cairo does not hesitate to

---

[19] For examples of 'the master manipulator' meme, see: Jordan Bates (2020), '12 psychological tactics Donald Trump uses to manipulate the masses', *High Existence*, 31 January, www.highexistence .com/12-psychological-tactics-donald-trump-uses-to-manipulate-the-masses/; Michael Kelly (2019), 'Donald Trump is a highly sophisticated master manipulator and a man motivated by division', *Irish Independent*, 28 June, 2019; Anna Skinner (2022), 'Trump's "complicated" tax records expose "alarming" hole in IRS', *Newsweek*, 22 December.

[20] Alberto Cairo (2020), *How Charts Lie*. New York: W. W. Norton.

[21] For more details of this, see the following chapter.

[22] Even the decision to depict Democrat support in grey, rather than in the customary blue, is strategic: grey is a less visually striking colour than blue, and certainly less striking than red. For a good discussion of the brightness of colour, see: Guy Deutscher (2011), *Through the Language Glass*. London: Arrow.

call it a lie. It seemed to show that the election result had been an overwhelming triumph for Trump. However, the map was based on the results for each county. By and large Trump's areas of victory at the sub-state or county level occurred in districts that were far less populated than the areas in which Clinton scored her victories. Clinton picked up many of her votes in densely populated cities. So, a map illustrating areas, not populations, that voted for the two candidates would show Trump conquering most of the land mass of the United States.

There would be nothing wrong with such a map had it been clearly and accurately labelled, but it was simply described as a representation of 'shares of the vote'. The unwary or enthusiastic Trump supporter could easily accept this as if it were a graphic representation of shares of the overall votes. No wonder Trump was pleased with the map: it was graphically misrepresenting, or manipulating, the shares of voting to suggest the untruth that Trump obtained an overwhelmingly higher proportion of the total popular vote.[23]

Trump had not devised and drawn up the map. The great manipulator was only distributing the graphically manipulated map: he had not personally invented the misleading labels and the colouring. This demonstrates something that we will be emphasising: namely, that statistical manipulation can be achieved verbally. The numbers can be correct, but what they are described as representing can be misleading. As we have seen, statistics are never just numbers; they are numbers which are said to be measuring particular phenomena. Consequently, you can manipulate statistics by mislabelling them, misleading people to think you are depicting one thing while you are actually depicting something else.

We can compare this map with the statistical charts that were pioneered in the nineteenth century. Florence Nightingale devised dramatic representations of the deaths in the British army. Her 'thin red line' showed graphically that the deaths of soldiers in peacetime Britain were greater in each age group than the average deaths of civilians. Nightingale had a political purpose behind her diagrams, for she sought to convince the army and the politicians to improve the sanitary conditions of the barracks. Nevertheless, she took care to ensure that her labels and titles were accurate just as she and Farr took care with the data they compiled about deaths in

---

[23] Alberto Cairo emphasises that Trump and the Republicans were not the only ones to present voting data in misleading charts and maps. He also gives examples of Democrats doing likewise for political advantage.

the army. It is true that she wanted her diagrams to shock the public, but only because the numbers in themselves were truly shocking.

Moreover, Nightingale fiercely criticised the statistics that the army had produced about deaths in Crimea. She pointed out discrepancies in the figures given about deaths on transport ships. The post-war figures were higher than those given by the surgeons serving on the ships at the time. She suspected that the post-war statistics had been 'dressed', which allowed the army to 'understate' the death figures in hospitals such as Scutari. As for using poor statistics for propaganda purposes, she dismissed an anonymous pamphlet which appeared to be a defence of the Army Medical Department, but which she said reproduced 'nearly every possible statistical blunder'.[24]

Her experiences of political and military pressures led Nightingale to champion independent statistics. The facts about statistical inconsistencies, not to mention statistical blunders committed to justify the unjustifiable, convinced her of the need to establish a military Statistical Department for the 'science of Sanitary statistics'.[25] By a Statistical Department, Nightingale meant an independent department that would be staffed by statisticians who would compile figures as accurately as possible. They would resist all pressure to 'dress' the numbers, or, as we would say today, to manipulate them.

The Statistician Claiming to Manipulate Data

The final example comes from a senior statistician claiming that modern statisticians are skilled at manipulating data. At the time of writing, Sir Ian Diamond holds the official post of being the United Kingdom's 'National Statistician'. In this role, he is the government's principal advisor on official statistics and also an advisor to the UK Statistics Authority (UKSA), whose official role is to oversee the quality of national statistics and to prevent their misuse (or what we are calling their 'manipulation'). In later chapters we will be looking in detail at the UKSA's role in combatting politicians who try to manipulate statistics.

One curious feature of the UKSA's battle against statistical manipulation is that its senior officers almost never use the words 'manipulation' or 'manipulate' in public, at least in the bad sense of the terms. They would

---

[24] Anonymous [Florence Nightingale] (1859), *A Contribution to the Sanitary History of The British Army During The Late War with Russia*, London: John W. Parker and Son, particularly pp. 4–6.

[25] Anonymous [Florence Nightingale] (1859), p. 12.

not in public accuse a politician of being a 'manipulator', let alone a 'master manipulator'. What they might say in private remains strictly private. Nevertheless, they do publicly use the phrase 'statistical manipulation' but in a positive sense. The Authority expects its senior statisticians to be experts in 'manipulating' statistics.[26]

In an interview, the national statistician was asked about changes in handling 'big data' over the course of his career. He replied that what we can now do on a smartphone is 'just unbelievable' compared with what could be done on computers when he was starting out as a statistician. He added: 'That means we can manipulate data in a way that we could only have dreamed of just a few years ago'.[27] He was not dreaming of misusing data. He was talking of handling data with scientific skill.

Positive Sense First

Whenever science advances dramatically, its vocabulary is likely to expand to keep pace with its discoveries and technical advances. New words will be invented and old words may acquire new meanings. The national statistician's comments might be thought to be an example of this. At the start of his career a statistician could only use machines for a limited number of tasks, so there would have been less need for a specific phrase to denote the handling of large data sets. As the handling of large data sets became available to every user of a mobile phone, and professional statisticians could work with enormous, complex data sets, then it is easy to imagine that the phrase 'manipulating data' could have been given a new and positive boost of meaning.

However plausible such an explanation might appear, it is incorrect. Previously, we chased the word 'statistics' back to its origins in the English language. Here we will do something similar for 'manipulate'. The *Oxford English Dictionary* is invaluable for giving the origins and different senses of words such as 'statistics' and 'manipulation'. Like 'statistics', 'manipulate' and 'manipulation' are not ancient terms but they entered the English language towards the end of the eighteenth century and became established in the first half of the nineteenth century. The words 'manipulate' and 'manipulation' came to English via French and are derived from the French word for hand (*main*), and ultimately from the Latin *manus*. The notion of statistical manipulation as *handling* large data sets fits well the etymological history of 'manipulation'.

---

[26] See below, p. 137.
[27] Sir Ian Diamond (2017), 'Ian Diamond: interview', *British Academy Review*, 31, 11–16, Autumn, www.thebritishacademy.ac.uk/documents/420/BAR31-03-Diamond.pdf.

The dictionary records several meanings of 'manipulation' and 'manipulate'. The two most prominent correspond to what could be said to be the positive and negative meanings of the words. What is interesting is that the positive sense is older than the negative. This is even true of the earliest, eighteenth-century uses of the words. The earliest use of 'manipulation' referred to a particular way of extracting silver from earth. This specific sense became obsolete in the early nineteenth century, when the meaning ceased to refer to a specific piece of machinery being used for a specific purpose but came to indicate handling things in general.

The positive sense was apparent because the general meaning of 'manipulate' meant more than just handling things, but handling them well. This positive meaning has persisted, as in its use by the British national statistician; and so has the connection with using the hands. Today the OED gives one sense of the verb 'manipulate', as to 'handle, especially with skill or dexterity' and 'to turn, reposition, reshape, etc., manually or by means of a tool or machine'. A nineteenth century example of this positive sense comes in the OED's illustrative quotation that skilled wood-turners 'can manipulate' the wood in their lathe. Today we see this positive sense reflected in the national statistician's comments, as he spoke approvingly about manipulating, or handling, large data sets.

There is also a therapeutic sense of the verb 'manipulated'. The OED quotes from the *British Medical Journal* of 1899, where an article declared that a skilled osteopath does not 'rub' or 'pat' their patients but 'manipulates' their bones. This positive, therapeutic sense has persisted: osteopaths still manipulate their patients' bones, and some doctors dextrously manipulate a patient's head to treat benign vertigo. *The Journal of Manipulative and Physiological Therapeutics* identifies itself as being dedicated to 'the advancement of health care principles and practices'.[28] No reputable social scientist would mistake the journal's focus or submit a paper which investigates how dictators manipulate their audiences by using dishonest techniques of persuasion.

Michael Faraday, the great chemist and pioneer of electromagnetism, deserves credit for establishing 'manipulation' in the English language in this positive sense. In 1827 he published a textbook for students entitled *Chemical Manipulation*.[29] He argued that chemistry and other empirical sciences comprised more than theories but are based on investigations and

---

[28] For the journal's aims and scope, see: www.jmptonline.org/content/aims.
[29] Michael Faraday (1827), *Chemical Manipulation: Being Instructions to Students in Chemistry*, London: W. Phillips.

demonstrations which need to be 'performed'. This performance 'may be properly enough expressed by the term "manipulation"'.[30] His textbook was devoted to showing the practical tasks required for such performances: how laboratories should be organised; how pieces of equipment should be operated; how they should be cleaned; the specific manual skills required for various demonstrations and so on.

Around the time that Faraday published his textbook, he delivered a series of lectures on manipulation to students. He apologised for using unfamiliar words but said that it was necessary: 'the word manipulation . . . though not usual in ordinary language, is so peculiarly expressive of the great object of these lectures, that I could not hesitate a moment to use it'. Faraday mentioned the etymological connection of 'manipulation' with *manus*, or hand, and said that this was entirely appropriate. By the term '*chemical manipulation* I wish you to understand that practice and habit of using the hands expertly in chemical investigation'.[31]

Faraday not only used 'manipulation' to denote his general topic of 'chemical manipulation', but he made subdivisions, such as 'pneumatic manipulation' which he used to describe the various practical and physical skills necessary for 'the management of gases'.[32] If different scientific skills and therapies can have their own forms of manipulation, then it is linguistically a short step from 'chemical manipulation' to 'pneumatic manipulation', and then to 'statistical manipulation'. However, this step was not taken immediately. There was to be a gap of some fifty years between Faraday's textbook and the phrase 'statistical manipulation' emerging in print.[33]

The phrase first appeared in 1878, in *A Manual of Anthropometry* by Charles Roberts, where it is used just once.[34] Roberts's book is a compilation of measurements of the human body, including skull measurements and claimed differences between races of the sort that would become politically notorious especially when used by fascists in the twentieth century. In an opening section, Roberts writes that he will be adopting

[30] Faraday (1827), p. iii.
[31] The quotation is taken from: Bence Jones (1870), *Faraday's Life and Letters*, vol. 1, London: Spottiswoode, p. 396, italics in original. Jones was quoting from Faraday's unpublished notes for the lectures.
[32] Faraday (1827), pp. 312ff.
[33] The OED does not give the first use of 'statistical manipulation' in English but English Corpora, using Google n-grams, notes the first use of the phrase in an English book, www.english-corpora .org/googlebooks/x.asp.
[34] Charles Roberts (1878), *A Manual of Anthropometry: a Guide to The Physical Examination and Measurement of the Human Body*, London: J. & A. Churchill, p. 26.

Quetelet's methods as 'the best' and 'only scientific method yet pro-
pounded' but he would be extending these methods because Quetelet
mostly used data from Belgians.[35]

Roberts declared that he would depart from Quetelet in another way.
He would be using feet and inches, not the metric measurements that
Quetelet used. Rees-Mogg would heartily approve. Roberts, however,
stated that he would not be using halves and quarters, as was customary
at that time, but he would be combining the decimal system of tenths with
the non-metric measures. He was doing this because 'the decimal system of
notation occupies less space in the chart, is most easily written down, and
is best adapted for subsequent arithmetical and *statistical manipulation*'.[36]

Here, in the first recorded English usage of 'statistical manipulation', the
author was using the term in a positive sense to mean the accurate,
scientific calculation of statistical data. In those days, calculation required
someone to laboriously write down the numbers to be added or subtracted,
and to write down the steps of calculation for the multiplication and
division of large numbers. To use Faraday's terminology, such calculations
would be manual tasks as well as mental ones. Following semantically in
the footsteps of Faraday, Roberts would have been confident that the
context in which he was using his new phrase would indicate that he
was describing something to be positively desired. Many years later
Diamond would likewise assume that his use of the same phrase would
not be misunderstood.

Routinely textbooks on methodology and statistics in psychology and
other behavioural sciences use the verb 'manipulate' and the noun
'manipulation' in this positive sense. *Research Methods and Statistics in
Psychology* is widely used by teachers of psychology in the USA and UK.
The book praises 'manipulation', especially when discussing experimen-
tation. The authors say that researchers in psychology achieve the 'goal of
science' when they 'manipulate variables in order to produce specific
behaviours'.[37] The spirit of Faraday is easy to detect: 'By controlling and

---

[35] Roberts (1878), p. 24. This may not have been entirely fair to Quetelet. True, he often used Belgian
data, but because of his influence in Belgium he was able to ensure the collection of the sort of data
that he required. In his *Treatise on Man*, Quetelet made good use of Scottish measurements,
particularly of chest girths: M. A. Quetelet (1842), *A Treatise on Man and the Development of his
Faculties*, Edinburgh: William and Robert Chambers.

[36] Roberts (1878), p. 26, emphasis added.

[37] Bernard C. Beins and Maureen A. McCarthy (2018), *Research Methods and Statistics in Psychology*,
second edition, Cambridge: Cambridge University Press, p. 12.

manipulating variables systematically, we can determine which variables influence behaviours that we are studying' (p. 158).[38]

Negative Sense Second

Today, the negative sense of 'manipulation' is the most popular sense of the word. When the journalist published his article criticising the Brexit bonus survey, he did not use the word to suggest that the survey was being conducted using all the correct scientific procedures. In ordinary language, if you say that someone manipulates people you are as likely as not to be criticising them, or at best grudgingly admiring them.[39] This might now be the primary meaning of the word but historically the negative sense entered English after the positive, scientific sense had been established. The OED defines this negative sense as: 'To manage, control, or influence in a subtle, devious, or underhand manner'. Only a technical statistician, using the phrase 'statistical manipulation', would mean something desirably scientific. The rest of us would use the phrase to indicate the illicit and non-scientific uses of statistical data.

The dictionary's earliest quotation of the negative meaning of 'manipulate' has a political dimension. It dates from 1862 and comes from Thomas Carlyle's history of Prussia. Carlyle was describing how a French diplomat, the Duke of Belleisle, cunningly intervened in the affairs of Prussia, having first got the 'electors manipulated, tickled to his purpose'.[40] Carlyle was suggesting that the Duke was deviously bending the electors to his political purposes. The OED illustrates this sense of 'manipulate' with other quotations, such as one from the psychoanalyst and social theorist Erich Fromm who, a century after Carlyle, referred to 'our thoughts, feelings and tastes manipulated by government and industry and the mass communications'.[41]

---

[38] Beins and McCarthy (2018), p. 158.
[39] See, for example: Bogdana Huma, Elizabeth Stokoe, and Rein Ove Sikveland (2021), 'Vocabularies of social influence: managing the moral accountability of influencing another', *British Journal of Social Psychology*, 60, 319–39. The researchers examine the moral implications of various words used in ordinary conversations to describe changes of opinion and they noted that speakers were reluctant to use 'manipulate' when talking about those that they knew.
[40] The OED makes a rare error in its citation for the quotation. The quotation comes in chapter xi of volume XII, not in chapter xi of volume III, of Carlyle's *History of Friedrich II of Prussia*.
[41] The full quotation is: 'the dreams of being independent masters of our lives ended when we began awakening to the fact that we have all become cogs in the bureaucratic machine with our thoughts, feelings and tastes manipulated by government and industry and the mass communications that they control': Erich Fromm (1979/2013), *To Have or to Be?*, London: Bloomsbury, p. 12.

The expansion of meaning from the positive sense to the negative was effected through a switch from the literal to the metaphorical. Faraday was predominately using 'manipulate' in a literal sense: hands were literally being used in many, if not most, of his tasks of chemical manipulation. He was saying that chemists quite literally need skills of handling equipment. By contrast, when Thomas Carlyle wrote that the Duke of Belleisle had manipulated and tickled the electors of Prussia, he was not saying that the Duke had literally gone round tickling or touching them. He had metaphorically handled them, or, rather, he had metaphorically mishandled them. In time, as this new meaning became established, so the negative meaning would come to be used literally. The reporter of the Brexit bonus survey was not saying that it was *as if* the data was being manipulated: he was saying that it *was* being manipulated.[42]

There is a further metaphorical element in the negative sense. In Fromm's quote, it is as if governments, industry and mass communications are not treating humans as humans, but instead they are using them as objects. Governments, industry and mass communications manipulate because they treat people like carpenters treat lumps of wood locked in their lathes: they are there to be controlled and shaped at will. What might be laudable in the handling of wood, chemicals and machinery becomes inappropriate in the handling of people.

The interests of lexicographers differ from those of social scientists. 'Manipulate', apart from its early, obsolete meanings, has been a transitive verb. In the earliest meanings, you did not need to specify what was being manipulated: if you said, 'the worker was manipulating' you would be understood by those in the mining business as referring to the extraction of silver using a particular piece of machinery. Today, you cannot just say that someone was manipulating – as a transitive verb, the word needs an object when it is used in the active voice. You need to specify who or what is being manipulated: you can't just manipulate.

The OED offers a number of examples where the object of 'manipulate' is information, rather than people. There is a quote from someone raising the possibility that a quotation has been manipulated; and from a speaker in the House of Commons saying that it might become possible for companies 'to manipulate their books'. The dictionary saw no reason to distinguish between the various objects of devious manipulation.

---

[42] The establishment of new literal senses of a word via metaphorical usage is a common occurrence. For a psychological analysis of this process, see: Sam Glucksberg (2001), *Understanding Figurative Language: from Metaphors to Idioms*, Oxford: Oxford University Press.

For social scientists the differences between manipulating people and information can be important for a simple reason. To adapt Faraday's terminology, performing these different forms of manipulation might involve the performance of very different sorts of action. For example, when Belleisle tickled and manipulated the electors of Prussia, he was manipulating them deviously through charm. The company director who is manipulating the company's books is not charming those books; nor does the person who manipulates a quotation for their own purposes charm the quotation. They may be using their manipulated information to persuade others deviously, even to charm them, but the actual manipulation of the information, including statistical information, involves very different kinds of action than directly manipulating people.[43] It is the same for someone who is able to manipulate a situation to their own advantage: there are as many ways of doing this as there are different sorts of situation, and many do not involve persuading anyone to change their opinion.[44]

There are also differences between an individual manipulating a quotation for their own interests and a company manipulating their books. The person who manipulates a quotation will be changing the words to suggest that the original speaker or writer was saying or implying something different from what they actually did.[45] When companies manipulate their book, numbers are at the centre of the action. This numerical manipulation is more like the statistical manipulations that we will be discussing, where official figures, including economic figures, are mishandled, mispresented or miscollected for political reasons. But, as we saw with our examples of the Brexit bonus survey or with Trump's red-covered map of the USA, it is never just a matter of numbers, for the numbers will be labelled. When companies manipulate their books, 'losses' may be turned into 'profits' or vice versa. Some numbers may disappear entirely, but none will be appearing in the books on their own without a verbal category. Thus, to manipulate the numbers is also to manipulate the categories.

There is another way that the manipulating of a company's books resembles the political manipulation of statistics. Both are likely to involve

---

[43] Michael Billig and Cristina Marinho (2017), *The Politics and Rhetoric of Commemoration*, London: Bloomsbury; Michael Billig and Cristina Marinho (2014), 'Manipulating information and manipulating people: examples from the 2004 Portuguese parliamentary celebration of the April Revolution', *Critical Discourse Studies*, 11, 158–74.

[44] William H. Riker (1986), *The Art of Political Manipulation*, New Haven: Yale University Press.

[45] Matthew S. McGlone (2005), 'Contextomy: the art of quoting out of context', *Media, Culture & Society*, 27, 511–22; see also the examples in Billig and Marinho (2014).

a team of professionals. The company, especially if it is a large one, will employ a team of auditors to prepare the books and maybe the directors will subtly convey to them the story that they would like the books to tell. The politician will enlist professional statisticians to do the numbers: we assume that Rees-Mogg was not personally compiling the data or composing the questions for the Brexit survey.

We will be arguing that the political manipulation of statistics typically involves an interrelated series of actions. It rarely consists of a single, isolated act, nor a single type of manipulative action. Politicians may manipulate statisticians, whether through charm, threats, etc.; statisticians may manipulate the numbers by mishandling the data and the labels; and politicians may seek to mislead their audiences with the help of their manipulated statistics. To produce the 'Brexit bonus' survey, the minister had to organise a team of statisticians who then devised and analysed the survey that was intended to produce statistics which the government would be able to use to mislead the public.

Faraday realised there was no single act of chemical manipulation, and he attempted to list some of its varieties. He appreciated that his list could never be complete – new discoveries would be made and there would always be new ways of performing old discoveries. No performance of a politician manipulating statistical information will be exactly like its predecessors. Each will have its own features, its individual political context and, above all, its specific combination of multiple actions. Even if social scientists want to compile a typology of all the different ways of manipulating statistics, they will need to observe individual episodes in their unique complexity.

Statistical Manipulation as a Research Practice

So far so good, one might think. There may be two very different meanings attached to 'manipulate', but in practice they will not be confused. The journalist criticising the Brexit survey and the national statistician were addressing two very different audiences and using their different senses in very different contexts. Sometimes two worlds can become intermixed. In the early years of the twenty-first century it became clear that many behavioural scientists were manipulating statistics in the bad sense of the term. The problem was so serious not because behavioural scientists were individually dishonest, but because the general research culture of the behavioural sciences was encouraging statistics to be widely manipulated.

David Spiegelhalter spoke perceptively about the problems in his 2017 presidential address to the Royal Statistical Society.[46] The crisis began in 2005 after an article had been published in a medical journal with the provocative title 'Why most published research findings are false'.[47] Part of the problem was that journals, especially in psychology but also in medical sciences, followed a policy of not publishing replications of already published studies, nor publishing studies which failed to find 'positive' results. Positive findings generally were those that were based on finding 'significant' statistical differences between the effects of variables that had been manipulated. 'Significant' normally meant that such statistical differences had a 5 per cent or less probability of being found by chance.

The result was that the magic 5 per cent levels of chance reported in the published studies could no longer be trusted. The practices that have come to be called 'p-hacking' (or probability hacking) were, for many years, standard ways for obtaining statistical results. Researchers, with the aim of producing publishable studies, would pack numerous testable measures into their research designs as an insurance policy in case their main hypotheses failed to produce significant differences. As Sir Ian Diamond said about the ease of analysing large data sets on mobile phones, hundreds of statistical tests can now be computed within minutes. If some of the secondary tests meet the probability level, then researchers can reconstruct their research reports around these findings, as if it had been their prime intention to test for the finding that they happened to find.

This was poor statistical practice because if you p-hack, then you are likely to obtain significant results by chance in 5 per cent of the statistical tests that you conduct. The problem was exacerbated because journals were not publishing replications and studies without significant results. This has led to what has been termed as 'the file drawer effect'.[48] Non-significant studies languishing in the bottom drawer cast doubt on the 'significant' findings published in the journals. If the unpublished, non-significant findings of essentially the same research were added to the

[46] Spiegelhalter (2017).
[47] John P. A. Ioannidis (2005), 'Why most published research findings are false', *PLOS Medicine*, 2, no. 8, article e124, https://doi.org/10.1371/journal.pmed.0020124.
[48] Megan L. Head, Luke Holman, Rob Lanfear, Andrew T. Kahn and Michael D. Jennions (2015), 'The extent and consequences of p-hacking in science', *PLOS Biology*, 13(3), e1002106, https://doi.org/10.1371/journal.pbio.1002106.

findings of the one published study, then the combined results would be unlikely to meet the statistical criteria for significance.[49]

The p-hacking scientists were not behaving dishonestly, but they were failing to question standard conventions of research. Stuart Ritchie, in his appropriately titled book *Scientific Fictions*, has claimed that the institutionalised procedures did not amount to 'outright fabrication and forgery', but something that was far more destructive of scientific integrity. The 'data manipulation' which behavioural scientists were practising was 'a sort of unconscious, or semi-conscious, massaging of data'.[50]

The more successfully that individual behavioural scientists obtained 'significant' results, the less likely they would be motivated to question the conventional practices. In consequence, there was 'statistical manipulation' in the negative sense without personal dishonesty but with personal ambition. It was a classic case of Campbell's law, which we have mentioned earlier.[51] A reasonable scientific measure of difference, namely a probability level of 5 per cent or less, was being corrupted because researchers were motivated to discover all sorts of ways to obtain research findings that met the magic criterion. They did this in order to publish in a culture of publish-or-die – not literally dying but metaphorically dying as a scientific researcher in the highly competitive world of modern science.

Here, we have been concentrating on statistical manipulation rather than open fabrication of results. However, it seems that the pressure to publish is encouraging scientific fraud, which is becoming an increasingly serious problem across the sciences, affecting physical, medical and behavioural sciences. *Nature* published a survey showing that even respectable journals are having to retract papers at a disturbing rate – that is, in effect, to admit that they are fraudulent and not to be trusted.[52] According to one distinguished neuroscientist, 'People are building careers on the back of this tidal wave of fraudulent science' and 'corruption is creeping into the system.'[53] If scientists are twisting their data and some are resorting to

[49] See: Spiegelhalter (2017) for a clear discussion of these issues.
[50] Stuart Ritchie (2020), *Scientific Fictions*, London: Vintage, p. 97. See also: Billig (2013), chapter 8, for a discussion why the routine statistical and rhetorical practices in psychology were leading to findings being systematically concealed and exaggerated.
[51] See above, pp. 24–5.
[52] Richard Van Noorden (2023), 'More than 10,000 research papers were retracted in 2023 – a new record', *Nature*, 624, 479–82, www.nature.com/articles/d41586-023-03974-8.
[53] Dorothy Bishop quoted in: Robin McKie (2024), '"The situation has become appalling": fake scientific papers push research credibility to crisis point', *Observer*, 3 February, www.theguardian.com/science/2024/feb/03/the-situation-has-become-appalling-fake-scientific-papers-push-research-credibility-to-crisis-point.

outright fabrication to advance their careers, then it is hardly surprising if we encounter politicians doing much the same.

Deception in Psychological Research

Alongside the corruption of statistics in the behavioural sciences, there is another related problem, especially in psychology: researchers have been manipulating and lying to those who participated in their research. If this seems to be taking us away from our central problem of statistical manipulation then please bear with us. Our diversion will lead back to one of our central themes: how to prevent statistical manipulation. First, we will see how not to prevent the manipulation of research participants. And that should set a negative example, telling us what we should not do if we want to prevent politicians from manipulating statistics.

One might expect that politicians will be constantly twisting the truth to their own advantage. As Hannah Arendt wrote: 'Truthfulness has never been counted among the political virtues, and lies have always been regarded as justifiable tools in political dealings'.[54] By contrast, truthfulness has always been counted among the scientific virtues. We would be shocked if we heard that Faraday manipulated the truth as freely as he manipulated his chemical equipment. In one recent survey, 74 per cent of respondents said that they would trust scientists, while only 9 per cent indicated that they would trust politicians.[55]

However, the behaviour of many behavioural scientists puts that trust in question. Experimental psychologists may claim to manipulate their variables and take this as a sign that they are following the procedures of science. But they also manipulate (in the bad sense) their participants, lying to them about the nature of the research before the study and lying to them during the research as they are manipulating (in the good sense) their variables. Some of the most famous and widely cited experiments in social psychology have involved experimenters telling their participants untruths.[56] It has been hard to calculate exactly the extent of deception

[54] Hannah Arendt (1967/1977), 'Truth and politics', in Hannah Arendt (ed.), *Between Past and Future*, Harmondsworth: Penguin, pp. 223–59, quote: p. 223.

[55] IPSOS (2023), 'Trust in politicians reaches its lowest score in 40 years', www.ipsos.com/en-uk/ipsos-trust-in-professions-veracity-index-2023.

[56] This includes the famous Milgram experiment in which participants were induced to deliver what they thought to be dangerous electric shocks to a victim; the Asch experiment on conformity; the Sherifs' experiment on inducing intergroup hostility; and Zimbardo's prison experiments in which participants acting as guards mistreated the participants acting as prisoners. For critical studies of the

in social psychological experiments, but, at a conservative estimate, it appears that the figures have consistently been over 50 per cent.[57] According to Alan Kimmel, the proportion may in fact be higher because investigators have tended only to include experiments with 'active deception' – those are experiments in which experimenters tell their participants downright untruths. However, as Kimmel suggests, this ignores experiments with 'passive deception' which occurs when experimenters deliberately mislead participants without actually telling them lies. As Kimmel puts it: 'with passive deception, a lie is not told; rather, a truth is left unspoken'.[58] If both forms of deception are taken into account, then between 60 and 70 per cent of research publications in social psychology use deception in one form or another.[59]

The distinction between active and passive deception is important for understanding how manipulating the truth might be seen to differ from downright lying. The word 'manipulate', in its negative sense, can cover cases where someone misleads by deviously implying an untruth without actually uttering that untruth. Some have said that this is the primary meaning of 'manipulation'.[60] The person who designed Trump's beloved

---

deception in these classic experiments, see: Diana Baumrind (2015), 'When the subjects become objects: the lies behind the Milgram legend', *Theory & Psychology*, 25, 690–95; Peter Lunt (2009), *Stanley Milgram*, London: Palgrave Macmillan; Stephen Gibson (2019), *Arguing, Obeying and Defying*, Cambridge: Cambridge University Press; Gina Perry (2013), 'Deception and illusion in Milgram's accounts of the obedience experiments', *Theoretical & Applied Ethics*, 2(2), 79–92; David Kaposi (2022), 'The second wave of critical engagement with Stanley Milgram's "obedience to authority" experiments: What did we learn?', *Social and Personality Psychology Compass*, https://doi .org/10.1111/spc3.12667; Gina Perry (2018), *The Lost Boys*, London: Scribe; Thibault le Texier, (2018). *L'histoire d'un mensonge*, Paris: La Découverte.

[57] There are differing figures about the exact percentages of social psychology experiments using deception and whether there has been a decline in recent years. One study suggests that the highest figures came in 1975 when 69 per cent of studies used deception: Romeo Vitelli (1988), 'The crisis issue assessed: an empirical analysis', *Basic and Applied Social Psychology*, 9, 301–9. For other estimations and discussions of the use of deception see: Allen, J. Kimmel (2001), 'Ethical trends in marketing and psychological research', *Ethics & Behavior*, 1, 131–49; Sandra D. Nicks, James H. Korn and Tina Mainieri (1997), 'The rise and fall of deception in social psychology and personality research, 1921 to 1994', *Ethics & Behavior*, 7, 69–77; Ralph Hertwig and Andreas Ormann (2008a), 'Deception in social psychological experiments: two misconceptions and a research agenda', *Social Psychology Quarterly*, 71, 3, 222–7; Ralph Hertwig and Andreas Ortmann (2008b), 'Deception in experiments: revisiting the arguments in its defence', *Ethics and Behaviour*, 18, 59–92; James, H. Korn (1997), *Illusions of Reality*, Albany: State University of New York Press.

[58] Allen J. Kimmel (2012), 'Deception in research', in S. J. Knapp (ed.), *APA Handbook of Ethics in Psychology*, vol. 2, APA: Washington DC, p. 402. See also: Benjamin E. Hilbig, Isabel Thielmann and Robert Böhm (2021), 'Bending our ethics code: avoidable deception and its justification in psychological research', *European Psychologist*, 27, 62–70.

[59] Kimmel (2001); Allen J. Kimmel (2011), 'Deception in psychological research – a necessary evil?', *The Psychologist*, 24, 580–85.

[60] See: Masia (2021); Maillat (2013); Didier Maillat and Oswald (2009); de Saussure (2013).

electoral map did not actually specify that the colours represented the overall number of voters, but they were misleading people to think that is what the colouring of the map meant.

In *Chemical Manipulation*, Faraday never considered the possibility that scientific manipulation could be routinely put into practice by devious and dishonest manipulation. Sometimes the lies themselves involve numbers and statistics. To give an example from a short study of persuasion, which was published in a major journal:[61] the authors used the noun 'manipulation' twenty-seven times, always in the positive sense. They did not use the words 'deceit', 'deception' or 'mislead', even when describing how they deceived and manipulated and misled their participants. They gave the participants 'false feedback' about whether they had changed their opinions during the experiment and whether other participants had done so. The falsities included fake numbers about fake research results. Some of the participants were informed that the results had shown that 88.6 per cent of people had changed their opinions during the experiment; and some of the participants were told that 12.2 per cent changed their opinions. The numbers were fake and had been decided upon before the study had started. Changing the false number was one of their experimental manipulations.

Opposing Manipulation and Deceit

Learned societies in psychology, such as the American Psychological Association (APA), seem to officially discourage, or even forbid, psychologists from using deceit in the conduct of their research. The APA's 'Ethical Principles of Psychologists and Code of Conduct' states in its subsection on Deception in Research: 'Psychologists do not conduct a study involving deception unless they have determined that the use of deceptive techniques is justified by the study's significant prospective scientific, educational, or applied value and that effective nondeceptive alternative procedures are not feasible'.[62]

Some psychologists have pointed to the discrepancy between the Code and the routine use of deception in published research.[63] They ask how this is possible. Clearly the Code is being bent, being manipulated. But this was always likely to happen because the Code was so worded that,

---

[61] Zakary Tormala, Victoria L. DeSensi, Joshua J. Clarkson and Derek D. Rucker (2009), 'Beyond attitude consensus: the social context of persuasion and resistance', *Journal of Experimental Social Psychology*, 45, 149–54.

[62] American Psychological Association (2017), 'Ethical Principles of Psychologists and Code of Conduct, Including 2010 and 2016 Amendments', www.apa.org/ethics/code#304. See particularly subsection 8.07: Deception in Research.

[63] Benjamin E. Hilbig et al. (2021); Hertwig and Ormann (2008a).

while appearing to discourage deceit in theory, it was permitting it to occur in practice. The Code justified using deceit if a study had 'significant prospective scientific, educational, or applied value'.[64] Every researcher is likely to believe that their own research will have significant scientific value, especially before they conduct the research. Who is going to say of their research 'I would like to give my participants some "false feedback"; it would make my manipulations so scientific; but really the whole project is so insignificant that I hesitate to do so'?

The discussions about the extent of deceit in psychological research, the crisis about the routine misuse of statistics in the behavioural sciences and also the updating of the APA's code of research practice in 2010 and 2016 were all taking place around the same time. This was the time when the regulatory bodies for official statistics were being established in both Britain and France. Later, we will be discussing these bodies and praising their attempts to expose and prevent the manipulation of official statistics.

When we discuss how these bodies were established, one thing emerges with clarity. They were intended to be independent bodies that made independent judgements. The regulatory bodies aimed to protect official statisticians from being manipulated by politicians, especially statisticians working in government ministries. They were not trade associations which were expected always to speak up on behalf of statisticians. If official statisticians produced poor statistics, the independent regulatory bodies would be expected to say so.

In short, the regulatory bodies were to be independent of those whom they regulated. The APA's Code of Conduct illustrates the weakness of self-regulation. Its prohibitions of deceit in research have had little effect on the level of deceit published in journals. The prohibitions are phrased with a huge proviso that allows the practice of deceit and the manipulation of participants. Researchers who practice deceit in the conduct of their research can always say in their own defence, especially to ethics commit-tees in their own university: 'I am following the APA's rules which permit deceit in this type of research.' We could say that the APA's rules are not only self-regulatory but they are self-manipulatory.

---

[64] Similar combinations of broad principles against deception, together with permissions to use deception in the cause of science can be found in other codes of psychology. See for example: British Psychological Society (2021), '7. Deception', *Code of Human Research Ethics*, p. 23. The BPS code also distinguishes between deliberately deceiving participants as compared with just keeping information from them, which is not identified as a form of deception or manipulation.

CHAPTER 4

Donald Trump
Master Manipulator

Sometimes journalists refer to Donald Trump as 'the master manipulator'. Popular magazines will publish semi-academic pieces which try to elucidate the master manipulator's manipulative skills. The writers even show a hint of admiration. Who would not envy someone who can set millions of people to think in his way and who is utterly unburdened by inhibition? In these lists, the skills of statistical manipulation do not sit alongside his considerable skills of manipulating people. No one thinks that Trump's forte is to be deftly devious with numbers.

He is known, especially by his political opponents, to be careless with the truth. The *Washington Post* kept a log on Trump's truthfulness during his presidency. It estimated that the president made 30,573 false or misleading claims and that his rate of telling untruths increased exponentially, from about six a day in 2017 to twenty-two a day in 2019.[1] Many of Trump's misleading claims made use of misleading numbers, but we are not going to attempt to track all of those instances.

Joel Best, a long-established and scholarly analyst of statistical manipulation, has written perceptively about the 'lies' that Trump told about Covid statistics.[2] There is no need for us to repeat here what Best has already done, and done well. Best connects the Trump administration's persistent and self-interested underestimation of deaths caused by Covid to Campbell's law about the corruption of statistical methods, which we discussed in Chapter 2.[3] Instead, we will concentrate on three topics which

---

[1] Glenn Kessler, Salvador Rizzo and Meg Kelly (2021), 'Trump's false or misleading claims total 30,573 over 4 years', *Washington Post*, 21 January; Glenn Kessler, Salvador Rizzo and Meg Kelly (2020), *Donald Trump and His Assault on Truth*, New York: Scribner.

[2] Joel Best (2021), 'How to lie with Coronavirus statistics: Campbell's Law and measuring the effects of COVID-19', *Numeracy*, 14, https://digitalcommons.usf.edu/numeracy/vol14/iss1/art6/. For a compilation of original documents, see: Jon Sternfield (2020), *Unprepared: America in the Time of Coronavirus*, New York: Bloomsbury.

[3] See above, pp. 24–5.

show up Trump's attitude towards statistics: the election that he won, unemployment figures and the election that he lost. Taken together these will show three key aspects of the way Trump mishandles numbers.

First, Trump believes that it is others – namely those who work in what he calls the 'phoney media' – who manipulate numbers. He sees himself as only trying to quote the 'real' numbers, whether these are the numbers of his own votes, the number of Covid victims or the rate of unemployment. Second, he gets these 'real' numbers from others, particularly from those on the outer edges of politics where conspiracy theories and other wild claims circulate unchecked. And third, there is Trump's own personal lack of restraint, including his tendency to deceive himself and to flatter himself.

By looking at particular examples, we will see Trump's hunger for numbers that fit his perspective, political interests and personal idiosyncrasies. In many ways he is the personification of manipulation freed from restraint. As far as statistical manipulation is concerned, he represents manipulation unbound.

An Election Won

Something curious happened less than three weeks after the 2016 US presidential election. The results of the election, which had been held on 8 November, were clear. According to the electoral rules, Donald Trump was the winner. As we saw previously, one aspect of the results rankled with him: his opponent gained almost three million votes more than he did. Because of the US's complicated electoral system, Clinton had gained her votes in the 'wrong' states, where large majorities brought no more Electoral College votes than small majorities would have done.

That was the end of the matter for the defeated candidate, but it wasn't for the victorious one. Several months into his presidency he was handing out maps of the United States which were principally coloured Republican red. The map was misleading, as we explained in the previous chapter.[4] On 27 November, after the election but before ascending to the presidency, Trump tweeted: 'In addition to winning the Electoral College in a landslide, I won the popular vote if you deduct the millions of people who voted illegally.'[5]

---

[4] See above, pp. 45–8.

[5] Donald J. Trump @realDonaldTrump (2016), X (formerly Twitter), 27 November, https://twitter.com/realDonaldTrump/status/802972944532209664. The tweet was widely reported on news channels and in newspapers. See, for example: CNN: Tom LoBianco, (2016), 'Trump falsely claims "millions of people who voted illegally" cost him popular vote', 28 November, https://edition.cnn.com/2016/11/27/politics/donald-trump-voter-fraud-popular-vote/index.html.

The description of his comparatively narrow Electoral College victory as a 'landslide' was stretching a point. Trump's comment about winning the popular vote is intriguing. He was not citing any evidence in his tweet. Nor was he using precise numbers. He was using the imprecise 'millions of people' which conveyed the rhetorical effect of 'hugeness'.[6] The president-elect was implying that there had been huge electoral fraud.

After Trump's tweet, several fact checkers traced the origins of his claim. The immediate source is disturbing. A few days before Trump's tweet the conspiracy broadcaster Alex Jones alleged on his radio programme *Infowars* that Trump won more votes than Clinton. Jones did not give a source for his claim, but fact checkers traced it to a right-winger called Gregg Phillips. When Phillips was asked to provide his evidence, he declined the invitation.[7] Before the election Trump had declared: 'I'm afraid the election is going to be rigged'.[8] This also followed a prior claim that Jones had made on *Infowars*.[9]

Alex Jones has been spreading his far-right conspiracy theories for a good number of years. He achieved particular notoriety for asserting that the 2010 massacre of twenty children at the Sandy Hook School in Connecticut never happened and that the parents had 'faked' their children's deaths. That led to the parents taking Jones to court. In November 2022 a Connecticut judge ordered Jones to pay punitive damages of $473 million on top of a judgement the previous month of almost one billion dollars against him.[10] Daniel Hellinger has written about Trump's attraction to conspiracy theories. He says that Trump did not create the environment in which conspiracy theorists flourish 'but he knew how to exploit' their ideas.[11]

---

[6] Michael Billig (2021), 'Uses of precise numbers and semi-magical round numbers in political discourse about Covid-19: examples from the government of the United Kingdom', *Discourse & Society*, 32, 542–58; Brendan T. Lawson (2023), *The Life of a Number*, Bristol: Bristol University Press.

[7] Andrew Restuccia (2016), 'Trump's baseless assertions of voter fraud called "stunning"', *Politico*, 27 November, www.politico.com/story/2016/11/trump-illegal-voting-clinton-231860; Arnie Seipel (2016), 'Trump makes unfounded claim that "millions" voted illegally for Clinton', *NPR*, 27 November, www.npr.org/2016/11/27/503506026/trump-makes-unfounded-claim-that-millions-voted-illegally-for-clinton.

[8] BBC News (2016), 2 August, www.bbc.co.uk/news/election-us-2016-36950083. Among the many newspaper reports of Trump's tweet, see: Reid J. Epstein (2016), 'Donald Trump: "I'm afraid the election is going to be rigged"', *Wall Street Journal*, 2 August.

[9] BBC News (2016), 2 August. The news also reported that Trump around this time had repeated Jones's description of Clinton as 'the devil'. See also: Reid J. Epstein (2016).

[10] Reuters (2022), 'Infowars host Alex Jones ordered to pay $473m more to Sandy Hook families', *Guardian*, 10 November, www.theguardian.com/us-news/2022/nov/10/alex-jones-conspiracy-theorist-sandy-hook-victims-hoax.

[11] Daniel C. Hellinger (2019), *Conspiracies and Conspiracy Theories in The Age of Trump*, Cham, Switzerland: Palgrave Macmillan, p. 82. For a general discussion of conspiracy theories, see: Jovan Byford (2011), *Conspiracy Theories*, Basingstoke: Palgrave Macmillan.

Nevertheless, what Trump did was strange. He had won the election and there was nothing more for him to gain on that front. When he claimed before the election that the results would be rigged, the polls were predicting a Clinton victory. So, Trump could have been preparing the ground to dispute a defeat. But after a victory? It didn't make much political sense. Besides he should have had more important things to think about, as he prepared himself to take the highest office in the land and arguably in the democratic world.

Deceiving Others or Deceiving Himself

A politician, who says something that is at variance with truth is not necessarily lying. It is possible to genuinely believe something that turns out to be false. Some philosophers claim that liars know when they are telling a lie because to lie is to intentionally deceive someone else.[12] Trump might know whether he genuinely believed that his votes in the 2016 election topped Clinton's, at least when her 'phoney' votes were subtracted. But the rest of us cannot know for certain. We have no access to his hidden thoughts. Even those who know Trump well and have worked closely with him can be unsure at times whether he truly believes what he says.

After the 2020 presidential election, which Trump lost to Biden, Trump vociferously and endlessly claimed that the election had been rigged and that he was the real winner. William Barr, Trump's former attorney general and loyal supporter, gave testimony to a closed session of the congressional inquiry that had been established to investigate Trump's responsibility for his supporters storming the Capitol in the hope of preventing the election result from being officially certified.[13] Barr told the inquiry that he repeatedly told Trump that his claims about the election were without foundation. According to Barr, Trump would become 'indignant' when he was contradicted. Barr reported: 'I was somewhat demoralized, because I thought, boy, if he really believes this stuff . . . he's become detached from reality.'[14] Even the president's close

---

[12] Sam Harris (2013), *Lying*, Opelousas, Louisiana: Four Elephants Press. Harry Frankfurt makes a similar point in his book on bullshitting: Harry G. Frankfurt (2005), *On Bullshit*, Princeton: Princeton University Press.

[13] For a discussion of 'stochastic terrorism' and the links between violent political language and violent actions, see: Kurt Braddock (2020), *Weaponized Words*, Cambridge: Cambridge University Press.

[14] Joan E. Greve (2022), 'Top aides repeatedly told Trump fraud claims were baseless, Jan 6 panel hears', *Guardian*, 13 June, www.theguardian.com/us-news/2022/jun/13/jan-6-house-committee-second-hearing-conspiracy-theories.

colleague could not tell whether Trump truly believed what he was saying or whether he was just using implausible theories as a means to have the results overturned. If Barr could not tell, then the rest of us should hesitate before claiming that we can read Trump's mind.

In the case of Trump, there is another possibility between deceitful lying and truthful belief: self-deceit. Perhaps Trump is a deceiver who is his own victim. Self-deceit seems complex, perplexing and yet thoroughly familiar. What if Trump is lying to convince himself that he is not lying? Was Trump, by hanging his favourite map so prominently in the White House, trying to convince himself that he really was the most popular politician in the United States? Surely those who voted for his opponent could not be proper Americans. By repeating the untruth was he trying to push from his own mind the troubling thought that his defeated opponent – the one who, in rally after rally, he said should be locked up – was really more popular than himself? For Trump, it must have been unthinkable.

Perhaps self-deceit is not particularly rare, being a form of repression by which uncomfortable thoughts are pushed from the mind.[15] And perhaps the political world is particularly prone to self-deceit. In modern times, politicians have to say so much and none want to believe that they are habitual liars. Self-deceit offers them a cheap shortcut to believing in their own honesty. Hannah Arendt, who understood more than a little about politicians and their lies, had interesting things to say about self-deceit. When politicians constantly have to adjust themselves and their fabrications to ever-changing circumstances, as happens so frequently in modern democratic conditions, then, according to Arendt, 'deception without self-deception' becomes 'well-nigh impossible'.[16]

Yet, in another regard, Trump is an extreme case, lacking the embarrassment and constraint to conceal his self-deceit. Some political analysts have alleged that flattery is a constant feature of political life, both in the past and present. Flattery is more than exaggerated praise, for the flatterer seeks to manipulate those whom they flatter.[17] Roni Danziger, an Israeli social scientist, notes that flatterers are engaged in something devious and self-interested for they hope to benefit from their exaggerated praise; but of

---

[15] For such a view of repression and self-persuasion, see: Michael Billig (1999), *Freudian Repression*, Cambridge: Cambridge University Press; Michael Billig, (2019), *More Examples, Less Theory*, chapter 4, Cambridge: Cambridge University Press.
[16] Hannah Arendt, (1967/1977), 'Truth and politics', in Hannah Arendt (ed.), *Between Past and Future*. Harmondsworth: Penguin. pp. 223–59; quote: p. 251.
[17] According to one analyst, flattery is praising in order to receive something in return: Willis Goth Regier (2007), *In Praise of Flattery*, Lincoln: University of Nebraska Press.

course they cannot reveal this to those whom they are praising.[18] Danziger cites the case of a junior minister in Binyamin Netanyahu's government who continually praised her leader in exaggerated terms: 'You are a great leader, even though some people in this country don't like to say so . . . but the truth must be told, you deserve this to be told'.[19]

This sort of excessive praise is recognisable in Trump's discourse, but with a difference: Trump's object of praise is not a political senior, but himself. Often he declares himself not just to be good at something, but to be the best ever: 'I'm the most transparent President in history'; 'no President has ever worked harder than me'; 'we've achieved more in this month alone than almost any President has achieved in eight years in office'; 'I have the greatest economy in the history of this country'; 'I am the least racist person there is anywhere in the world'; and the statistically impossible 'I've completed more promises than I've made'.[20]

Unsurprisingly, Trump is not shy about quoting praise from others. During a press conference held late September 2018 in advance of the impending G20 Summit, the president was talking about China and his good relations with President Xi. He quoted Michael Pillsbury, the veteran Washington right-wing commentator who was developing a growing fondness for conspiracy theories. Trump told journalists that he had heard Pillsbury saying that 'China has total respect for Donald Trump and for Donald Trump's very, very large brain'.[21]

Is Trump trying to persuade others of his very, very large brain and being the hardest working president in history – especially since critics have publicly claimed the opposite? And is he also persuading himself, turning any self-doubt into self-flattery, thereby deceiving himself? Just by

[18] Roni Danziger (2020), 'The pragmatics of flattery: the strategic use of solidarity-oriented actions', *Journal of Pragmatics*, 170, 413–25; Roni Danziger (2021), 'The democratic king: the role of ritualized flattery in political discourse', *Discourse & Society*, 32, 645–65; Zohar Kampf and Roni Danziger (2019), '"You dribble faster than Messi and jump higher than Jordan": the art of complimenting and praising in political discourse', *Journal of Politeness Research*, 15, 1–23.

[19] Danziger (2021), p. 651. It has been argued that strong male leaders are particularly prone to flattery, thereby possibly revealing their underlying weaknesses: Anne Applebaum (2020), *Twilight of Democracy*, London: Allen Lane; Ruth Ben-Ghiat (2020), *Strongmen*, London: Profile Books.

[20] Kessler et al. (2020), pp. 41–5 and 163. For the 'least racist' boast, see: *Guardian Video* (2019) 30 July, www.theguardian.com/us-news/video/2019/jul/30/trump-claims-least-racist-person-in-the-world.

[21] For a video of these comments, see: the BBC News (2018), 27 September, www.bbc.co.uk/news/av/world-us-canada-45664690. For an analysis and background information on Michael Pillsbury, see: Ben Schreckinger and Daniel Lippman (2018), 'The China hawk who captured Trump's "very, very large brain"', *Politico*, 2 February, www.politico.com/story/2018/11/30/trump-china-xi-jinping-g20-michael-pillsbury-1034610.

watching 'the very, very large brain' video, we cannot tell. But there is another video of public self-praise which is a bit more revealing.

In September 2018 Trump addressed the United Nations.[22] He began by recounting how the previous year he had warned the UN of the threats facing 'our world'. Wearing his most serious face, Trump said he now stood before the United Nations 'to share the extraordinary progress we've made'. Then, still with his serious face, he continued: 'In less than two years my administration has accomplished more than almost any administration in the history of our country'.

He uttered another word – 'America's' – but then was distracted as an audible rumble of laughter spread across the auditorium. Trump showed none of the behaviour expected of a person who is being laughed *at*, rather than being laughed *with*. He gave his first smile of the speech as he paused and said 'so true', as if agreeing with the laughers. Someone who believes that they are being laughed *at* is likely to go serious and maybe forcefully, even aggressively, restate the opinion that was being mocked. Or a speaker might just grimly continue, ignoring the mockery, as did Sergei Lavrov, the Russian foreign minister in 2022 when addressing an international gathering shortly after Russian forces invaded Ukraine. He had just mentioned 'the war, which we are trying to stop, which was launched against us', when the rumble of laughter spread.[23]

Henri Bergson wrote that laughter can demand a 'momentary anaesthesia of the heart'.[24] Trump seemed to have spontaneously assumed that the laughing audience could not have possibly anaesthetised their hearts against him, not even momentarily. 'Didn't expect that reaction but that's OK,' he declared next, with his smile becoming even wider. Trump was displaying no recognition that parts of the audience might have been mocking his implausible bragging.

He was giving signs of protective self-deception. It was as if he believed that some of the foreigners in the audience had unexpectedly shown their agreement by laughing happily, and now he was agreeing with them. His facial expression, bodily stance and words ('but that's OK') show that his spontaneous reaction was not a fabricated deceit. If there was deceit, it was Trump deceiving himself. Then he continued with the statement that he

---

[22] Full videos are available on YouTube, for example: www.youtube.com/watch?v=-z4y8OJxlK8.
[23] Lavrov did not smile or say 'so true', but he continued, grim faced, ignoring the laughter: www.bbc .co.uk/news/av/world-europe-64848508.
[24] Henri Bergson (1900), *Laughter*, London: Macmillan, p. 5.

had started. It was another boast: 'America's economy is booming like never before. . .' This time there was no laughing.

Self-flattery is troublesome concept. The self-flatterer has to provide the flattery that the flattered self desperately wishes to hear, but the self-flatterer cannot openly admit to others or to themselves that this is their wish. If flattery is a form of manipulation, then self-flattery must also be a strange form of manipulation – the manipulation of the self by the self, maintained, as Trump showed at the UN, by a protective wall of self-deceit. No wonder some found Trump's UN performance extraordinarily funny. There is no contradiction in finding it hilarious and deeply disturbing.

Manipulating Statistics: What It Means According to the Trumps

After a brief diversion into the darker depths of self-deception, it is now back to the manipulation of statistics and how Trump has put the manipulation of statistics to work in the interest of political advantage, as well as self-deceit and self-flattery. The first issue is not that Trump personally manipulates statistics or that he takes up the manipulations of others, but that he has a very ordinary concept of what it means to manipulate statistics, or, in his words, to produce 'phoney numbers'.

Perhaps the clearest account of Trump's concept of statistical manipulation has been provided by his loyal eldest son, Donald Trump Junior. At the time of writing Donald Junior is the executive vice-president of the Trump Foundation. His political views are similar to those of his father – certainly no milder. He actively campaigned for his father in the successful 2016 presidential campaign and in the unsuccessful 2020 one. As soon as the 2020 results were declared, Donald Junior was voicing his father's view that the election had been stolen. Donald Junior tweeted: 'The best thing for America's future is for Donald Trump to go to total war over this election to expose all of the fraud, cheating, dead/no longer in state voters, that has been going on for far too long.'[25] 'Total war' says much about the son's politics.

The example of Trump Junior's idea of statistical manipulation comes from the 2016 campaign, when he was discussing the official unemployment statistics for the USA. For a good number of years, Donald Senior had been dismissing the unemployment figures that the Bureau of Labor

---

[25] Chantal da Silva (2020), '"Reckless" and "stupid": Trump Jr calls for "total war" over election results', *Independent*, 6 November, www.independent.co.uk/news/world/americas/us-election-2020/trump-jr-election-results-war-b1634841.html. Da Silva reports that the post was quickly hidden by Twitter, which warned that 'some or all of the content shared in this Tweet is disputed and might be misleading about an election or other civic process'.

Statistics (BLS) regularly publishes. The Bureau describes itself as 'the principal fact-finding agency in the broad field of labor economics and statistics and serves as part of the US Federal Statistical System'.[26]

The Bureau's unemployment figures were comparatively low during the Obama administration. Again and again, Donald Senior indicated that he did not believe the Bureau's numbers. The *Washington Post* documented nineteen separate occasions when Trump had dismissed the BLS numbers: they were 'phoney numbers' (September 2012); 'unemployment is a totally phoney number' (May 2014); 'phoney statistics' (August 2015), and so on.[27]

Sometimes Trump compared the phoney numbers with the 'real' ones: 'Our real unemployment is anywhere from 18 to 20 per cent. Don't believe the 5.6. Don't believe it.' (June 2015). In September 2015, he said that he had seen figures of 24 and 42 per cent unemployed.[28] In a talk given to the Detroit Economic Club in August 2016, Trump said that 'one in five American households do not have a single member in the labour force' and that these are 'the real unemployment numbers'.[29]

Such categorical assertions about 'phoney' and 'real' figures do not provide any indication how the apparent manipulation of unemployment statistics might have occurred. Donald Junior, however, was more specific in an interview that he gave to CNN in July 2016.[30] He was asked about his father's views on the Bureau's unemployment figures. In criticising the official unemployment figures for being too low, the son indicated how the statistical error occurred: 'The way we actually measure unemployment is after x number of months if someone can't find a job, congratulations, they're miraculously off' and 'that doesn't count' in the unemployment numbers.

In other words, if someone who has been classified as unemployed cannot find a job within 'x' number of months, then they are removed from the figures of the unemployed. Donald Junior continued: 'These are artificial numbers' and 'these are numbers that are massaged to make the

---

[26] US Bureau of Labor Statistics: www.bls.gov/bls/about-bls.htm.
[27] Christopher Ingraham (2017), '19 times Trump called jobs numbers "fake" before they made him look good', *Washington Post*, 10 March, www.washingtonpost.com/news/wonk/wp/2017/03/10/19-times-trump-called-the-jobs-numbers-fake-before-they-made-him-look-good/. See also: Tim Harford (2021), *How to Make the World Add Up*, London: Bridge Street Press, pp. 144f.
[28] Ingraham (2017).
[29] J. Brian Charles (2016), 'Transcript of Donald Trump's economic policy speech to Detroit Economic Club', *The Hill*, 8 August, https://thehill.com/blogs/pundits-blog/campaign/290777-transcript-of-donald-trumps-economic-policy-speech-to-detroit/.
[30] For details see: Eugene C. Emery Jr. (2016), 'Donald Trump Jr. says unemployment rates are manipulated for political purposes', *PolitiFact*, 25 July, www.politifact.com/factchecks/2016/jul/25/donald-trump-jr/donald-trump-jr-says-unemployment-rates-are-manipu/.

existing economy look good, to make this administration look good when, in fact, it's a total disaster.'

First, we should note that Donald Junior does not actually use the term 'manipulated'. He says that the official numbers are 'massaged' by omitting the long-term unemployed. The magazine *PolitiFact* published a report with the headline 'Donald Trump Jr. says unemployment rates are manipulated for political purposes'.[31] The headline is followed by the 'massaged' quotation in the subheading. In this context, 'manipulated' and 'massaged' are being treated as being synonymous: manipulating numbers is understood to be the same as massaging them.[32]

According to Donald Junior, the errors in the BLS figures did not occur by chance. The numbers were being deliberately manipulated/massaged downwards for the specific political purpose of making the administration look good. His father had been saying much the same for a long time. Donald Junior was implying that skilled statisticians are well placed to manipulate/massage data. He was not suggesting that the statisticians had simply made up the low numbers and then published them. Quite the reverse. Donald Junior was accusing the statisticians at the Bureau of Labor Statistics of knowingly misusing statistical procedures to produce the figures that the administration desired.

Donald Junior was going further than just calling the numbers that he didn't like 'phoney numbers'. He was accusing professional statisticians of using biased methodology: the statisticians were deliberately removing the unemployed from the category of 'unemployed' after x months. Following Donald Junior's interview, his father said much the same. In December 2016, Trump, as president-elect, told supporters at a rally held in Des Moines:

> The unemployment number, as you know, is totally fiction. If you look for a job for six months and then you give up, they consider you give up. You just give up. You go home. You say, "Darling, I can't get a job." They consider you statistically employed. It's not the way. But don't worry about it because it's going to take care of itself pretty quickly.[33]

[31] Emery (2016).
[32] In Chapter 3, we quoted Stuart Ritchie about the institutional manipulation of data by social psychologists. Ritchie there uses 'massaging' data as a synonym for 'manipulating' data. Stuart Ritchie (2020), *Scientific Fictions*, London: Vintage, p. 97. The two terms are not equivalent in all contexts. When the object of manipulating/massaging is a person, the equivalence does not hold: to manipulate a person is not the same as massaging someone, except perhaps in therapeutic contexts.
[33] Glenn Kessler (2016), 'Donald Trump still does not understand the unemployment rate', *Washington Post*, 12 December, www.washingtonpost.com/news/fact-checker/wp/2016/12/12/donald-trump-still-does-not-understand-the-unemployment-rate/.

The father's words were more vivid than the son's. In one regard, they are numerically more precise: the unemployed are removed after 'six months' rather than 'x months'. There is a statistical difference between what father and son say. According to the son, after x months the unemployed simply disappear from the category 'unemployed'. His father says that after six months they are put onto the list of the 'statistically employed'.

Statistically the father has upped the stakes, for his uncalculated calculation is the more extreme. If the long-term unemployed are registered as employed, rather than just disappearing from the unemployment figures, then the total proportion of employed people rises more sharply than when the unemployed just disappear from the numbers of unemployed. In that case, the Bureau would be producing even 'phonier' numbers.

The president-elect's comment 'It's not the way' points in the same direction as some of his son's remarks. Neither Trump is openly dismissing all statistics, as if statistical thinking is by its nature alien to them. They do not dispute that it is possible to count the number of unemployed people. By implication both are saying that dishonest statistical practices should be replaced by honest ones. As Trump Senior implies, there is a way.

Manipulating Numbers, Degrading Statistics

To say that Donald Trump Junior might have understood what it means to manipulate or massage data does not mean he was correct about the unemployment figures. For good statistical reasons, he and his father were both incorrect in what they were saying. Donald Senior may have been talking with all his customary self-confidence, but he was revealing the limits of his statistical knowledge.

The term 'unemployed' is part of ordinary language. If people were asked whether someone who has not worked for so long that they have given up all hope of getting a job is unemployed or not, they are likely to answer 'Yes they are unemployed'. When statistics are measuring complex macroeconomic processes such as gross domestic product or the effects of raising the interest rate, then non-specialists have less chance of recognising poor or biased methodologies. But when their own lives are touched then people can have a much better idea of what the numbers should mean, and that includes being employed or being unemployed.[34] The public would

---

[34] Johnny Runge and Nathan Hudson (2020), 'Public understanding of economics and economic statistics', Economic Statistics Centre of Excellence, Occasional Paper No. 3. Regarding unemployment, the authors state that the British public have a fairly good understanding of

understand that the long-term unemployed should not be removed from the unemployment figures.

In accusing the statisticians at the Bureau of making statistical errors, the Trumps were making their own errors. Both spoke as if the BLS produces a single unemployment figure which deliberately underestimates the real rates of unemployment. This is inaccurate. The Bureau recognises that there are different ways of calculating unemployment and that each method has its strengths and weaknesses. Consequently, each month the BLS publishes six different figures, each using a different way of calculating unemployment. It labels the six figures for unemployment: U-1, U-2, U-3, U-4, U-5 and U-6. U-1 consistently produces the lowest unemployment figure and U-6 produces the highest.

U-3 is the figure that the two Donalds were complaining about. For historical reasons this figure is sometimes called the 'official unemployment' rate. By keeping this measure constant, cross-temporal comparisons can be made with figures from the past. There is nothing unusual about this. Statisticians often persist with methods of measurement that they know can be improved. They will judge that the benefits of spotting trends across time outweigh the losses that arise from using measures with obvious defects.[35] The BLS deals with the dilemma by making available the results from six ways of measuring unemployment.

The differences between the measures relate to the basic question who should be included and who should not be included as unemployed. The Bureau identifies a group whom they call 'persons marginally attached to the labour force'. These include those who are not working nor looking for work, but who indicate that they want to work, are available for work and that they 'have looked for work sometime in the past 12 months'. A subsection of this group are 'discouraged workers' who have given up looking for a work-related reason, for example those who say there are no jobs in their area or that they have previously been unable to find work.[36]

The categories U-4, U-5 and U-6 include these 'discouraged workers'. These are the long-term unemployed, whom Donald Junior claimed were

unemployment as a concept, but 'considerable nuances exist, especially in relation to public understanding of its measurement' (p. 8).

[35] Daniel Mügge and Lukas Linsi (2021), 'The national accounting paradox: how statistical norms corrode international economic data', *European Journal of International Relations*, 27, 403–27. See also the excellent work of Joel Best, who for a number of years has written critically about statistics and its social uses: Joel Best (2021a), *Damned Lies and Statistics*, Berkeley: University of California Press; Joel Best (2021b), 'Promoting bad statistics', *Society*, 38(3), 10–15.

[36] Bureau of Labor Statistics: www.bls.gov/news.release/empsit.t15.htm.

'miraculously' off the figures after x months, or after six months according to his father. The correct figure is twelve months but they are not automatically removed. One of the criteria for being included as 'marginally attached to the labour force' or being 'a discouraged worker' is that the person reports that they have looked for a job within the past twelve months.[37]

Thus, Donald Senior is incorrect when he says 'if you look for a job for six months and then you give up', they consider you employed. In fact, the BLS categorises such a person as unemployed in U-4, U-5 and U-6, so long as the last time they looked for job is not more than a year ago. When Trump's son says that if someone 'can't find a job', they're miraculously off the list of unemployed, he also is wrong. To say that someone 'can't find a job' is to imply that they are looking for one, or have looked for one very recently. When someone says 'I can't find my glasses, phone or hat', they are implying that they are looking for, or have just looked for, the said articles. Consequently, the person 'who can't find a job' is likely to be classed by the BLS as 'unemployed'.

There are good reasons for doubting that the prime concern of the Trumps was to produce as accurate figures as possible. They seem to have focussed on the disadvantages of measures that were politically inconvenient to them, and overlooked the disadvantages of alternative measures that produce more politically convenient numbers. Earlier, we mentioned that when in 2015 Trump senior dismissed the Bureau's figures, he said that he had seen figures of 24 and 42 per cent unemployed. He did not criticise these higher figures, not even the implausible 42 per cent.

The magazine *PolitiFact* published a piece about the origins of that 42 per cent figure.[38] David Stockman, President Ronald Reagan's former budget director, calculated this high unemployment figure. The number was not based on calculating the proportion of unemployed individuals in the working-age population, but on the proportion of available working hours that were actually worked. Stockman had written that there were 210 million Americans between the ages of 16 and 68; and that if you assume that each of those was able to hold down a full-time job, there would be a total of 420 billion potential working hours. According to Stockman, the Bureau of Labor Statistics in 2014 recorded that only

[37] Bureau of Labor Statistics: www.bls.gov/cps/cps_htgm.htm#nilf.

[38] Louis Jacobson (2016), 'Donald Trump repeats pants on fire claim that unemployment rate could be 42 per cent', *PolitiFact*, 11 February, www.politifact.com/factchecks/2016/feb/11/donald-trump/donald-trump-repeats-pants-fire-claim-unemployment/.

240 billion hours had been worked and that left, Stockman said, 42 per cent of the notional possible hours of work unworked.

PolitiFact points out that Stockman's figure of 210 million possible workers includes those who were not looking for work, such as early retirees and students, or those who could not work, such as those with disabilities or full-time carers. Listing such people as unemployed would transgress ordinary understanding every bit as much as listing those who could not find a job as being employed. Moreover, Stockman's 42 per cent referred to the notional proportion of unworked hours, not to people. Anyone concerned with the accuracy of statistics, rather than with political advantage, would not have treated the 42 per cent as if it referred to the proportion of unemployed people.

That is not the end of the story. When Donald Senior became president, he could have dropped the U-3 measure as the official rate and given prominence to U-6 instead, on the grounds that it 'solved' the 'discouraged workers' problem. However, he did not make this change, which would have increased the unemployment rate. Instead, he did something very different – something that constituted poor statistical judgment.

About six weeks after Trump took office in 2017, the Bureau published the February job figures which showed that unemployment had fallen. Sean Spicer, Trump's spokesperson, seemed fully prepared for a question on the figures at the White House press conference. A journalist from CNBC, the consumer news and business channel, asked Spicer: 'Does the President believe that this jobs report was an accurate and a fair way to measure the economy?' Spicer replied: 'I talked to the President prior to this, and he said to quote him very clearly. They may have been phoney in the past, but it's very real now.'[39]

If previously Trump thought that the Bureau's way of measuring unemployment was unsatisfactory, then it would still be unsatisfactory for exactly the same methodological reasons. It is poor statistical thinking to declare that a methodology has suddenly shifted from being unsatisfactory to being satisfactory without offering a reason why that could have happened. A statistical methodology cannot go from being inaccurate to accurate simply because the political interests of the president have changed. That is not how official statistics work, or rather, how they should work.

Here was a president who was showing that he was not bothered about statistical niceties. He was uninhibitedly motivated by the politics of

---

[39] Bourree Lam (2017), 'After a good jobs report, Trump now believes economic data', *Atlantic*, 17 March, www.theatlantic.com/business/archive/2017/03/trump-spicer-jobs-report/519273/.

advantage and disadvantage. Far from caring about the statistics, he seemed to be flattering himself on his statistical illiteracy. It is as if he had instructed his press secretary to say 'the President doesn't care what you think; he doesn't care about the statistical details; the figures are now real because he says they are'. That is, of course, not a statistical argument, although at the time it might have been a popular one.

The Election Lost: Trump's Statistical Claims

Trump's claims about the 2016 election were just a prelude. Back then he asserted that he had obtained more overall votes than Hillary Clinton, at least if you subtracted her 'millions' of phoney votes. After the 2020 election he had a political reason to add to his personal reasons. Just distributing a red-coloured map would never achieve his purpose of having the election result officially reversed.

Immediately after the 2020 results were declared, Trump was declaring that he was the real winner and that the election had been stolen. This conviction came before any theory about how the election had been manipulated. Just over two weeks after the election, he had plenty of theories. On 18 November he tweeted:

> This was a rigged election. No Republican Poll Watchers allowed, voting machine "glitches" all over the place (meaning they got caught cheating!), voting after election ended, and so much more![40]

He and his supporters needed explanations – any would do. In the early months after the election there was an explanatory chaos, as explanation after explanation was voiced with the same certainty. All these claims were statistical to the extent that they referred to the way that numbers had allegedly been counted, or rather miscounted. In addition, some of the claims were also statistical because they relied on statistical arguments for showing why everyone should recognise that the election had been stolen. We will deal with these doubly statistical claims first. Then we will discuss the claims that relied on visual, rather than directly statistical, evidence for the alleged miscounting.

Claiming that the election result had been manipulated became part of the means for manipulating the figures. Trump supporters, especially those on the outer edges of the political right, did not take long to come up with

---

[40] Donald J. Trump @realDonaldTrump (2020), X (formerly Twitter), 18 November, https://twitter .com/realDonaldTrump/status/1329064787142172673.

statistically based reasons for disputing the results of the election. We are fortunate that a team of statistically minded political scientists from Stanford University and the University of Chicago – Andrew Eggers, Haritz Garro and Justin Grimmer – have tested the main statistical arguments of those claiming the election to have been stolen. Eggers and his colleagues published their report in *Proceedings of the National Academy of Sciences*. Their conclusions were clear: 'In each case, we find that the purportedly anomalous fact is either not a fact or not anomalous'.[41]

An example of a statistical claim that spread rapidly in right-wing circles was one made by Bill Binney, a former member of the National Security Agency. Binney calls himself 'Constitutional Patriot' when tweeting his support for various right-wing causes and conspiracy theories.[42] On 19 December 2020, Binney tweeted why the election had been a fraud:

> With 212 Million registered voters and 66.2% voting, 140.344 M[illion] voted. Now if Trump got 74 M[illion], that leaves only 66.344 M[illion] for Biden. These numbers don't add up to what we are being told. Lies and more Lies![43]

Binney's rhetoric is one of absolute confidence. He doesn't say 'I think there may be an anomaly here, can anyone spot an error in my calculations?' He presents the numbers as unambiguous truths. His uses conspiratorial rhetoric: we are being told 'lies and more lies'. The plot to unseat the president was deliberate.

Binney starts with the assumption that Trump's votes are genuine and Biden's are not. From a purely statistical point of view, the numbers that Binney cites could just as well be used to support the opposite conclusion. If Biden got 81 million that would leave only 59.344 million for Trump. So, Trump's 74 million must be wrong, a gross overestimation. Binney's calculations cannot be used to prove that Trump's votes must be genuine and Biden's cannot be. No proof can assume the very proposition that it seeks to prove.

Binney's numbers spread rapidly on the far right. The day after his tweet, the conspiracy theory site *Gateway Pundit* contained an article

---

[41] Andrew C. Eggers, Haritz Garro, and Justin Grimmer (2021), 'No evidence for systematic voter fraud: A guide to statistical claims about the 2020 election', *PNAS*, 118 (45), www.pnas.org/doi/10.1073/pnas.2103619118; with Appendix 01 which can be accessed through the article.
[42] Binney has appeared on Alex Jones's conspiratorial *Infowars*. For details, see: Timothy Johnson (2018), 'Alex Jones tries and fails to pass off a publicly available document as the House GOP's secret Russia memo', *Media Matters for America*, 23 January, www.mediamatters.org/alex-jones/alex-jones-tries-and-fails-pass-publicly-available-document-house-gops-secret-russia.
[43] Bill Binney @Bill_Binney (2020), X (formerly Twitter), 19 December, https://twitter.com/Bill_Binney/status/1340106702167961602.

entitled 'REVEALED: "Simple math" shows Biden claims 13 MILLION more votes than there were eligible voters who voted in 2020 election'.[44] The subheading was 'The 2020 election will go down as the most corrupt US election in history'. The conclusion was highlighted in bold red type:

> If President Trump won 74 million votes, then that leaves only 67.5 million votes remaining for Biden. This means 13 million duplicate or made up ballots were created and counted for Biden!

Ten days later, Binney's calculations and confident rhetoric received the ultimate support. The former president tweeted:

> The United States had more votes than it had people voting, by a lot. This travesty cannot be allowed to stand. It was a Rigged Election, one not even fit for third world countries![45]

Within days of Trump's tweet, Reuters press agency published an article written by its staff writers, identifying Binney's statistical error.[46] The maths was not as simple as the conspiracy site stated. Apparently, Binney had taken the voting figure of 66.2 per cent from an article in the *Washington Post*. The article had not been clear what this figure represented: whether it was 66.2 per cent of those registered to vote or 66.2 per cent of the American population of voting age. The difference is important because not all the population of voting age are registered voters; 66.2 per cent of the voting age population is a much larger number than 66.2 per cent of registered voters.

The *Washington Post* confirmed that its percentage referred to the proportion of the total voting age population that voted in the 2020 election. As Eggers and his colleagues confirmed in the supplement to their *PNAS* paper, the combined number of votes officially ascribed to Biden and Trump match 66.2 per cent of the total US population of voting age. Seen in this light, the apparent anomaly disappears: there were not more votes than people voting.

At the same time as Binney announced his so-called proof, Charlie Kirk, a conservative radio host, was trying another statistical argument. He tweeted in December 2020: 'Does anyone else have a hard time

---

[44] Joe Hoft (2020), 'REVEALED: "Simple math" shows Biden claims 13 MILLION more votes than there were eligible voters who voted in 2020 election', *Gateway Pundit*, 20 December, www.thegatewaypundit.com/2020/12/breaking-huge-simple-math-shows-biden-claims-13-million-votes-eligible-voters-voted-2020-election/.

[45] Donald J Trump @realDonaldTrump, 2020, X (formerly Twitter), 30 December, https://twitter.com/realdonaldtrump/status/1344367336715857921.

[46] Reuters Factcheck (2021), 'Claim that turnout numbers prove U.S. election fraud uses wrong figures', 4 January, www.reuters.com/article/uk-factcheck-13-million-votes-idUSKBN2970JQ.

believing Joe Biden won a record-high number of votes despite winning a record-low number of counties?'[47] Eggers and his colleagues point out that Kirk's question could be turned around. If Trump won so few votes, how could he have legitimately won so many counties? Just like Binney, Kirk was using the assumption that Trump's votes were genuine and Biden's votes were questionable, in order to prove that same assumption.[48]

Moreover, as we have seen, there was a good reason why Trump won so many counties and so few votes: Trump's counties tended to have fewer voters both in 2016 and 2020. Eggers and his colleagues showed that, if you took the population numbers of counties into account, then no one who understood the statistics should have any problem recognising that it was possible for Biden to win a record number of votes despite losing so many counties.

Some of the evidence that Eggers and his colleagues tested was more statistically sophisticated than the Kirk and Binney claims. In December 2020, the Trump team produced an anonymous report of statistical analyses that seemed to support the claim that Biden won a disproportionate number of votes – 5.6 per cent more votes – when Dominion vote-counting machines were being used. The report claimed that this was evidence of fraud.[49] The idea was that the Dominion voting machines had been rigged to transfer a proportion of Trump votes to Biden. This notion became highly cited by Trump supporters, including Trump's lawyers and far-right sites in general. Trump himself quoted the conspiracy site of One America News Network ('@OANN'), when he tweeted in capital letters: 'STATES USING DOMINION VOTING SYSTEMS SWITCHED 435,000 VOTES FROM TRUMP TO BIDEN'.[50]

---

[47] Charlie Kirk @charliekirk11 (2020), 'Does anyone else have a hard time believing Joe Biden won a record-high number of votes despite winning a record-low number of counties?', X (formerly Twitter), 20 December, https://twitter.com/charliekirk11/status/1340692425635979266?lang=en.

[48] Eggers et al. (2021).

[49] DataScience in Coordination with BASEDMedia (2020), 'Evidence of Fraud in Conjunction with Use of Dominion BMD Machines', PartyofTrump.com, 17 December, https://thepartyoftrump.com/media/FraudInCountiesUsingDominionVotingMachines.pdf.

[50] Donald J. Trump @realDonaldTrump (2020), X (formerly Twitter), 12 November: https://twitter.com/realDonaldTrump/status/1326926226888544256.The following day Factcheck.org published a critique of Trump's tweet: Rem Rieder (2020), 'Trump tweets conspiracy theory about deleted votes', Factcheck.org, 13 November, www.factcheck.org/2020/11/trump-tweets-conspiracy-theory-about-deleted-votes/.This was not the only time that Trump has quoted One American News Network. See: Mythili Sampathkumar (2017), 'Donald Trump's false claim about UK crime rate seems to have come from conspiracy theorist news network', Independent, 21 October, www.the-independent.com/news/world/americas/us-politics/trump-uk-crime-rate-oann-where-from-report-conspiracy-theories-a8012136.html.

Eggers and his colleagues examined the statistics in the anonymous Trump-supporting report. They found numerous faults. They said it p-hacked, failed to compare Dominion voting machines directly with other voting machines, and ignored that the biggest predictor of the Biden voting figures in 2020: namely Clinton's share of the vote in 2016.[51] If counties that voted Clinton in 2016 were heavily populated and used voting machines, including Dominion machines, then there would be an innocent explanation for the relationship between Dominion machines and voting for Biden. When the team re-ran the data, controlling for the effect of Clinton's share of the 2020 vote, they found no statistical evidence that the use of Dominion machines, when compared with other voting machines, demonstrated an increase in Biden's share of the 2020 vote.[52]

Trump's lawyers took their argument about the Dominion machines to court in many of the states that had used those counting machines. One by one the courts rejected the argument. The most famous legal case was to come later, more than two years after the election. In April 2023, Dominion Voting Machines, the company producing the machines, brought a civil case again Fox News. It claimed that Fox News had damaged its business by widely publicising the untruth that the company had programmed its machines to transfer Trump votes to Biden. Dominion won its case and, in the settlement, Fox News agreed to pay Dominion damages of $787.5 million, and there was a possibility of further legal actions to come.[53] Of course, convinced believers in conspiracies would take this as proof that the courts were phoney courts, not that the Dominion machines operated properly.

Visual Evidence of Miscounting: Seeing is Disbelieving

Among the hotchpotch of numbers and theories, supporters of Trump claimed to have found visual evidence of electoral fraud in the state of Georgia. There was, they claimed, film of the theft that you could see with your own eyes. Georgia was important because Biden had won the state

---

[51] On p-hacking, see: Chapter 3, pp. 57–8.

[52] Eggers et al. (2021), Appendix 01, pp. 9–13. See particularly: Table 6, 'No Evidence Dominion/Hart machines increase in Biden's turnout', and Table 7, 'Dominion machines do not cause an increase in vote share for Biden', p. 13.

[53] Martin Pengelly (2023), 'Dominion wants "accountability" over Fox News election lies, co-founder says', *Guardian*, 1 May, www.theguardian.com/us-news/2023/may/01/fox-news-dominion-lawsuits-trump-election-lies; Guardian staff (2023), 'The legal problems still overshadowing Fox News after its Dominion settlement', *Guardian*, 19 April, www.theguardian.com/media/2023/apr/19/the-legal-problems-still-overshadowing-fox-news-after-its-dominion-settlement.

narrowly by less than 12,000 votes. The result was so close that the Georgia secretary of state announced a full re-count by hand. This was completed by 19 November, and Biden's victory in Georgia was confirmed.

Trump's team went to court to have the results overturned and the state's sixteen Electoral College votes transferred to Trump. In early December 2020, a case was heard by the Georgia Senate Judiciary subcommittee. Even by then, forty such cases had been dismissed by courts across America.[54] The case that the Trump team brought to the Georgia subcommittee did not appear to have been carefully prepared in advance. The team were intending to present the sort of evidence about corrupted ballot-counting machines, dead people voting, illegal immigrants and so on that had already been rejected by courts in other states. However, on 3 December the Trump-supporting legal team took a new path. They introduced a lawyer and Trump supporter, Jacki Pick, to take the subcommittee through key video evidence.

The evidence was taken from the surveillance video recording of the count in one county, Fulton County. Pick said in her evidence that the team had only received the fourteen hours of film late the previous night. They only had time to watch two of the fourteen hours. Nevertheless, she showed a short extract of the video to the subcommittee. Her evidence and the film that she showed to the subcommittee is publicly available.[55]

The footage is grainy, hard to see and even harder to interpret. The video shown to the subcommittee shows film from four cameras, which had been positioned in the counting room. All four were presented to the subcommittee playing simultaneously on a split screen divided four ways. Pick was providing a commentary of what can be seen in the footage from the four cameras. Basically she tells a conspiratorial story. In the late evening 'one person who was working the polls' told 'everyone to leave on the basis that they were going to stop counting'. And she points out that you can see most people, including the election observers from the Republican Party, leaving the room. Because the recording is without sound, you cannot hear what was said.

---

[54] For an account of the courts rejecting Trump team's cases following the election, see: Jacob Shamsian and Sonam Sheth (2021), 'Trump and his allies filed more than 40 lawsuits challenging the 2020 election results. All of them failed', *Insider*, February 21, www .businessinsider.com/trump-campaign-lawsuits-election-results-2020-11?r=US&IR=T.

[55] On the internet, particularly on YouTube, there are a number of recordings of Pick's evidence along with the film that she was presenting to the hearing. See, for instance: www.youtube.com/watch? v=hRCXUNOwOjw&t=1987s.

She guides the subcommittee to watch what happened at 11.00 pm. She does not present the video first and then give her interpretation. She gives the interpretation first, thereby guiding the audience to what they should be looking for: 'What you're going to see happened about eleven o'clock is, once everyone has gone, the coast is clear, they're going to pull the ballots out of from underneath a table, watch this table'. Of course, the video cannot present visual evidence that the election officials were thinking that 'the coast is clear' – that statement is a dramatic addition, giving rhetorical colouring to the wordless video.

Pick's story is that once the coast is clear, the remaining election officials pull out from beneath a table 'suitcases' filled with ballots. Pick asks a rhetorical question: 'Is it normal to store suitcases of ballots under a table?' The choice of the word 'suitcases' is semantically significant. It helps to convey that something very untoward was happening, because ballots are not normally stored in suitcases. The audience could see on the imperfect footage objects that look very much like suitcases. Pick says: 'I saw four suitcases come out from underneath the table' and she asks another rhetorical question: 'So what are these ballots doing there separated from all the other ballots?'

In answering her own question Pick introduces numerical issues. The ballots are taken out of the suitcases, straightened out and run through counting machines: 'These machines can process about 3,000 ballots an hour so you do the math. How many ballots went through those two machines when there was no one there?' She proposes a figure of 18,000 ballots. She points out that this number 'is beyond the margin of victory in this race'. Here are the illegal, surplus votes without which Biden would not have won Georgia.

Rudy Giuliani, Trump's lawyer, thought the video record provided insurmountable proof of electoral fraud. The same day that Pick gave her presentation, Giuliani tweeted:

> The video tape doesn't lie. Fulton County Democrats stole the election. It's now beyond doubt. Go to the tape![56]

Giuliani also appeared before the Georgia senate subcommittee. In his comments to the subcommittee, Giuliani was certain that the video unambiguously proved electoral fraud:

---

[56] Rudy W. Giuliani @RudyGiuliani (2020), X (formerly Twitter), 3 December, https://archive.is/ ykw1q#selection-2781.0-2811.12. Fulton County was the country in which the videoed count took place.

I don't have to be a genius to figure out that those votes are not legitimate votes. You don't put legitimate votes under a table, wait until you throw the opposition out and in the middle of the night, count them.[57]

With the video evidence, you can see it with your own eyes. Except that you can't.

Giuliani was tweeting and saying that anyone who sees the video will see the theft, for the camera and the videotape that it records cannot lie. The truism is true: the video, like numbers, cannot lie. However, the producers of film and numbers can lie. A videotape can be arranged in such a way that it is designed to mislead. The producers of propaganda films can manipulate recordings to make speakers appear to say what they did not say. Certainly the Trump team produced such films during the 2020 election campaign.[58]

Giuliani was tweeting with a purpose: he wanted the courts and the public to treat the tape as if it were revealing the clear truth – as if anyone seeing the film would automatically see the theft. But if the tape were so unambiguous why did the Trump team in Georgia need to recruit Jacki Pick to give a running commentary on the short extracts that were shown? And could you be certain that the short extracts taken from fourteen or so hours of recording showed what really happened? Giuliani was not letting the video speak for itself because, in claiming that it did, he was tweeting his support for Pick's interpretation. Even if cameras can't tell lies, interpreters can persuade themselves that they have seen exactly what they are desperate to see and believe.[59]

For the Trump team, Pick's suitcase story was their story of stories. Trump travelled to Georgia two days after Pick's evidence in order to speak to a mass rally. It was his first public rally since he had lost the election. Predictably he spoke about how he had won the election but it had been

---

[57] A clip of Giuliani saying that the video was a 'smoking gun' can be found at: https://twitter.com/cspan/status/1539323922025312256.

[58] One of the most notorious films depicted Trump's chief medical advisor, Anthony Fauci, appearing to praise Trump. Fauci complained because he had actually been praising his own research team, but clever intercutting made it seem that Trump was the object of the praise: www.youtube.com/watch?v=emnCFyi5cuQ. See: Lauren Aratani (2020), 'Anthony Fauci criticises Donald Trump for using his words out of context', *Guardian*, 11 October: www.theguardian.com/us-news/2020/oct/11/anthony-fauci-criticises-donald-trump-for-using-his-words-out-of-context. See also: Daniel Strauss (2020), 'Donald Trump campaign repeatedly doctoring videos for social media ads', 4 September, www.theguardian.com/us-news/2020/sep/04/donald-trump-campaign-doctoring-joe-biden-videos-manipulated-media-twitter.

[59] Later that day Giuliani tweeted, citing 'rampant voter fraud' and asking whether we are 'going to let Democrats steal the election in front of our faces'. Rudy W. Giuliani @RudyGiuliani (2020), X (formerly Twitter), 3 December, https://twitter.com/RudyGiuliani/status/1334982029117714432.

stolen from him: 'We got seventy-four million-plus and they're trying to convince us that we lost. We didn't lose'. As a proficient public speaker in control of his adoring audience, Trump knew how to pause so that the crowd could chant 'Stop the steal! Stop the steal!'[60]

Trump mentioned the suitcases as evidence of the steal. He said that 'people are walking in with suitcases and putting them under a table'. Following Trump's speech, the suitcase story went viral; newspapers across the world covered the story, but not always in the way that Trump and his supporters would have wished.[61]

One reason for the sceptical press was the way that the senior Georgia election officials responded. They stressed that Pick had shown only a small portion of the video and that this gave a distorted view of what occurred. On the day of Pick's presentation, Gabriel Sterling, the state's voting implementation manager and himself a Republican who had voted for Trump, tweeted that Pick's '90 second video' had shown 'normal ballot processing'.[62]

In an interview, Sterling dismissed Trump's claims of voter fraud as 'fantastical, unreasonable' and 'lacking in any factual reality'. As for Giuliani appearing before the Georgia subcommittee, Sterling said 'he had looked them in the eye and lied'.[63] *Factcheck.org* interviewed Sterling and he denied that the video had shown 'suitcases'. They were, he said, just the standard ballot containers which the state used for securing ballots, especially postal and military ballots that had to be kept separate from other ballots. Sterling said that the containers had been opened earlier in the night and they had not been surreptitiously introduced into the building; they had been 'put in there about an hour earlier', as the full surveillance video would show.

---

[60] For analyses of the ways that proficient public speakers use rhetorical devices and intonation to indicate when their supporters should applaud, cheer or even chant a slogan, see the classic work of Max Atkinson (1984), *Our Masters' Voices*, London: Methuen. See also: John Heritage and David Greatbach (1986), 'Generating applause: a study of rhetoric and response at party political conferences', *American Journal of Sociology*, 92, 110–57; Peter Bull (2002), *Communication Under the Microscope*, Hove: Routledge.

[61] In the UK, the right-wing *Sun* and left-of-centre *Guardian* covered the story, saying that Giuliani's tweet and the video proved nothing: Nicole Darrah (2020), *Sun*, 'NO "SMOKING GUN" Vid released by Rudy Giuliani to "prove voter fraud" shows NOTHING unusual', 4 December: www .thesun.co.uk/news/13389973/georgia-trump-giuliani-voter-fraud-video-claims-investigation/; Oliver Laughland (2020), 'Trump rails against election result at rally ahead of crucial Georgia Senate runoff', *Guardian*, 6 December, www.theguardian.com/us-news/2020/dec/06/trump-rails-against-election-result-at-rally-ahead-of-crucial-georgia-senate-runoff.

[62] Gabriel Sterling @GabrielSterling (2020), X (formerly Twitter), 4 December, https://twitter.com/ GabrielSterling/status/1334825233610633217.

[63] For the Sterling interview, see: www.youtube.com/watch?v=NwKZYE_Yi94.

The *Factcheck* team also undermined Pick's mathematics. They asked an election monitor, who wished to remain anonymous, about the numbers of ballots that had actually been processed during the suspicious period. His figure was much lower than Pick's – less than 10,000, and thus less than Biden's overall winning margin in Georgia. It was not that either Pick or the monitor had made an error when they calculated the numbers. Like the grainy video itself, Pick's maths was also an interpretation, not an accurate description of the number of votes that had actually been counted.

Master Manipulator Fails to Manipulate

That was not the end of the story. On 2 January 2021, after the Georgia Senate's subcommittee inquiry had finished, Trump phoned the secretary of state for Georgia, Brad Raffensperger. The call also included Trump's chief of staff Mark Meadows and the conservative attorney Cleta Mitchell, as well as Ryan Germany, the Georgia state lawyer responsible for the conduct of the election. A transcript of the call was published in the *Washington Post* a few days later.[64]

Trump had a specific reason for calling Raffensperger. He wanted to put pressure on him to find sufficient extra Trump votes for Trump to be declared the winner of the state. One more vote than Biden would be sufficient, the president reassured Raffensperger throughout the call. The call became the subject of a potential criminal inquiry in Georgia, and at the time of writing Trump faces criminal charges in Georgia.

Numbers slip in and out of the call. Trump constantly tells Raffensperger that all he needed was for 11,780 more votes to be found. That was nothing because 'I think I probably did win it by half a million'. He offered up reason after reason as supposed evidence that there had been electoral fraud. There were 200,000 forged signatures. The number of people who were turned away from voting because someone else had already voted in their name was more than 50,000. Then there were 4,502 people voting who were not registered to vote; and 18,325 voted without having a proper address. According to Trump, 'dead people voted, and I think the number is close to 5,000 people'.

Then there was Fulton County, where 18,000 votes, all for Biden, were registered by the fraudulent scanner who had emptied the room of voters

---

[64] For the transcript, see: Amy Gardner and Paulina Firozi (2021), 'Here's the full transcript and audio of the call between Trump and Raffensperger', *Washington Post*, 5 January, www.washingtonpost .com/politics/trump-raffensperger-call-transcript-georgia-vote/2021/01/03/2768e0cc-4ddd-11eb-83e3-322644d82356_story.html.

and then fetched out the suitcases. Trump was certain the ballots had not been put in proper containers: 'They weren't in an official voter box; they were in what looked to be suitcases or trunks, suitcases, but they weren't in voter boxes'. His overall conclusion was clear: 'The bottom line is, when you add it all up and then you start adding, you know, 300,000 fake ballots, many, many times above the 11,779'.

Trump delivered a whole buffet of complaints and numbers which he asserted rather than justified. He also mentioned that 'we have a big issue with Dominion in other states and perhaps in yours', but he wasn't bringing it up. Raffensperger had told him that it couldn't be an issue in Georgia. Because of the closeness of the vote, the election officials had also done a hand count which showed very similar figures to the numbers for the voting machines.

Here we see the pragmatics of Trump's reasoning: if it works, use it; if it doesn't, drop it, at least for the moment. Raffensperger and Germany tried to take Trump through the numbers. At one point, Raffensperger told the president that 'the data you have is wrong'; only two dead people voted, not 5,000. Regarding, the Fulton County video, Raffensnperger countered Trump: 'it's extremely unfortunate that Rudy Giuliani or his people, they sliced and diced that video and took it out of context'. The whole video, he said, showed that nothing untoward had occurred in the counting room.

When it became apparent that neither Brad Raffensperger nor Ryan Germany were going to find the extra votes, Trump turned to threat. Addressing Raffensperger, he said that shredding ballots, or Dominion subtracting Trump votes, was 'a criminal offence'. If Raffensperger let that happen that was 'a big risk to you and to Ryan, your lawyer', and they would be involved in the criminal offence:

> I'm notifying you that you're letting it happen. So look. All I want to do is this. I just want to find 11,780 votes, which is one more than we have because we won the state.

Note how Trump switches from saying that the Georgia lawyers were committing criminal acts to saying that all he wants is for them to find 11,780 votes. The unspoken implication is that if they do this thing that he is asking for, then they will be free from the risk of being found guilty of criminal acts.[65]

---

[65] Certainly Raffensperger in his biography thought that Trump issued threats: Brad Raffensperger (2021), *Integrity Counts*, Forefront Books.

Trump's threat was potentially the criminal act. At the time of writing, we do not know how the court case in Georgia will proceed, even if it will proceed. Nor do we know whether Trump will be the Republican candidate in 2024; and certainly we cannot tell whether he will return to the presidency.

To their great credit, both Raffensperger and Germany stood firm in the face of pressure from the man who was still legally the president of the United States. Trump was not managing to persuade them to do with the voting numbers what he wanted them to do. The master manipulator was failing to manipulate.

Opinions, Facts and Democracy

We might suppose that as time passes, and as we get further from 2020, so the claims about electoral fraud will fade and normal politics will return. That might be too optimistic – as if Trump were a sudden explosion of unbound danger which will disappear as fast as it appeared. However, there are longer trends that made the emergence of Trump possible and that will ensure that his legacy might continue, especially if his third bid for the presidency is successful. The evidence is worrying, especially in relation to beliefs about the fairness of elections and confidence in official results.

The warnings of Hannah Arendt, who had lived in a country that turned from democracy to dictatorship, should give pause for thought. When facts become a matter of opinion, then, in Arendt's view, democracy becomes weakened, for there is little to hold a people together.[66] We might add that the danger is greater when those facts that have become opinions are the results of elections. There will be no facts that defeated candidates need accept except their own opinion whether the defeat was really a defeat. If they regularly deceive themselves, then there will be little to shake their opinion that the election had been stolen from them. There need be no limit to their self-deceit. In this context, the claim that everything has been manipulated becomes the means and justification for them to try to manipulate the results.

Public opinion polls suggest that in the United States people, especially Republican supporters, continue to believe that presidential elections are unfair and that votes are not properly counted. This is more than an effect

[66] Hannah Arendt (1967/1977), 'Truth and politics', in Hannah Arendt (ed.), *Between Past and Future*, Harmondsworth: Penguin, pp. 300f.

of the 2020 election. Four years earlier, after the 2016 election, Trump had voiced his doubts on the legality of the votes for Hillary Clinton. An opinion poll conducted at that time found that 44 per cent of Clinton voters thought that the votes had not been accurately counted in 2016. The vast majority of Trump voters believed that the votes had been counted accurately, with just under 10 per cent thinking they had not been.[67]

Move on four years, and the figures have flipped. Trump voters now are the disbelievers. Following the 2020 election a poll recorded that 68 per cent of Republicans thought that the election had been 'rigged'.[68] Since then this figure has remained more or less constant, although at the time of writing it is only three years since the election, and therefore too soon to tell whether the figure will drop in time. However, there has been one small but detectable change. Of the Republicans who believe that the election had been wrongly counted, almost half now believe that there is no 'solid evidence' to back this up.[69]

We have an interesting but worrying situation. The Republican supporters tend to believe in the theft of the 2020 election. Almost half of these believers in the theft acknowledge a lack of evidence to support this belief. It is as if the belief is so important to them that it does not need to rest on solid evidence. The other half believe that there is solid evidence. As we have seen, the 'solid evidence' is not so solid, although on the fringes of extreme politics the so-called evidence is vociferously held to be rock solid.

Those who believe in the solidity of the evidence were possibly the sorts of people who got their news from Fox News. During the legal case with Dominion, Fox News were required to release emails and WhatsApp messages that their executives and broadcasters had sent to each other. These private communications revealed that for the most part the executives and broadcasters did not believe the stories about election theft that they were publicly broadcasting. The company felt that it needed to

---

[67] Hellinger (2019), Table 4.4, p. 126.
[68] Chris Kahn (2020), 'Half of Republicans say Biden won because of a "rigged" election: Reuters/Ipsos poll Reuters Nov 18', www.reuters.com/article/us-usa-election-poll/half-of-republicans-say-biden-won-because-of-a-rigged-election-reuters-ipsos-poll-idUSKBN27Y1AJ. See also: Gordon Pennycook and David G. Rand (2021), 'Examining false beliefs about voter fraud in the wake of the 2020 Presidential Election', *The Harvard Kennedy School Misinformation Review*, 11 January, https://misinforeview.hks.harvard.edu/article/research-note-examining-false-beliefs-about-voter-fraud-in-the-wake-of-the-2020-presidential-election/.
[69] Alison Durkee (2023) 'Republicans increasingly realize there's no evidence of election fraud—but most still think 2020 election was stolen anyway, Poll Finds', *Forbes*, 14 March, www.forbes.com/sites/alisondurkee/2023/03/14/republicans-increasingly-realize-theres-no-evidence-of-election-fraud-but-most-still-think-2020-election-was-stolen-anyway-poll-finds/.

continue with such stories for commercial reasons. The executives feared that otherwise Fox News might lose a significant proportion of its audience.[70]

A factual belief that does not require solid evidence is potentially a self-deceptive belief. The believers might protect their beliefs and themselves by dismissing any embarrassing facts as 'phoney'. Against this, strong statistical analyses, such as those conducted by Eggers and his colleagues, are politically weak. No matter what numerical arguments are produced, the committed believers will dismiss the numbers that they do not like. If you believe that there was a powerful conspiracy to steal something as massive as a presidential election, then it does not take a great leap of faith to believe that the conspirators have the power to commission a few academics to produce some fancy numbers and airy theories to deny the theft.

As Arendt wrote, democracy is threatened when facts become opinions. She might have added that democracy is especially threatened when it is electoral results that are reduced to being matters of opinion. And that threat is further amplified when those who believe in the story of electoral theft remain convinced even if they recognise that there is no solid evidence. The dangers then become all the greater if those same believers imagine with unshakeable certainty that they represent the true beating heart of their nation.

---

[70] See for example: Sarah Ellison, Paul Farhi and Jeremy Barr (2023), 'Fox News feared losing viewers by airing truth about election, documents show', *Washington Post*, 17 February, www.washingtonpost.com/media/2023/02/17/fox-news-dominion-ratings-fear/; Jeremy W. Peters and Katie Robertson (2023), 'Fox stars privately expressed disbelief about election fraud claims "crazy stuff"', *New York Times*, 16 February, updated 24 April, www.nytimes.com/2023/02/16/business/media/fox-dominion-lawsuit.html; Jonathan Freedland (2023), 'Fox News and its audience became hooked on lies – now they can't break the habit', *Guardian*, 21 April, www.theguardian.com/commentisfree/2023/apr/21/fox-news-audience-lies-dominion-trial-donald-trump.

CHAPTER 5

Manipulating Statistics and Statisticians

The statistical manipulation of official data is typically, but not exclusively, tied to the exercise of power. We saw in the previous chapter how Trump used the power of the presidency when he attempted to reverse the results of the presidential election of 2020. His statistical manipulation was chaotic as he lashed out at election officials and official statisticians. By contrast, governments which manipulate their official statistics often do so in disciplined ways. Because their ministers are not proficient statisticians, they may try to manipulate their statisticians to manipulate the data for them.

We will be discussing how governments might manipulate official statistics, and we will present four examples to show how this manipulation can be played out in practice. Two of the examples occurred in communist autocracies and two in capitalist democracies. We will be suggesting that behind the manipulation of official statistics, there are usually networks of power and a series of interrelated, but different, actions. A government minister may commission the production of manipulated statistics; the minister's statisticians may have to manipulate the data, so that the minister can then manipulate the public with the manipulated statistics. Sometimes the statisticians cooperate and sometimes they do not.

Pali Lehohla, who was South Africa's statistician-general between 2000 and 2017, has written about the problems facing official statisticians in the modern world.[1] According to Lehohla, the position of senior statistician has grown more politically precarious in the past twenty-five years. It does not matter whether statisticians are working in autocracies,

---

[1] Pali Lehohla (2022), 'When your number's up: Bloodbath intensifies for statisticians for being bearers of bad news', *Independent Online*, 26 November, www.iol.co.za/business-report/opinion/when-your-numbers-up-bloodbath-intensifies-for-statisticians-for-being-bearers-of-bad-news-2667d8db-d512-41ce-b704-a73abef5706d. For a critical account of the development of statistical agencies in South Africa from the apartheid era to today, see: Juliette Alenda-Demoutiez (2022), 'White, democratic, technocratic: the political charge behind official statistics in South Africa', *Review of International Political Economy*, 29, 44–64.

semi-democracies or full democracies, they can still directly face the demands of those with political power. To quote Lehohla on the sacking of chief statisticians, 'the last decade has seen more living ghosts in the graveyard of statistics' than at any other time in the past seventy years. Lehohla was using 'graveyard' metaphorically, but he was aware that in Stalinist Russia the graveyards of statisticians were not metaphorical.

We offer a schematic guide which suggests that there are three stages to this sort of statistical manipulation by politicians. Our four examples have not been handpicked to confirm this guide. In fact, none of the four neatly progresses from stage one through to stage three. A schematic guide is not a theory or a model and certainly not a law. It suggests what observers should look out for, but not necessarily expect to find. At root, our guide points to the possible conflict between professional statisticians and the exercise of political power. Sometimes there is conflict, and sometimes governments succeed in recruiting the statisticians to do their murky numerical business. It is seldom simple.

National Statistics and National Politicians

In the nineteenth century, the state was the big producer of numbers through things like censuses, registrations of lives and deaths and so on. Today, states produce numbers on a grander scale, but in a highly quantified world they are no longer virtually the only producers of them.[2] Every large commercial organisation will generate its own statistical numbers – whether to show the balance of profits and losses, the perform-ance of employees, the happiness of customers, and so on. It is the same for educational, medical and financial organisations. We live as if there is a measure to evaluate every human quality, every type of success or failure, and every gain or cost. No wonder it has been said that modern life is dominated by 'a tyranny of metrics'.[3]

The etymological origin of the word 'statistics', coming from 'state', may be largely forgotten today, but politically it has not been outgrown. There are now 'official' national statistics for economic outputs, national debts, costs of living, educational performances, rates of international trading, crimes, unemployment and many, many more numbers. All the areas of life, in which politicians have traditionally played important roles

---

[2] Wendy Espeland and Mitchell Stevens (1998), 'Commensuration as a social process', *Annual Review of Sociology*. 24, 313–43; Wendy Espeland and Mitchell Stevens (2008), 'A sociology of quantification', *European Journal of Sociology*, 49, 401–36.
[3] Jerry Z. Muller (2018), *The Tyranny of Metrics*, Princeton: Princeton University Press.

are now regularly quantified by the state; the costs of policies are routinely calculated before their implementation and their effects are measured afterwards. Such is the entanglement between politics, power and statistics.

When a nation wants a census – and these days all nations do – then it will organise its own, choosing how to count its population, just as the nations did in the nineteenth century. When international organisations want to calculate the world's population, they have to add together the totals from the differently conducted national censuses of the world's nations. Some of the censuses will be known to be less rigorous than others for a variety of reasons, not least because some countries can afford rigorous censuses and some cannot. This can lead to the publication of precise-looking calculations that are known to be imprecise. In November 2022, the United Nations announced that the world's population had now passed eight billion, and indulged in the statistical fiction that the eight billionth person was potentially identifiable.[4]

Every recognised independent nation – whether massive or tiny, democratic or autocratic, wealthy or poor – now has a national agency for producing its own statistics. The Statistics Division of the United Nations lists these agencies.[5] China, the most populous nation in the world with almost one and half billion inhabitants, has its National Bureau of Statistics, while Tuvalu, the tiny Pacific island with a population of around 12,000, has its Central Statistics Division.

The United Nations also presents the statistical agencies' self-descriptions. Most of them appear keen to describe their own histories, statistical missions and achievements. One self-description that crops up again and again is that the agency is independent and free from government control. Some of the claims are hard to accept at face value. The Statistical Centre of Iran describes itself as 'an independent organization and completely free from political interference'; its mission is 'Independence and Impartiality in Statistical Production'.[6] Russia is, to use the ambivalent phrase of Putin and his ministers, 'a managed democracy'.[7] Its statistical agency ambivalently describes itself as 'an independent government agency under the supervision of the Government'.[8]

---

[4] BBC News (2022), 'World's population is now 8 billion, according to UN', 15 November, www.bbc.co.uk/newsround/63632981.

[5] United Nations Statistics Division: https://unstats.un.org/unsd/dnss/cp/searchcp.aspx.

[6] United Nations Statistics Division: https://unstats.un.org/unsd/dnss/docViewer.aspx?docID=595#start.

[7] Stephen Holmes and Ivan Krastev (2012), 'Putinism under siege: an autopsy of managed democracy', *Journal of Democracy*, 23(3), 33–45.

[8] United Nations Statistics Division: https://unstats.un.org/unsd/dnss/docViewer.aspx?docID=645#start.

It is not only statistical organisations in undemocratic or semi-democratic countries that describe themselves in potentially problematic ways. The Argentinian Instituto Nacional de Estadística y Censos (INDEC) claims that since its foundation in 1968, it has preserved 'in all cases its independence'.[9] Argentina provides one of the four examples discussed later in this chapter. It would be a bit optimistic to count the example as an instance where the agency preserved its independence.

Sometimes the assertions of independence carry hints that politicians have exerted power over statisticians, even in the most established of democracies. Statistics Netherlands gives a brief résumé of its history. In January 2004, it became 'an autonomous agency', and, as a result, there is 'no longer a hierarchical relationship between the Minister of Economic Affairs and the organisation'.[10] The brief description does not say how in the past ministers might have compromised the agency's autonomy; nor whether occasionally governments still try to do so.

The political motives of Dutch government ministers would not have substantially altered since 2004. They will still want to gain, exercise and maintain power. Perhaps now the statisticians may be given more protection. Even so, that does not mean that it has become absolutely impossible for a minister to put pressure on the statisticians to come up with the numerical goods that will help them remain in power.

Three Stages of Statistical Manipulation

We have constructed a schematic guide to emphasise that the political manipulation of statistics is seldom based on a single action. Instead there is likely to be a series of interrelated acts which are performed within a wider political context. The guide identifies three possible stages. First, government ministers might manipulate their statisticians to produce manipulated statistics. Then, the statisticians might duly oblige by manipulating the numbers; and thirdly the ministers might publicly use those manipulated statistics to manipulate their audiences. Different acts of manipulation will be occurring; some of them will be publicly performed while others will take place behind closed doors.

The schematic guide is presented in Figure 5.1. It is not a theory or a model which stipulates what must happens whenever statistical

---

[9] United Nations Statistics Division: https://unstats.un.org/unsd/dnss/docViewer.aspx?docID=530#start.
[10] United Nations Statistics Division: https://unstats.un.org/unsd/dnss/docViewer.aspx?docID=516#start.

	STAGE 1	STAGE 2	STAGE 3
MANIPULATOR	Government leader or member of government	Official statisticians	Government leader or member of government
OBJECT OF MANIPULATION	Official statistician(s)	Official statistics	Typically, public of own nation; sometimes other governments or international organisations
MEANS OF MANIPULATION	Appointing supportive statisticians; influencing official statisticians by bribery, coercion, appeals to patriotism etc.	Raising or lowering numbers to fit demands made in Stage 1, and achieved by changing measures, labels of measures, data collection etc.	Government leader/members citing manipulated figures which official statisticians produced in Stage 2
TYPE OF MANIPULATION	Manipulating people	Manipulating information	Manipulating people
CONTEXT OF MANIPULATION	Interpersonal, private communication	Act of manipulation behind closed doors; results published publicly, or privately sent to government	Public when addressed to nation in speeches, televised interviews etc.; or behind closed doors in government negotiations

Figure 5.1   Three Stages of Manipulating Official Statistics: A Schematic Guide

manipulation occurs. It is a guide for examining examples, rather than a rigid theoretical system. It may help observers to note what might be going on, especially if key acts have to be inferred because they occur away from the public gaze, including the gaze of academic observers.

Later in the chapter, we will be presenting our four examples. None of the examples show the acts of statistical manipulation running in neatly organised stages. Actual political and statistical activity is more messily complex than a schematic guide might depict. Paradoxically, a schematic guide can help us to show this.

We use the guide to stress that statistical manipulation involves more than a trained statistician sitting alone at a computer, changing and ordering numbers in potentially misleading ways. We must ask what might have led a professional statistician to the point of manipulating figures. Were they manipulated by a governmental ministers or were they willingly helping out the minister? There may be much that we do not know and cannot find out.

Stage 1

The schematic guide starts with the motives and actions of politicians rather than those of statisticians. The first stage depicts governing politicians exercising their powers over the nation's official statisticians. Some observers have suggested that members of autocratic governments are more likely to be in a position to exercise this power than ministers in democracies.[11] In democracies, government ministers may have to use subtler methods of persuasion if they want their statisticians to produce the sort of numbers that the government wants. But our two examples from autocracies – Stalin's Russia and contemporary China – reveal ministerial sophistication; and our two examples from democracies show that statisticians in these states can face crude threats.

Stage 1 provides a convenient way of examining a specific act of statistical manipulation, considered in isolation. However, it may not always be the right place to start because acts of manipulation always take place within a wider political, historical and cultural context. If we want to discover why a group of official statisticians may be enthusiastically manipulating a particular set of official statistics for their ministerial bosses, we would need to go back further in time.

Stages 2 and 3

These two stages can be discussed briefly here, because the later chapters in the book will be presenting in detail examples of numbers being manipulated by official statisticians (Stage 2) and of politicians publicly using these manipulated numbers for political purposes (Stage 3).

The second stage involves statisticians, engaging their professional skills in their places of work. There are many ways in which they can use methods to distort official numbers. They might be constructing measures

[11] Roberto Aragão and Lukas Linsi (2022), 'Many shades of wrong: what governments do when they manipulate statistics', *Review of International Political Economy*, 29, 88–113; Luis R. Martinez (2021), 'How much should we trust the dictator's GDP growth estimates?', working paper, Becker Friedman Institute, University of Chicago, https://bfi.uchicago.edu/wp-content/uploads/2021/07/BFI_WP_2021–78.pdf.

that do not properly measure what they are claiming to be measuring. Or they might not be using proper samples of respondents but might be treating a biased sample as if it were a representative sample. Or they might be inappropriately comparing two samples that are so different that they cannot be compared. There are all sorts of things that statisticians can do to influence the production of numbers, whether with the aim of raising or lowering measurements. In the case of manipulation, the primary aim is not to obtain the most accurate measurement possible but to obtain politically desirable numbers.

The acts of planning the collection of data then analysing and interpreting the numbers are likely to occur behind closed doors, either in face-to-face meetings or online meetings between fellow professionals, or at one senior statistician's computer. Such acts, thus, are generally enacted beyond the public gaze. The decisions taken at these meetings can become public information, especially if, as often happens, statisticians publish their methods and results. Not all might be revealed: some key information might either be published in an uninterpretable manner, or simply not be published at all because the governing politicians do not like what the statisticians found or do not want to broadcast how they found what they did.

If governing politicians have persuaded their statisticians to produce politically advantageous numbers, it is unlikely that the numbers will simply remain hidden in a data file: the politicians will seek to use the numbers for political gain. This is the third stage. Normally we can expect the politician to use their desired numbers in their public rhetoric: for instance, while boasting of achievements in televised speeches and interviews, or while fending off challenges from the opposition in parliamentary debates, or when campaigning to be returned to power. However, this final stage might not occur if the statisticians have failed to produce sufficiently suitable numbers. Then, the numbers might remain unreleased. One of our examples is Stalin's unreleased 1937 census of the Soviet Union.

Because of the constant possibility of manipulation, fact-checking organisations and national agencies for the maintenance of statistical standards are so important in democracies. In autocracies, governments have greater powers to protect themselves and their obedient statisticians from challenge. They can outlaw fact-checking organisations as enemies of the state. Given that official statistics always involve the use of categories, governing politicians can behave like Lewis Carroll's Humpty-Dumpty:

> "When I use a word," Humpty Dumpty said in rather a scornful tone, "it means just what I choose it to mean — neither more nor less."

"The question is," said Alice, "whether you can make words mean so many different things."

"The question is," said Humpty Dumpty, "which is to be master – that's all."[12]

When I use a number, says the modern manipulative politician in a democracy or the undemocratic leader of an autocracy, it means just what I say it does. I have my statisticians to back me up. The only question is who is to be master – that's all.

Stalin, the Missing Census and the Missing Statisticians

The story of the Soviet census of 1937 is the story of a missing census. It is also the story of Stalin's brutal treatment of his statisticians. As Pali Lehohla wrote in his essay on the vagaries of being a statistician, the missing census showed quite literally that 'failure to deliver a politically expected number can be fatal to the statistician'.[13]

The census was conducted in early January of that year, having been ordered by Stalin the previous year. The results were never officially published. Details about what happened to the statistics and the statisticians were concealed at the time, and what the regime said publicly about the census cannot be trusted. Even with the opening of the archives, following the Soviet collapse, any historical account of the lost census will contain gaps.

This short section on the census does not reveal anything new. We are relying on some historical and demographic works, published in English as well as some translations of primary texts.[14] The historical works include Catherine Merridale's superb essay on the census.[15] She is the author of

[12] Lewis Carroll (1871/2019), *Through the Looking-Glass*, Orinda: Sea Wolf Press, p. 64.
[13] Lehohla (2022).
[14] On the history of the 1937 Census, see: James von Geldern (2016), 'The lost census: subject essay', *Seventeen Moments in Soviet History: an Online Archive of Primary Sources*, Michigan State University https://soviethistory.msu.edu/1939-2/the-lost-census/; R. W. Davies, Mark Harrison, Oleg Khlevniuk and Stephen G. Wheatcroft (2018), *The Industrialisation of Soviet Russia*, Vol. 7, London: Palgrave Macmillan; Holubnychy's 1960 account of Soviet statistics remains worth reading, despite having been published just seven years after Stalin's death, well before the opening of the Soviet archives: Vsevolod Holubnychy, V. (1960), 'Government statistical observation in the USSR: 1917–1957', *American Slavic and East European Review*, 19, 28–41. Reimund Mink includes a useful account of the Census in chapter 5 of his book on official statistics: Reimund Mink (2023), *Official Statistics – a Plaything of Politics?* Cham, Switzerland: Springer, pp. 89–103.
[15] Catherine Merridale (1996), 'The 1937 census and the limits of Stalinist rule', *The Historical Journal*, 39, 225–40.

several beautifully written histories, in which she displays deep knowledge of Russia's past and of the myths Russians continue to hold about that past.[16] We will also be relying on Mark Tolts's invaluable statistical work, particularly when discussing the details of Russia's censuses during the Soviet era.

Where to start this brief account of Stalin and the manipulation of the census? Unlike a formal theory or schematic guide, events in the social world rarely have a clearly defined beginning. The manipulation of statistics is not like a three-person relay race, in which the first baton holder only begins running after hearing the clear crack of a starting pistol and then hands on the baton to the second-stage runner. But even the starting pistol is not the beginning of a runner's race: there is the taking-up of the starting position, and before that the warm-up exercises, the walking out into the stadium, not to mention the months of training. How is it possible to pinpoint exactly where the first stage for any ultimate success or failure actually began?

Regarding the 1937 Soviet census, we must mention the previous one, conducted in 1926 and planned before Stalin had fully established himself as the ruler of the USSR. The census recorded the total population of the USSR as more than 147 million, or to be precise: 147,027,915. This was to prove a source of statistical problems for Stalin.

Stalin's stated aim was to show that he was building a socialist society that could be scientifically demonstrated to be superior to capitalist societies. A new census, ten years after the previous one, should provide evidence that the Bolshevik vision was being realised. A growth in the population would show the improving health of the new Soviets and that life was improving throughout the USSR's huge territory. Stalin, it seems, pushed for a new question to be added to the census: respondents would be asked about their religious beliefs. The leader was hoping to demonstrate statistically that the majority of the population no longer needed the 'opium of the masses', but they would willingly identify themselves as atheists.

The new census posed problems for many of the senior statisticians in the Central Statistical Office (TsUNKhU). Ivan Kraval headed the Office and was placed in charge of organising the new census. Since the early 1930s Kraval had been supplying the regime with projections about the growth of the USSR's population. It seems that Kraval had been sending

---

[16] Catherine Merridale (2013), *Red Fortress*, Harmondsworth: Penguin; Catherine Merridale (2017), *Lenin on the Train*, Harmondsworth: Penguin.

his projections directly to Stalin and to Molotov, then serving as the chairman of the Council of People's Commissars and later to become minister of foreign affairs. The population projections that Kraval sent upwards to his leaders had included estimates from 1933.

This year was significant because 1933 was the year of the great famine in the USSR. The famine had arisen principally from the policy to 'collectivise' farming and to forcibly remove independent, better-off peasants, or kulaks, from their lands. Sudden collectivisation led to a disastrous loss of agricultural productivity, especially in Ukraine and Kazakhstan where many kulaks lived. The food shortages resulted in mass starvation and loss of life, and this was enhanced by loss of life among those kulaks who resisted collectivisation and were punished violently.

It should have been obvious to Stalin in 1936 that a new census would reflect the depredations that the USSR had suffered during the previous three years. It should have been obvious, but for one fact. The projections that Kraval had been sending Stalin and Molotov had been manipulated to hide the effects of the famine and to show a steady increase in the population. To quote Catherine Merridale, the head statistician had 'chosen to mask the extent of demographic shortfalls and disasters in the 1930s, possibly on the principle that the messenger would be the first to be shot'.[17]

Kraval and his colleagues had been statistically manipulating their projections upwards as a matter of course without specific directions from the country's leader. But, of course, the statisticians were reacting to the general atmosphere of political fear and control. They did not need direct orders, but what they were doing was a response to Stalin's power over them and over other administrators of the state. Their statistical manipulation may have been designed to forestall greater trouble, but it led to precisely the trouble that they feared.

Because of the difficulties in designing the questions for the census and in recruiting the immense number of enumerators required to administer the survey, the census was delayed from 1936 to January 1937. It is said that Stalin took a great interest in the design of the questions in the census and commented on successive drafts.[18] The Communist newspaper *Pravda* was bullish in promoting the census. It declared that the census was a matter of great economic and political significance. Lenin had loved accurate data and comrade Stalin's 'attitude towards statistical data is well-known'. According to the paper only bourgeois and petty bourgeois politicians feared statistics.[19]

---

[17] Merridale (1996), p. 225.   [18] Mink (2023), pp. 96–7.   [19] Merridale (1996), p. 230.

Kraval feared the statistics that the survey would produce. He ordered the statisticians under his command not to divulge any results. He knew that the census figures would be well below the projections that had been based on the 1926 census, and that had taken into account estimations of normal population growth and had largely ignored the mass famine. The estimated figures for 1933 had been between 165 and 167 million. Kraval had been estimating that the figures for 1936–7 should be higher than in 1933 – somewhere around 170 million.

However, the 1937 figures were showing the total population to be only around the 162 million mark (162,039,470 to be precise). This was noticeably below the estimate for 1933 and, if published, it would have provided the public with evidence about the effects of famine and persecution on the total population. Worst of all, the numbers revealed by the census would be evidence pointing at the failure of Comrade Stalin's policies.

Stalin, however, did not think that the figures were providing evidence of his own failures. In his mind they revealed the treachery of his leading statisticians. Certainly the census had statistical and methodological weaknesses. The statisticians had left openings for double counting. Citizens who were not staying at their family home could be counted both at that home and also at the house where they were staying – a possibility all too likely over the celebrations for the Orthodox Christmas when the census was conducted. But this error would lead to an overestimation of the population. The statisticians might have justified increasing numbers on the grounds that the enumerators failed to reach and count remote rural and mountainous populations in the depths of winter.[20] But it would have been dangerous to admit faults in the conduct of the census. Possibly, the statisticians missed opportunities to manipulate their totals further upwards. They were not new to the business of inflating estimations, but they were facing a political leader who was demanding an impossibility. Stalin wanted specific numerical results from his statisticians but he insisted that they produce these numbers without manipulation or scientific cheating. He believed that it was possible to do both things because the benefits of Marxism were scientifically necessary and therefore scientifically demonstrable.

It did not take long for the worst private fears of the head statistician to be confirmed publicly. The leadership announced that the census, projected for January 1937, had been cancelled because of 'the deliberate

---

[20] Mark Tolts (1995), 'The Soviet censuses of 1937 and 1939: some problems of data evaluation', paper presented at the International Conference on Soviet Population in the 1920s and 1930s, www.academia.edu/1522451.

distortion on the part of the enemies of the people'.[21] In December 1938 the party publication *Bol'shevik* mentioned the errors in the design of the 1937 census and declared that they were not innocent mistakes. There were signs of deliberate, anti-government sabotage. According to *Bol'shevik*, the census 'was conducted with violations of government instructions, with the grossest violations of elementary principles of statistical science' because 'enemies of the people set themselves the goal of distorting the real number of the population'.[22] An inquiry into the census was announced and it concluded that the Statistics Office had been penetrated by 'a group of spies' and that Kraval had consciously or unconsciously permitted their activities.[23]

Being identified as an enemy of the people was in those days tantamount to a sentence of death. So it proved for the statisticians. Kraval and some of his top colleagues, such as his deputies Kurman and Kvitkin, immediately disappeared. They were almost certainly executed without even a show trial. This was a dangerous time for senior administrators and party bureaucrats. Hannah Arendt describes 1936 as having marked the start of the 'gigantic super-purge which in nearly two years liquidated the existing administration'.[24]

The Statistics Office was not closed down following its so-called failure with the 1937 census, but replacements were found to take the places of those who had been denounced, removed and never seen again. Like other bureaucrats, who were denounced and then disappeared, they are likely to have been shot out of sight. Here surely was the final stage of the missing 1937 census. Nevertheless, it was not the final stage of the statistical manipulation.

In fact, we might see the tragic end of the 1937 census not as a final stage at all. We could view it as the first stage of the replacement census of 1939. On 29 November 1938, *Pravda* announced in a lead article that there would be a census in the following year. It quoted what Comrade Stalin had told the 13th Party Congress:

> No construction work, no government work, no planning work is conceivable without accurate calculation. But calculation is inconceivable without statistics. Without statistics, calculation cannot move forward even a single step.[25]

[21] Holubnychy (1960), p. 38.
[22] *Bol'shevik* (1938), 'Duty of the whole people', 23–24 December, https://soviethistory.msu.edu/1939-2/the-lost-census/the-lost-census-texts/duty-of-the-whole-people/.
[23] Davies et al. (2018), pp. 140–41.
[24] Hannah Arendt (1951/1973), *The Origins of Totalitarianism*, Orlando: Harcourt Brace, p. 394.
[25] *Pravda* (1938), 'A most important government task', 29 November, p. 1. For translation of original, see: https://soviethistory.msu.edu/1939-2/the-lost-census/the-lost-census-texts/a-most-important-government-task/.

Pravda made clear the connection between ideology and a growing population, when it declared:

> With the years of Soviet authority, our country has become a wealthy and mighty socialist power. In the Soviet Union the population is growing with extraordinary speed.[26]

In the eighteenth century, Voltaire wrote in *Candide* that the British had executed Admiral Byng, after losing the Battle of Minorca, *pour encourager les autres* (to encourage the others). This would have been an extreme method of encouraging the other admirals to do better in future naval battles. The execution of Kraval and his assistants might seem to indicate paranoid politics, rather than pragmatic policy. However, behind the executions there also lay a manipulative and ideological logic.[27]

The Statistics Office, now headed by Vladimir Starovsky, had a new set of senior statisticians who had been 'encouraged' in the most extreme way to produce the desired numbers. Comrade Stalin was helping them to appreciate just what they had to do. Weeks after the census, he announced at the 18th Party Congress on 10 March 1939 that the total Soviet population numbered 170,000,000. Stalin's speech to the Party Congress might appear at first sight to be a classic third-stage boast: he was trumpeting the manipulated numbers as a great achievement, thereby publicly hiding the truth of his political failures. Such a boast, one might think, should have followed the manipulation of the census numbers by the statisticians responsible for calculating the population.

In his speech Stalin was doing more than treating manipulated numbers as if they were statistical facts. He was also doing something sinister. Mark Tolts has suggested that Stalin was announcing the results of the census before the statisticians could have possibly calculated the actual numbers.[28] Not just boasting to a mass audience, his message was also being directed at his statisticians. He was threatening them, telling them the numbers they must find.

If Stalin's new statisticians were *les autres* to be encouraged by the execution of their predecessors, then Voltaire's ironic words scarcely describe the terror under which the statisticians of 1939 were operating. Starovsky and his colleagues met their immediate target, declaring the total

---

[26] *Pravda* (1938), 29 November.
[27] Stephen Kotkin writes in his biography of Stalin that the dictator 'was brilliantly adept at administration and manipulation' (p. 419). According to Kotkin, the key to Stalin's political brutality lay in his commitment to hard-line revolutionary Marxism: Stephen Kotkin (2015), *Stalin*, vol. 1, London: Penguin.
[28] Tolts (1995).

population of the USSR to be 170,557,093. They thereby avoided being branded as enemies of the people. According to Tolts's calculations, their figure is likely to have involved a manipulated inflation by at least three million. The populations of famine-depleted Ukraine and Kazakhstan were exaggerated at a rate well above the average exaggeration for the rest of the USSR.[29]

After Starovsky's success in manipulating the statistics from the 1939 census, Stalin kept him in post as chief statistician. Starovsky continued to oversee the production of politically acceptable numbers, so much so that he survived professionally to take charge of the 1959 census of the USSR. This was the first census after the death of Stalin.

We started this section by saying that we were going to tell the story of Stalin's missing census of 1937. But to understand why it was suppressed, it was necessary to go back to the earlier statistical manipulations of 1933, when fear made senior statisticians overestimate the population of the USSR. Statistical manipulation rarely involves a single self-contained act and the missing census led to further statistical manipulations in the 1939 census. To understand a single episode in this sequence – such as the missing census – we need to look backwards to earlier events and forward to future ones. There is no simple Stage 1 and Stage 3. Instead, there are interlocking series of actions, involving the brutal power of government, statisticians trying to oblige that power by manipulating official figures, and, in retaliation, the government executing some of those statisticians.

China: Manipulating Local Statistics

China is very much a centralised society, where power flows down from the Communist Party and its leader to the provinces and the regions of the country. The party and its leader like to present an image of a society in which the various levels of government all slot together in harmonious unity. The National Bureau of Statistics (NBS), China's official statistical agency, fits nationally and regionally into this top-down society. Officially it serves the Party, its leader as well as the government, and it coordinates the production of official statistics at all levels of this huge country. The

---

[29] Tolts (1995); Mark Tolts (2019), 'The results of the 1939 Soviet census: two problems of adequacy', *Demographic Review*, 7, 100–17. Mark Tolts reports that the 1939 Soviet census for Kazakhstan was blatantly distorted. Officially it was reported that the population of Russians outnumbered Kazakhs but according to Tolts's re-recalculation the reverse was true: Mark Tolts (2006), 'Ethnic composition of Kazakhstan on the eve of the Second World War: re-evaluation of the 1939 Soviet census result', *Central Asian Survey*, 25 (1–2), 143–8.

image might look perfect, but the relations between statisticians and their political bosses are seldom straightforward. In modern China, senior statisticians have been in the uncomfortable situation of being caught up in problems relating to the fabrication of statistical data. The story that we are telling about the publication of targets and the manipulation of statistics bears out something that Donald Campbell wrote in the 1970. He claimed that the political corruption of statistical measures would occur wherever politicians sought to show that they were meeting targets, whether in a capitalist or a communist society.[30]

Look at any of NBS's major documents and you will find in the opening paragraph the Bureau paying a standard tribute to the regime. To give an example: at the end of February 2023, NBS published a statistical communiqué about the economic and social development of the country. NBS declared that the previous year had been 'of great importance' because the National Congress of the Communist Party had outlined 'a grand blueprint for building a modern socialist country'. The opening of the communiqué went on: under 'the strong leadership of the CPC Central Committee with Comrade Xi Jinping at its core … all regions and departments fully implemented the decisions and arrangements made by the CPC Central Committee'. The rest of the communiqué was designed to illustrate this achievement with an assortment of statistical tables and ascending graphs.[31]

Most of NBS's important documents start with similar wording. The Bureau's interim economic report for 2022 carried good statistical news about the economy recovering after Covid-19. The report started with a tribute: all regions and departments were following the strong leadership of the Party with Xi at its core.[32] The difference was that the 'departments' in the phrase 'all regions and departments' did not refer to geographical departments but to government departments which had provided information for the surveys. The government departments are also arranged top-down from the central ministry down through the regions and layers of local government.

---

[30] Donald T. Campbell (1979), 'Assessing the impact of planned social change', *Evaluation and Program Planning*, 2, 67–90.
[31] National Bureau of Statistics of China (2023), 'Statistical communiqué of the People's Republic of China on the 2022 national economic and social development', www.stats.gov.cn/english/PressRelease/202302/t20230227_1918979.html. The NBS website publishes its documents in both Chinese and English. Our quotations come from the official English versions.
[32] National Bureau of Statistics of China (2022), 'National economy showed sound momentum of recovery in the first three quarters', press release 24 October, www.stats.gov.cn/english/PressRelease/202210/t20221024_1889500.html.

This interim economic report, like the economic and social development report, was organised to provide good-news statistics. It was as if each of China's thirty-one provinces, as well as their regions and even the lower levels of counties and village/townships, were publishing through the NBS their own versions of good-news data. So were the various levels of ministerial departments. Everyone seemed to be marching together in fulfilment of the leader's strong leadership.

However, there was a statistical cloud to upset the serene sky: data fabrication. Fabricating statistics was serious enough that a specific law was passed in 1996 making it a punishable offence.[33] In 2009 *China Daily*, an English-language Chinese newspaper, published several articles on proposed revisions to strengthen the law and to increase the penalties for offences. According to the paper, the government and NBS were jointly drafting new provisions to impose severe penalties on officials who 'intervene in government statistical work and manipulate or fabricate data'.[34] There was a need 'to crack down on rampant cheating in statistics by some local governments'.[35]

The new penalties failed to solve the problem of statistical manipulation. Ten years later *China Daily* reported that the National Bureau was urging the country to impose even stronger punishments for statistical fraud.[36] The Bureau held a special conference in 2020 to address the issue because statistical fabrication had occurred in several of China's provinces. The actions of whistle-blowers had brought the offences to light. In one province, the deputy Party leader was expelled from the Party and from public office for a series of offences that included the fabrication of data.[37]

The dismissed provincial Party chief would not have manufactured his own statistics. He would need his local branch of NBS to produce the numbers for him, and then he could send them upwards to central government while his local NBS passed the numbers onto the central NBS. We do not know how the local Party leaders might have prevailed on

---

[33] For an updated version of the law, see: National Bureau of Statistics of China (2022), 'Statistics Law of the People's Republic of China', www.stats.gov.cn/english/LF/SL/201209/t20120921_27177 .html.

[34] *China Daily* (2009a), 'China revises statistics law to curb data falsification', 26 June, www .chinadaily.com.cn/china/2009-06/27/content_8330256.htm.

[35] *China Daily* (2009b), 'Statistics and lies', 30 April, www.chinadaily.com.cn/cndy/2009-04/30/ content_7731763.htm.

[36] *China Daily* (2019), 'Ensuring authenticity of data focus of draft statistics law', 10 October, https:// global.chinadaily.com.cn/a/201910/10/WS5d9e78e8a310cf3e3556f8ed.html.

[37] For details see: *Global Times* (2020), 'China gets tougher on statistical fabrication to ensure data quality for macro fine-tuning and scientific policymaking', 1 June, www.globaltimes.cn/page/ 202206/1267161.shtml.

their statisticians to fabricate the numbers. Did the local statisticians see it as part of their job to support the local Party leaders and so need little persuasion? Did they share a strong regional identity and a sense of distance from the central leadership? Or were the local statisticians threatened with dismissal if they did not comply? Perhaps they were encouraged by the prospect of promotion if the whole region enjoyed political success. We do not know, but in each case something had to happen behind closed doors.

China Daily, when it called statistical fabrication 'rampant' in some local governments, had been quoting a leading central politician.[38] The basic problem was structural. The government required data to show that the economy was progressing and local leaders would often have good reasons for boosting their data.[39] Towards the end of each year, the central government and its departments set targets for the coming year. Then, with these central targets in mind, the provinces and provincial regions set their own targets. The leaders of the local governments would have vested interests in seeing that the figures which are returned demonstrate that they have successfully met their targets.[40]

There is evidence that boosting figures was common at local levels. A team of four academic statisticians, three from Fudan University in Shanghai and one from Yale University in the States, examined whether some local governments met their economic targets by manipulating the numbers.[41] Using 'the discontinuity method', the researchers asked whether there was anything suspicious about the spread of the economic data that the provinces and regions were returning between 2002 and 2015. The researchers found that statistics indicating that targets had been narrowly missed were between four and five times less frequent than those indicating that targets had been narrowly achieved. This would not have been expected by chance. It strongly suggested that the local politicians were boosting near-miss numbers to push them over the target line.

The comments of central politicians and newspapers, as well as academic researchers, seemed to be combining to condemn fabrication as a

[38] *Global Times* (2020). See also: Carsten A. Holz (2014), 'The quality of China's GDP statistics', *China Economic Review*, 30, 309–38.

[39] Dmitriy Plekhanov (2017), 'Quality of China's official statistics: a brief review of academic perspectives', *Copenhagen Journal of Asian Studies*, 35, 76–101.

[40] Xia Chen, Qiang Cheng, Ying Hao and Qiang Liu (2020), 'GDP growth incentives and earnings management: evidence from China', *Review of Accounting Studies*, 25, 1002–39.

[41] Lyu Changjiang, Kemin Wang, Frank Zhang and Zhang Xin (2018), 'GDP management to meet or beat growth targets', *Journal of Accounting and Economics*, 66, 318–38.

local, not a central, problem. In such an authoritarian society, with its image of a strong central government, there are vested interests in project-ing problems onto the local government and away from the central leadership. If the public seems to distrust the centre's statistics, then it needs to be informed that the faults lie in the localities. In 2009, when *China Daily* reported about rampant statistical cheating by some local governments, the paper implied that centrally produced statistics did not have this problem. But sometimes the public might be sceptical about central statistical claims. *China Daily* denied that increasing the penalties for statistical fabrication had anything to do with the mistaken and 'widespread public scepticism about the inflated average salary of urban workers' which NBS had released earlier that month.[42]

Local leaders might be blamed for having an interest in being seen to meet their yearly targets. However, central ministers might have corres-ponding motives. Repeated failure to meet targets would expose a central minister to the prospect of dismissal by the leadership. In addition, the statistics of centre and periphery cannot be easily separated. The central ministries, in collecting figures for the whole country, would typically rely on figures that were collected locally. The central NSB, when computing figures for the overall gross domestic product (GDP), relies substantially on using figures collected by the local statisticians.[43] Even if the central statisticians strongly suspected that the data had been manipulated and even if they augmented it with measures that were centrally collected, they could not dispense with the local data. Indeed, some central ministers might not wish to dispense with them, if that was their route to being seen to have met their national targets.

The central government would have a vested interest in not finding data fabrication at the centre of government. It would then be looking else-where for the manipulation of data; and this in itself would be a way of manipulating the data about manipulation. Take the Fudan–Yale study as an illustration. The authors write that they used GDP data to measure economic output because this data is 'publicly available and can be collected without much effort'.[44] The GDP figures and target figures for the whole of China would have been just as available as the data for the

---

[42] *China Daily* (2009b), 30 April.
[43] Thomas G. Rawski (2001), 'What is happening to China's GDP statistics?', *China Economic Review*, 12, 347–54; Chen et al. (2020); Wei Chen, Xilu Chen, Chang-Tai Hsieh and Zheng Song (2019), 'A forensic analysis of China's national accounts', Working Paper no. 25754, National Bureau of Economic Research, Cambridge, Mass.
[44] Lyu et al. (2018), p. 330.

provinces and regions. The 'discontinuity method' could have been used to check whether the departmental ministers and their central statisticians had been manipulating their national figures to show that targets were being met. However, the Fudan–Yale team did not do this. They looked for manipulation in the provinces.[45]

More generally, this shows what can happen when a statistical bureau seeks to do the bidding of a strong central government. It can get too close to power for comfort. This does not mean that it will be forced to fabricate data crudely, but there will be some statistical investigations to avoid for political reasons. As the fictional detective Sherlock Holmes once said, sometimes it is the dog that doesn't bark that provides the clue.[46] Similarly, sometimes the surveys that aren't conducted provide the statistical clue that the surveys that have been conducted may not be all they appear to be.

Argentina: the Price of Prices

Statistical manipulation is not confined to autocracies. Democratic governments can use their powers to try to control statisticians and to induce them to infringe the principles of good statistical practice. Our first democratic example comes from Argentina and it concerns the county's inflation figures during the first decade of the twenty-first century. This example throws open a door that is normally kept closed. Through this door, we can see a minister aggressively threatening a statistician. It is not an edifying sight.

This is the story of Graciela Bevacqua as told in an interview which was published in *Significance*, the magazine of the Royal Statistical Society.[47] Bevacqua worked at the Instituto Nacional de Estadística y Censos (INDEC), Argentina's national agency for statistics. She was based in the department that calculated the country's consumer price index (CPI), and she ultimately rose to become the leader of the Consumer Price Index Group. As Bevacqua told her interviewer, 'this was a rewarding time'.[48]

---

[45] In this case, the corruption of the method, and thereby the manipulation of statistics, does not of itself follow quite the way that Campbell (1967) predicted. It follows from the non-usage of the method to check on the targets of the most powerful, rather than on its usage.

[46] Arthur Conan Doyle (1892/1989), 'Silver blaze', in A. C. Doyle (ed.), *Sherlock Holmes: The Complete Stories*, London: Wordsworth.

[47] Alicia Carriquiry (2012), 'Graciela Bevacqua: a life in statistics', *Significance*, 9(6), 34–6. Alicia Carriquiry is a Uruguayan statistician, who currently works as Distinguished Professor of Statistics at Iowa State University.

[48] Ibid., p. 34.

But it wasn't to last. In 2005 Nestor Kirchner, who headed a left-leaning government, appointed Guillermo Moreno as the minister for domestic trade. Moreno wanted to reduce Argentina's official rate of inflation – itself a laudable ambition. However, he wanted to do this by pressuring the statisticians to reduce the CPI figures that were published each month. As such, Moreno's solution was methodological, and thus statistically manipulative, rather than being based on reducing the actual price of goods.

The story starts with a meeting that took place behind closed doors. Shortly after Moreno was appointed, he summoned Bevacqua and her immediate superior to his office. Bevacqua became worried as she entered the room: 'He had put on classical music, and I thought it was because he didn't want people outside to hear what he was going to say'. The minister began with a 'tirade' about how the CPI affected people's morale and that the index needed to be changed, in order to 'increase confidence in the economic outlook'.[49] Alicia Carriquiry, the author of the *Significance* story, commented that the minister was 'demanding' that the figures should be more 'favourable to the government'.[50] Here was the start of a classic Stage 1 as portrayed in our schematic guide.[51]

Bevacqua recounted how Moreno tried to manipulate her. First he played the patriotic card, telling her and her statisticians that 'the patriotic thing to do was to report a low CPI'. They were, after all, national servants who should serve the interests of the nation. When this appeal failed, Bevacqua said that she was 'permanently harassed', as Moreno would phone her almost daily, shouting his demands down the phone: 'There was no stopping his bullying,' she told *Significance*.[52]

He made two demands in particular. First, all the statisticians, who worked in her group to calculate the consumer price index, should always round numbers down, never round them up. This was not a minor adjustment because of the volume of calculations being made each month

---

[49] Ibid.   [50] Ibid.
[51] Celia Lury and Ana Gross provide an interesting account of Moreno and the Argentinian CPI. Because they are interested in 'statactivism', or public activism relating to statistics, their account starts in 2007 with the public controversy, unlike our account that begins a year earlier: Celia Lury and Ana Gross (2014), 'The downs and ups of the consumer price index in Argentina: from national statistics to big data', *Partecipazione & Conflitto*, 7, 258–77, http://siba-ese.unisalento.it/index.php/paco/article/view/14153. For the concept of 'statactivism', see: Isabelle Bruno, Emmanuel Didier and Tommaso Vitale (2014), 'Statactivism: forms of action between disclosure and affirmation', *Open Journal of Sociopolitical Studies*, 7, 198–220, https://papers.ssrn.com/sol3/papers.cfm?abstract_id=2466882.
[52] Carriquiry (2012), p. 35.

to extract a single figure from the prices of a large number of different commodities. Carriquiry pointed out that the effect of always rounding down could over a year halve the inflation figure from twenty-five per cent to twelve per cent.[53]

Second, Moreno demanded to know who the retailers supplying INDEC with information about their prices were. To calculate the CPI, INDEC received information each month from selected retailers in the greater Bueno Aires area about the price of specific items that the statisticians had chosen to represent the cost of living. Non-luxury food items were an important part of this measure, but it also included items such as the cost of holidays. Bevacqua and her colleagues knew that if they passed on the information to the minister, they would be divulging information that had been given to them with the assurance of confidentiality.

In addition, the statisticians strongly suspected that Moreno wanted this information so that he could pressurise the retailers to lower the prices on their monthly returns to INDEC. In short, Moreno was attempting a double manipulation: he was aiming to manipulate the statisticians so that he could then manipulate their respondents. An earlier article on the *Significance* website in May 2012 reported that retailers felt threatened and intimidated to report lower prices than they were actually charging.[54] This particularly affected travel agents. Because there were so few of them in the Buenos Aires area, the minister did not need information from the statisticians to find out who they were.

Colleagues outside Argentina told Bevacqua that Moreno's methods were more typical of an authoritarian dictatorship than a democratically elected government. She stood firm against him for a while, but her resistance did not last long. In January 2007 she was suspended from her post and, along with others, she was dismissed. Many of INDEC's statisticians were involved in public protests against Moreno and there was a series of brief strikes.[55] The director of INDEC resigned in March. Bevacqua immediately noticed a difference in the CPI figures, for the rise in prices was halved. Moreno must have successfully pressured the remaining statisticians in the CPI group to manipulate the data.

It is not altogether clear why Moreno acted in this way. Certainly he was personally ambitious and would have been delighted if he became known

---

[53] Ibid.
[54] Cecilia T. Lanata Briones and Claudia Daniel (2020), 'Inflation in Argentina: a controversial figure', *Significance*, 17, 30–5.
[55] See: Lury and Gross (2014) for details of the public protests.

as the man who solved Argentina's runaway inflation – even if he only did so by manipulating the published numbers. Some analysts have suggested that Moreno had economic reasons for lowering the rate of inflation by manipulating the figures. Joseph Kadane, an American statistician working at Carnegie Mellon University, wrote an article for the *Los Angeles Times*, pointing out that Argentina had issued a number of government bonds in the early 2000s. Banks and other institutions who bought the bonds expected the government to repay them with interest within a stipulated period, otherwise the debt would increase. The value of some of these bonds was linked to the rate of inflation. That meant, as Kadane explained, that if the government lowered the official rate of inflation, then it would owe its creditors less.[56]

It did not stop there. Moreno continued to be able to publish diminishing CPI figures, whether these figures were produced by statisticians within INDEC or whether Moreno was hiring outside contractors to manipulate the official numbers. It is said that he made an agreement with retailers to cap the prices of basic goods in their returns to INDEC.[57] What is clear, however, is that Moreno continued to pursue Bevacqua and some of her colleagues, who were privately producing and publishing estimates of the CPI which showed the rates to be far higher than the official ones. Moreno threatened to prosecute anyone who issued statistical figures that diverged from the official ones.

In fact, the Argentinian government levied hefty fines on Bevacqua, and brought criminal charges against her and her colleagues for compiling independent price indices.[58] International statisticians declared this to be a threat to freedom of speech, because by law all statisticians had to agree with the government's figures and any alternative calculation was criminal. The fines were not negligible, with some of the independent statistical agencies being fined sums equivalent to half a million US dollars. Bevacqua was fined, then prosecuted for a civil offence along with one of her colleagues. When the case came to court in 2012, it was dismissed by the judge. Moreno simply raised the stakes. He threatened Bevacqua with

[56] Joseph B. Kadane (2013), 'Numbers racket in Argentina', *Los Angeles Times*, 30 January, www.latimes.com/opinion/la-xpm-2013-jan-30-la-oe-0130-kandane-argentina-inflation-censorship-20130130-story.html.
[57] *The Economist* (2012), 'The price of cooking the books', 25 February, www.economist.com/the-americas/2012/02/25/the-price-of-cooking-the-books.
[58] William Seltzer and Joseph B. Kadane (2012), 'Politics and statistics collide in Argentina', *Amstat News*, 1 December, 7–8.

a further prosecution, this time for a criminal offence that carried the possibility of a lengthy prison sentence.

Internationally, there was a great deal of support for the persecuted Argentinian statisticians. The American Statistical Association (ASA) even appealed to the United Nations to intervene in what it called 'the systematic intimidation and violation of the free speech and scientific freedom rights of the statisticians.[59] In August 2015, *Amstat News*, the official magazine of the ASA, announced that the 'long ordeal' of Graciela Bevacqua and her colleagues was coming to an end, as a judge had ruled in her favour on the criminal charges.[60]

By this time the Kirchners were out of power and a new government had been elected. As if by magic, the inflation figures started rising again. There has been increasing evidence to show that the government had been systematically manipulating the inflation figures between 2007 and 2011.[61] In 2014, following pressure from the International Monetary Fund, the Argentinian government conceded that the official figures for the CPI had been manipulated for a good number of years.[62]

The evidence from Alberto Cavallo and his colleagues, who have been pioneering a new way of measuring consumer prices, has been particularly important. Instead of using returns from selected retailers within a specified area, they monitor the prices which major national supermarkets publish daily on their webpages. This produces a far greater amount of data than the traditional method and it saves the need for making decisions about what is an 'average' consumption of an 'average' household. All the prices are recorded automatically, and, given the enormous amount of data generated, Cavallo has named his method the Billion Prices Project (BPP). Like all methods that measure complex social phenomena, the BPP is not perfect: it relies on supermarket prices and it excludes the prices of small retailers, including local bakers.

[59] Seltzer and Kadane (2012).

[60] *Amstat News* (2015), 'Argentine mathematician cleared on charges of publishing alternative price indexes magazine', 1 August, https://magazine.amstat.org/blog/2015/08/01/argentine-mathematician/.

[61] See, for example: Aragão and Linsi (2022); Alberto Cavallo, Guillermo Cruces and Ricardo Perez-Truglia (2017), 'Inflation expectations, learning, and supermarket prices: evidence from survey experiments', *American Economic Journal: Macroeconomics*, 9(3), 1–35; Ariel Coremberg (2014), 'Measuring Argentina's GDP growth: myths and facts', *World Economics*, 15(1), 1–31, https://arklems.files.wordpress.com/2011/10/wec-151_coremberg-1.pdf.

[62] *International Business Times News* (2014), 'Argentina finally owns up to its real inflation rate', 15 February.

Cavallo compared the results from his new method with the official national figures of inflation in Brazil, Chile, Columbia, Venezuela and Argentina. He found that in four of these five countries, his new method, based on its wide and continual sampling, showed broad agreement with the traditional ways of measuring consumer prices. The exception was Argentina between 2007 and 2011 – the heyday of Moreno. Cavallo concluded that 'the results for Argentina . . . confirm the suspicion that the government is manipulating the official inflation series'.[63] He suggested that the government was only reporting a fraction of the real inflation rate.

As for Moreno, he resigned from his post in late 2013 and then he resigned from the Justicialist Party. The following year he was prosecuted for abusing his authority as a minister by illegally trying to suppress independent estimates of inflation. He was found guilty. In a curious turn of fate, this political bully, who had threatened statisticians so intemperately, entered the delicate world of diplomacy, becoming for a while an economic attaché at Argentina's embassy in Rome.

Moreno's foray into the diplomacy did little to diminish his reputation as a bully or free him from his unfulfilled political ambitions. In 2022 he was found guilty of threatening behaviour and was given a suspended prison sentence of two years, as well as being disqualified from holding public office for six months.[64] His political dreams have persisted undiminished. He heads his own small political party, the Principles and Values Party, which declares its admiration for strong leaders such as Juan Perón and Donald Trump.[65]

In 2021 Moreno stood as a presidential pre-candidate, but he failed to attract enough votes to progress to later rounds. He has announced that he will stand again. It is too simple to say that he has so little support that he could never succeed in a presidential election. In today's volatile political world, unpopular populists on the threshold of old age have suddenly been transformed into handsome popular populists. Moreno can hope to follow

---

[63] Alberto Cavallo (2013), 'Online and official price indexes: measuring Argentina's inflation', *Journal of Monetary Economics*, 60, 152–65, p. 163. See also: Cavallo, Cruces and Perez-Truglia (2017).

[64] See: Archyde (2020), '"Helmet or gloves?" a new oral trial begins against Guillermo Moreno', 13 March, www.archyde.com/helmet-or-gloves-a-new-oral-trial-begins-against-guillermo-moreno/; *The Nation View* (2022), 'Guillermo Moreno sentenced for threats in newspapers: "Everything within the law, nothing outside the law"', 6 July, https://thenationview.com/politics/57340.html. For an earlier incident, see: Benedict Mander (2013), 'Argentina: guillotine for Guillermo?', *Financial Times*, 23 September, www.ft.com/content/ccba7377-b29f-3fe7-91e5-4bb265c77170.

[65] On Moreno's party and his presidential ambitions, see: *CE Noticias Financieras English*, (2023), '"You were willing to vote for an unhinged marginal", Guillermo Moreno's unusual spot with references to Milei', 12 May.

his hero Trump. He seems to dream that the goddess of fortune will plant a kiss on the cheek of an elderly, Argentinian bully. There will be statisticians around the world hoping that she doesn't.

Greece: Starting or Stopping Statistical Fraud

Our second example of statistical manipulation in a democratic country comes from Greece – the country which is often called the birthplace of democracy (but only if you discount ancient slaves, foreigners and women). This second example has many of the same characteristics as the Argentinian case. They both feature a high-ranking statistician who encountered intense pressures from their government to manipulate national, economic statistics. Both statisticians faced criminal prosecution when they refused to comply. And for their stance, both received strong support from senior statisticians across the world. The second democratic example, however, is certainly not a mere repetition of the first.

Our story of the Argentinian case was based around the story of Graciela Bevacqua, a courageous statistician who stood against the bullying behaviour of a government minister. Our account of the Greek manipulation also centres around the story of an individual statistician, Andreas Georgiou. He also resisted political pressure to produce dishonest statistics. Nevertheless, the two stories are very different. The Argentinian case seemed perfect for illustrating our schematic guide, or at least the first stage of the guide. We see Bevacqua working happily, compiling the consumer price index to the best of her and her team's ability. Then suddenly there is a minister threatening her if she doesn't fiddle the figures. There is a clear opening act in the drama.

In the Georgiou story, there is no opening stage, and our understanding of the manipulation does not depend on us identifying the precise moment when it all started. It is much more than a story between two individuals. It is the story of a senior statistician joining a statistical agency where the manipulation of official statistics about the national debt has become endemic. We do not know exactly when the agency's manipulation of the national debt started. Moreover, the production of the manipulated numbers may have occurred in Greece but it took place in an international context.

As new statistical evidence has emerged, so the starting date of the manipulation has been pushed back in time. Even today, more than twenty-five years later, there is no identifiable moment when all observers will say 'that's exactly when Greek economic statistics started to be manipulated'. We are not going to say when, in our view, the first stage began. When statistical manipulation has become routinely accepted by politicians and statisticians, the precise starting moment is not necessarily the most important issue. Discovering when it started will not tell us how endemic manipulation can be undone, nor what might be necessary to prevent a future repetition.

So, our story of Georgiou will not begin at the statistical start, because everyone agrees he only arrived after the manipulation had become routine. His story has been told a number of times. Like Bevacqua, he gave his side of the dispute in an interview with *Significance*.[66] Reimund Mink, who served at various times as an economic advisor to the International Monetary Fund, the World Bank and the European Central Bank, has written a very sympathetic account of his fellow high flyer.[67] There are other good accounts of the injustices that Georgiou experienced.[68]

The parlous state of the Greek economy provides the background for Georgiou's story. At the end of the last century and in the opening years of the new millennium, many Greeks, on the left and the right, believed that joining the European Union and then joining the Eurozone offered a way out of what seemed to be an ever-deepening economic hole. However, the European Union stipulated that any member state had to fulfil a number of economic conditions for membership of the EU and then to join the Eurozone. Part of these conditions referred to a member country's ratio of debt and expenditure to GDP. A member country with too high a debt and too large an expenditure would have to remain outside the common European currency.

When the Eurozone started in January 1999, Greece was officially judged not to have met the economic preconditions. Greece was officially informed that it needed to wait until its debt-to-GDP ratio improved before it could join. Almost immediately the figures improved and Greece joined the Eurozone at the start of 2001. Nevertheless, suspicions

---

[66] Robert Langkjær-Bain (2017), 'The trials of a statistician', *Significance*, 14(4), 14–19. Mink (2023) suggests that Georgiou had been actively courted by some senior members of the Greek government.
[67] Mink (2023), chapter 7.
[68] Megan Greene (2017), 'By convicting an honest statistician, Greece condemns itself', *Politico*, 2 August, www.politico.eu/article/greece-andreas-georgiou-elstat-by-convicting-an-honest-statistician-greece-condemns-itself/; Miranda Xafa (2021), 'Andreas Georgiou: a travesty of justice', *World Economics Journal*, 21 April, www.world-economics-journal.com/Papers/The-Case-of-Andreas-Georgiou-A-Travesty-of-Justice.aspx; International Statistical Institute (2019), 'Court proceedings against Andreas Georgiou, former President of ELSTAT', www.isi-web.org/files/docs/statements-and-letters/2019-11_court-proceedings-against-andreas-georgiou.pdf.

circulated whether the debt figures had actually improved or whether they had been manipulated by the National Statistical Service of Greece (NSSG). It is possible also that the European Community was so keen for countries to join the Eurozone that it was not checking submissions as carefully as it should have been.[69] A report on Greece delivered to the European Parliament in 2010 made a revealing admission in a footnote: 'debt data reported by Member States are not scrutinised by Eurostat [the official statistical office of the European Union] or any other Commission service'.[70]

Eurostat started keeping a closer watch on the deficit and debt ratios that the Greek government was submitting. It also re-examined past figures, pushing the problems back in time. In 2004 Eurostat published a report, announcing that it was necessary to revise upwards Greece's debt statistics from 2000 to 2003. According to the report, Greece's official statistical agency had failed to report accurately the extent of government spending; indeed, military expenditure had not been included.[71]

Eurostat then looked at the figures from 1997 to 1999, declaring that NSSG had seriously underestimated the county's overall deficit in those years. The problem, according to Eurostat, was long standing and that NSSG had been systematically using methodologies that underestimated the national debt, omitted some forms of governmental spending, and overestimated the amount of tax that was being collected. Again it is possible to suspect that Eurostat was wishing to exonerate itself and to put the blame firmly on the Greek statisticians and the Greek government; it was not blaming European enthusiasm for the Eurozone and an unwillingness to check the statistical returns of countries that were applying to join the zone.[72]

Reimund Mink has written that Eurostat had 'reservations' about the Greek data for many years. Mink explains that 'having reservations' is a 'technical terms for doubting the quality and accuracy of official statistics'.[73] More direct, less diplomatic language would soon be used. A 2014 report by one of the European Parliament's committees used neither

[69] Aragão and Linsi, (2020).

[70] European Commission (2010), 'Report on Greek Government deficit and debt statistics', Brussels: European Commission, fn. 1, p.3, https://ec.europa.eu/eurostat/documents/4187653/6404656/ COM_2010_report_greek/c8523cfa-d3c1–4954-8ea1–64bb11e59b3a.

[71] Eurostat (2004), 'Report on the revision of the Greek government deficit and debt figures', 22 November, https://ec.europa.eu/eurostat/web/products-eurostat-news/-/greece.

[72] Aragão and Linsi (2020).   [73] Mink (2023), p. 144.

diplomatic nor technical language, but directly criticised 'statistical fraud in Greece'.[74]

By this time, the NSSG no longer existed. A report from the European Commission had pointed an accusing finger at NSSG, judging that its problems went deeper than poor methodological choices. After all, no competent statistician could accidentally forget to include military costs from an estimate of governmental expenditure. The EC's report claimed that the Greek set-up did not 'guarantee the independence, integrity and accountability of the national statistical authorities'.[75] It recommended that NSSG should be closed down and a new statistical agency established. In 2010 ELSTAT (Hellenic Statistical Authority) was formed and was looking to appoint its first director.

Andreas Georgiou, a Greek economist, had lived in the United States for more than thirty years, and was working for the IMF. Greece had just negotiated a €110 billion bailout, based on debt figures that had been produced before Georgiou's appointment. Having taken up the post to head up ELSTAT, Georgiou realised that there were serious problems with those and other figures, and one of his first priorities was to produce figures that were more accurate. Within months, he was revising the national debt upwards, and he continued to revise upwards for the next couple of years. The European Commission accepted Georgiou's figures, but inside Greece there were fierce criticisms that he was not serving the nation's best interests, and even that he was still serving the interests of his old employer, the IMF.

In 2011, the government began investigating ELSTAT's new figures with a view to criminal prosecution. Georgiou told *Significance* he did not take this too seriously – he thought it was just politics. But he was wrong: the prosecution, when it came in 2013, was serious. Along with two senior colleagues Georgiou was accused of 'complicity against the state'. It was alleged that he had artificially inflated the size of Greece's 2009 deficit statistics, thereby costing Greece around 171 billion euros. He was also accused of 'violation of duty' because he did not convene ELSTAT's board to approve the statistics that had been prepared. It was claimed that Georgiou continued to do work for the IMF while at ELSTAT.[76]

[74] European Parliament (2014), 'Report – A7–2024-0149)', 28 February, www.europarl.europa.eu/ doceo/document/A-7-2014-0149_EN.html?redirect. The French version used equally direct language.
[75] European Commission (2010).
[76] For a complete list of charges, see the report in *Amstat* (2021), 'Eight Years of Government Persecution of Greek Statistician', 8 October, www.amstat.org/news-listing/2021/10/08/eight-years-of-government-persecution-of-greek-statistician.

The first charge was particularly serious: complicity against the state was analogous to treason and carried a maximum punishment of life imprisonment. There followed a disturbing farce. Each time the charge was brought to court, it was thrown out by a judge. Back would come the government prosecutor with a renewed charge, which would be thrown out in its turn. Statisticians across the world expressed their support for Georgiou, with the International Statistics Institute being particularly vocal. The Institute stood firmly behind him, protesting against his mistreatment. For instance, in August 2021, the Institute wrote: 'we demand an end to the now 10-year persecution of Andreas Georgiou and his full exoneration'.[77] As one professor of statistics at the London Business School wrote, you would imagine that Georgiou's crime would have involved falsifying national economic data, rather than being prosecuted for trying to correct the economic falsifications.[78]

When Georgiou entered the world of Greek official statistics he was entering a culture of manipulation and falsification. It involved more than politicians telling statisticians that it was their patriotic duty to lie for their country, as Moreno was telling Bevacqua. In Greece, the lying, the production of statistics and the protestations of patriotic duty were entangled. Clearly many of the statisticians in NSSG had cooperated in manipulating the debt figures because they believed this was the way to help the nation. The creation of ELSTAT was not entirely a fresh start. It would have been impossible to have run ELSTAT with completely new staff who had no experience of working on official statistics. Many of the staff from the old NSSG were taken on by the new agency.

Georgiou said in his *Significance* interview that some colleagues, even close colleagues with whom he worked, suspected his loyalties. They believed that his attempts to present the economic statistics as accurately as possible would cost the nation billions of euros that it could ill afford. The country was rife with rumours and conspiracy theories. Some believed that Georgiou was still working for the IMF, and that the IMF was seeking to destroy Greece as an independent nation. Some of these believers were statisticians in ELSTAT. The statistics may have been corrupted but the believers considered that it was in the interests of the nation to treat them as if they were genuine. To use a phrase that Stalin would have recognised,

---

[77] International Association for Official Statistics (2021), 'ISI and IAOS Letter of Support for Andreas Georgiou', 8 August.

[78] Michael G. Jacobides (2016), 'Greece needs to be honest about the numbers', *Harvard Business Review*, 25 September, https://hbr.org/2016/09/greece-needs-to-be-honest-about-the-numbers. Mink (2023) makes a very similar point, pp. 153f.

only enemies of the state would question those numbers; and as enemies of the state they should be prosecuted.

Georgiou might have been distrusted by his colleagues, but the feeling was mutual. The state had charged Georgiou with violating his duty because he did not submit the figures for Greece's deficit to ELSTAT's board for approval. In his defence, Georgiou said he had stopped convening the board after police informed him that one of its members was hacking into his emails and then was circulating the emails to the other board members. Hacking emails in this way was a criminal offence, but again, the Greek state was prosecuting the victim of crime.

After five years in post Georgiou had enough. He resigned and returned to the United States, where he opted for the quieter life of teaching statistics and ethics at his old *alma mater*, Amherst College. He taught his students about the travails of statisticians. He told them about the statisticians that Stalin had killed because he was unhappy with the census results. When asked whether he knew about Stalin and the statisticians before he took the ELSTAT position, Georgiou did not answer directly. He said that he 'didn't know then how risky this job could be'.[79]

A politics that involves fraud – including, of course, statistical fraud – is a dangerous politics, for it defrauds its supporters. It raises hopes that cannot be directly fulfilled, just as Eurostat by ignoring statistical error was raising hope in Greece. It is better to admit openly the weaknesses of a national, or international, economy and to propose radical changes to remedy those weaknesses than to look for scapegoats. Self-deluding conspiracy theories will be the result if politicians, with the support of their statisticians, promote the idea that all would be well economically if only the IMF had not secretly placed an unpatriotic agent to head the Greek statistical service.

When statistical manipulation becomes endemic for political purposes, then the lesson of the Georgiou story is that only politics can right the statistical wrongs. A statistician working alone is more likely to be prosecuted than succeed in turning things around. The Greek story underlines that matters can spread so far that national politics on its own may be insufficient. Internationally there needed to be a change of direction in European politics and in Eurostat's choice of calculations.

One of the most heartening features of the Bevacqua and Georgiou stories was the international support that they received, especially from professional organisations like the International Statistical Institute. The

---

[79] Mink (2023), p. 153.

Institute traces its history back to Quetelet's International Congresses of Statistics in the nineteenth century. During his lifetime, Quetelet became disillusioned by the narrowly national perspectives of his fellow statisticians. He would surely have been proud of the Institute's international support for its threatened colleagues.

This points to the possibilities that are open to those statisticians who stand against the manipulation of their skills. We must look beyond treating such statisticians as if they can only be heroic but isolated figures. Instead, we should seek to examine how statisticians might collectively protect their craft; and ask what sorts of institutional structures might help them to combat politically motivated forces that demand dishonest numbers. Regarding our four examples, there are two related questions that we have not asked so far. What was absent in Greece and Argentina – not to mention in Stalin's USSR and in China today – that might have made it more difficult for the governments to have manipulated the statisticians? And might that absent element protect the statisticians of tomorrow?

CHAPTER 6

Establishing a Statistical Authority in Britain

Here, we make a switch. Previously we have been examining how politicians manipulate their statisticians – how they might pressure statisticians to come up with politically advantageous numbers, or, in the case of Donald Trump, to pressure those in charge of counting electoral votes to produce the numbers that he wanted. As we have seen, there are a variety of ways that politicians can manipulate statisticians to manipulate statistics. In autocratic societies the pressures can be brutal, but they can also be tough in democracies, as the examples from Greece and Argentina showed. The recalcitrant statistician who refuses to manipulate the numbers can face bullying, threats of dismissal, prosecution and, perhaps most corrupting of all, promises of promotion.

In this chapter and in the following one, we are moving from such horror stories to asking what can be done, at least in democracies, to make it harder for politicians to control official statisticians. The Greek and Argentinian examples showed senior statisticians, like Georgiou and Bevacqua, finding themselves isolated and placed in the precarious position of facing a powerful politician one-to-one. There were no legally constituted, intermediate institutions to which they could appeal and draw support from. Instead, when the statisticians tried to resist, their political boss acted to have them prosecuted as criminals. There was little difference between the actions of these ministers working in a democratic state and those in an autocratic one.

We will be asking what sort of institutions can be created in democratic countries to act as a buffer between government and statisticians, and thereby make it harder for elected politicians to manipulate the official statistics. We will be looking at the United Kingdom Statistics Authority (UKSA) which was founded as a regulatory agency for statistics. Then, in the following chapter, we will be turning to France and L'Autorité de la statistique publique (the Authority for Public Statistics: ASP), which functions in a similar way to the UKSA. Both bodies were established towards the end of the first decade of the twenty-first century. Significantly both bodies have 'Authority' in their official title, for both are legally empowered to deliver authoritative judgments about official statistics. Both of these agencies operate by appearing to remove official statistics from politics.

Before we do this, there is one explanation for the Greek and Argentinian cases that must be put aside. Both countries had experienced autocratic rule within living memory. Consequently, it might be assumed that it was the residual remains of an undemocratic political culture that led to the bullying behaviour. However, political bullies can be found in long-standing democracies, as our earlier analysis of Donald Trump showed.[1] There cannot be a nation – whether democratic, semi-democratic or autocratic – in which governing ministers have always resisted the temptation to twist the numbers to fit their politics. British politicians, who would have considered themselves to be the very personification of an old democratic culture, have tried to control the production and interpretation of national statistics. In doing so, they were acting in ways that were not totally dissimilar to what can be observed in China today.

We hope to show some of the difficulties of working in a regulatory agency of statistics. The task demands diplomacy as well as good statistical judgement. The senior officers in such agencies have to work with, not against, democratically elected politicians, yet they must assert their statistical independence in the face of political power. Good statistics always involves matching words appropriately with numbers. Those whose job is to expose the wrong numbers matched with the right words, or the wrong words matched with the right numbers, must also be skilled in matching statistical judgements with appropriately effective diplomacy. We will see how this leads to the virtual disappearance of the word 'manipulation' in the official language of the British and French statistical agencies.[2]

Coy about the Past

The obvious way to start would be with the beginning of the UKSA as an institution. The lazy way of doing this would be to go to the UKSA's website and tap on the 'About us' link which, as on most institutional

---

[1] See above, Chapter 4.
[2] The English noun 'manipulation' and verb 'manipulate' have their direct equivalents in French: *la manipulation* and *manipuler*. The French noun and verb have negative and positive meanings, like their English equivalents (see: Chapter 3). That makes it easier for us to compare the language that UKSA and ASP use, and the language that they do not use.

websites, is easy to find. And then give a tap on the subsection link: 'About our history'. But the UKSA has no such button. Its 'About us' subsections are very much rooted in the present. They tell the link-tapper what 'we' are doing now, not why 'we' were established in the first place. The UKSA's 'About us' section starts with its single sentence about the Authority's history: 'The UK Statistics Authority was established under the Statistics and Registration Service Act 2007'.[3] And then 'About us' moves quickly to the present. We are told that the Authority 'has a statutory objective of promoting and safeguarding the production and publication of official statistics that 'serve the public good''. The Authority would appear coy about its past.

This might seem a bit curious, but the websites of other British public agencies which regulate standards are similar.[4] There is a reason why national regulatory agencies of this type would not wish to make a fuss about their origins. They need to be seen to operate impartially and to be above politics. For example, the Competition and Markets Authority must make decisions about whether a particular takeover by an independent company or a particular policy proposed by the government threatens to create a monopoly. The Authority needs to come to its judgement on the facts of the case, not whether it supports the government's policies. It is the same for the UKSA: it must stick to the statistics and avoid the politics.

It is prudent, therefore, for the UKSA to avoid stressing on its website, or elsewhere, that it was created by politics. It must not say words to the effect that the Labour government in its great wisdom decided to bring in the 2007 Act to ensure the good standing of British statistics. Any hint of such a statement about the past would immediately cast suspicion over the Authority's present impartiality. No British statistical authority could act like the Chinese Bureau of Statistics, which, as we discussed in the previous chapter, heads all important communiqués with praising the Party and its leader.

Significantly, the agencies which openly, even proudly, present their history tend to be those that did not originate in political decisions. Some agencies developed from the efforts of specific industries to regulate themselves. For example, the Advertising Standards Agency grew out of

---

[3] United Kingdom Statistics Authority (2024), 'About the Authority', https://uksa.statisticsauthority .gov.uk/about-the-authority/.

[4] To give just two examples: the websites of the Food Standards Agency and of the Competition and Markets Authority are similar. They both say almost nothing about the past history of the agency. See: www.food.gov.uk and www.gov.uk/government/organisations/competition-and-markets-authority.

the advertising industry's own attempts to regulate what could be said in advertisements and what was not permitted. Today on its website the Agency has a section about its history. It says that 'we're very proud of our colourful history that stretches out over half a century'.[5]

The UKSA's website does not completely eradicate its own history. In fact, the website has archived some fascinating accounts of the Authority's origins, written by several of the leading figures of the early days.[6] The site, however, does not advertise these papers or make it easy for casual visitors to find them. To access this archive, you have to have an idea of what you are looking for. Having found these accounts, we will be using them for irreplaceable details about the UKSA's history.

The UKSA's Early History

The UKSA's archived histories recount how in the early 1980s Margaret Thatcher, the right-wing Conservative prime minister, commissioned the business executive Derek Rayner to write a report on the state of official statistics in Britain. Rayner was a great admirer of Thatcher and her politics. He duly obliged and his report recommended that the statistical services should be cut back. He proposed that statistics should not be collected for their own sake, but only if the government needed those figures in order to govern.

In effect, Rayner was proposing that the collection and dissemination of official statistics should be firmly under the government's control. If the government did not wish to collect statistics on a particular matter, or if it preferred not to publish the numbers that had been collected, then it should be free to do so. It was as if the government owned the official

---

[5] Advertising Standards Agency, www.asa.org.uk/about-asa-and-cap/our-history.html. In Chapter 3 we touched on some of the problems with self-regulation when we discussed how the American Psychological Association dealt with psychologists using deception in the conduct of research. See: pp. 61–2.

[6] UKSA's early history is discussed by its first Head of Assessment, Richard Alldritt, and his deputy, Richard Laux. See: Richard Alldritt (2008), 'Methodology, assessment and service delivery', talk given to GSS Methodology Conference, 23 June, https://uksa.statisticsauthority.gov.uk/news/speech-by-richard-alldritt-head-of-assessment-of-the-uk-statistics-authority-to-the-2008-gss-methodology-conference/; Richard Laux, Richard Alldritt, and Ross Young (2008), 'Independence for UK official statistics: the new UK Statistics Authority', https://uksa.statisticsauthority.gov.uk/publication/independence-for-uk-official-statistics-the-new-uk-statistics-authority/; Richard Laux and Richard Alldritt (2011), 'The UK statistical service in 20 years' time', talk given at 58th World Congress of the International Statistical Institute, Dublin, 21–26 August, https://uksa.statisticsauthority.gov.uk/wp-content/uploads/tempdocs/the-uk-statistical-service-in-20-years-time.pdf; Richard Laux and Mark Pont (2012), 'Enhancing the impact of assessment', talk given at European Conference on Quality in Official Statistics, Athens, 29 May to 1 June, https://uksa.statisticsauthority.gov.uk/wp-content/uploads/tempdocs/enhancing-the-impact-of-assessment.pdf.

statistics and that it should be able to do what it liked with them. In British statistical circles, Rayner's recommendations became known as 'The Rayner Doctrine' or 'Raynerism'.[7] The Chinese Communist Party leader has power over official statistics, both the statistics that are gathered and those that are not gathered. So long as it remained in power, the British government was aspiring to exercise the sort of power over statistics that the Party leaders held in China. The major difference between what is advocated by Raynerism and what is practised in China is not statistical. It is that the statistics-controlling government in Britain was daily criticised in the media, and could be removed by regular, free elections, while the statistics-controlling party in China faces neither daily criticism nor regular, free elections.

Thatcher accepted Rayner's report and she rewarded its author by elevating him to a peerage. He sat in the House of Lords as Baron Rayner and, of course, he supported the Conservatives. He also supported Thatcher's attempt to put into practice one of his recommendations: to make national statistics more similar to a profit-making, free-market business than it had been. At one stage, even Parliament had to pay for using national statistics, as a later statistician at the library of the House of Commons was to reveal.[8] The UKSA's archived histories indicate that Britain's official statisticians had serious concerns about the effects that 'Raynerism' would have on the standard of UK statistics.

If that had been the end of the story, then there would have been no UKSA, nor any other independent institution with the legal mandate to oversee and regulate national statistics. However, in democracies a political move in one direction is often countered by a move in the opposite direction. This is what happened in relation to the politics of British statistics. The general election of 1997 was won by the Labour Party, headed by Tony Blair. As one of the UKSA's archived histories points out, the Labour Party's election manifesto contained a pledge to establish 'an independent national statistical service'.[9] Out went 'Raynerism', and in came a policy to free official statistics from governmental control.

The proposals about statistics were part of a wider policy that led the new government to do something that few governments do – namely, to hand over power from the government to independent organisations.

[7] For details, see: Laux, Alldritt and Young (2008).
[8] Georgina Sturge (2022), *Bad Data*, London: Bridge Street Press, p. 123.
[9] Laux, Alldritt and Young (2008).

In one of his first acts as the new chancellor of the exchequer, the government minister responsible for economic issues, Gordon Brown gave the governor of the Bank of England the responsibility for setting the Bank's lending rate. Previously, this decision had been firmly in the hands of the chancellor. Brown's thinking was that technical decisions should be removed from politicians and put into the hands of experts.

The same principle applied to statisticians. It should be the statisticians, rather than the politicians, who should have the authority to pronounce on what constituted good and bad statistical practice. Most importantly, governments should not have the right to hide statistics from the public's eyes, just because they did not like the look of those statistics. By this move, the United Kingdom was moving away from the statistical organisations of Greece, Argentina, the People's Republic of China and, indeed, from those of most other nation states.

Towards the Foundation of the UKSA

During the age of Raynerism, British statistics did not enjoy a good reputation. Both at home and abroad many suspected that the British government was interfering with the country's official statistics.[10] This suspicion was reflected in 'The good statistics guide' that the *Economist* magazine published in 1991.[11] By this time Margaret Thatcher, the architect of Raynerism, had been replaced by her party as prime minister, and John Major was now leading the Conservative administration. The change of leader had not affected the organisation of official statistics when the *Economist* delivered its nasty little shock.

To compile its guide the magazine had assembled a panel of expert statisticians 'from various countries'. The magazine asked these unnamed statisticians to rate the reliability of the official statistics produced by ten democratic countries all of which were members of the OECD (Organisation for Economic Co-operation and Development). Canada came out top of the list, followed by Australia and Sweden.[12] Italy was bottom of the ten with the least trusted statistics. Britain came just one place above Italy and the magazine quoted one of its economic experts saying that Britain's figures 'often taste of fudge'.

---

[10] Ibid.   [11] Anonymous (1991), 'The good statistics guide', *Economist*, 7 September.
[12] The *Toronto Star* proudly reported: 'When it comes to numbers, no one in the world beats Statistics Canada', *The Toronto Star*, 8 September 1991.

Two years later, the *Economist* updated its good statistics guide.[13] Canada continued to top the list, but this time Belgium and Spain were at the bottom. Britain's position had improved from ninth to sixth, but it still remained in the bottom half of the table. This was not a desirable place for Britain to occupy. As the magazine commented, intelligent discussion of economic policy is 'hobbled unless the users of official statistics trust the gatherers'. Clearly something had to be done to improve the reputation of British statistics.

Shortly after coming to power in 1997, Labour set about trying to remedy the problem of Britain's distrusted numbers. The new government published a consultative paper or what in the curious language of British bureaucracy is officially called a 'Green Paper'. It invited the public to submit their views on proposals to restructure the organisation of statistics. The Green Paper contained a preface by the new prime minister. Blair wrote that a reform of the statistical services was one of the key elements of the government's plans to 'clean up politics'.

The main part of the Green Paper began with a declaration that 'reliable official statistics are a cornerstone of democracy'.[14] The purpose of the government's new proposals was to ensure that the production and presentation of official statistics should 'be *free from political interference*, and to be seen as such' (emphasis in the original).[15] The implication was clear: the previous administration had been interfering with the production and presentation of statistics. Although the writers of the Green Paper did not state this quite so blatantly, they came very close. In its section on 'The need for change', the Green Paper quoted the two articles in the *Economist* and it included the tasting of fudge quotation. The Green Paper also quoted from the second *Economist* piece which said that, despite Britain's improved position in the table, there was still 'the lingering suspicion that statistics … in Britain are subject to political meddling'.[16]

The second *Economist* piece also gave a cogent reason why British statistics might have been particularly prone to political meddling. The countries with the most trusted statistics had centralised statistical agencies. By contrast, in the United States and Britain official statisticians were scattered in different government departments where they might find themselves working closely with ministers. As we saw in the Argentinian

---

[13] Anonymous (1993), 'Snakes and adders', *Economist*, 11 September.
[14] 'Statistics: a Matter of Trust. A consultation document' (1998), Presented to Parliament by the Economic Secretary to the Treasury by Command of Her Majesty, February. The quotation about statistics as the cornerstone of democracy comes in Section 1.1.
[15] 'Statistics: a Matter of Trust', Section 1.5.   [16] 'Statistics: a Matter of Trust', Section 3.2.

example and will see later in examples from Britain and France, this is a situation which can expose small groups of statisticians to undue political pressures. By no means all the pressures are threatening, as they were in the Argentinian case. Even so, some statisticians may become all too eager to please a minister with whom they are working closely. The *Economist* illustrated this with a colourful quotation from an unidentified European statistician:

> Living under the same roof as an attractive person of the opposite sex can generate impure thoughts. Cohabitation with a ministry can raise problems of independence.[17]

The chairman of the Statistics Users' Council, who was a Labour MP, used the very same quotation in the British parliament. Unlike the *Economist*, he identified the quote's author: Georges Als who served from 1963 until 1990 as the director of the Luxembourg's Central Service of Statistics and Economics.[18]

In those days senior statisticians were almost exclusively male, and Als's quotation rings with the sexist and social assumptions of that time, particularly assumptions held by successful men working at high levels in masculine environments. Als was using his semi-humorous metaphor to highlight what can happen when small groups of statisticians cohabit the same office building as their minister. A minister can try to bully a statistician as happened in Argentina. More commonly, and more insidiously, is what Andreas Georgiou found in Greece, where statisticians wanted to please their powerful political boss by producing politically desirable numbers.

When they work side by side, it is easier for the minister to tempt and cajole the statistician. In such conditions, the statisticians may, indeed, have impure thoughts. The impurities may take different forms: impure numbers shackled to pure words; impure words shackled to pure numbers; impure numbers and impure words shackled together. Whatever form the impurities take, the politician and statistician, who are cooperating to produce such impurities, will be aware of what they are doing.

Complaining of Political Manipulation

Gordon Brown wanted the Labour government to introduce legislation to create an independent statistical agency which would have the authority to

---

[17] *Economist* (1993), 11 September. The article in the *Economist* does not identify the author of the quotation.
[18] Ian Maclean, MP (1998), 'Memorandum to the Select Committee of the Treasury', 22 July. See report in Hansard, https://publications.parliament.uk/pa/cm199798/cmselect/cmtreasy/976/8102703.htm.

pass judgement on the quality of official statistics and, most importantly, on the interpretation of statistics by politicians. For example, the agency would be empowered to judge whether the data for assessing the cost of living had been collected and analysed appropriately, and whether politicians were interpreting those numbers correctly. Such judgements should be statistical, not political.

The intention was to create the agency as part of the Office for National Statistics (ONS), but it would remain operationally separate from the other parts. This was necessary because the agency would be regulating the statistics produced by the ONS. In the language of the British civil service, it would operate 'at arm's length'. The phrase 'at arm's length' denotes an organisation that is independent of government departments and is directly accountable to Parliament rather than to a specific minister.[19] The agency would, it was hoped, make it harder for ministers and their statisticians to manipulate the production and interpretation of statistics. In consequence, the public would place greater trust in official statistics, at least so long as it trusted the agency to do its job.

Despite Brown's enthusiasm for the project, creating the statistical agency was not Tony Blair's top priority. It was said that Blair enjoyed deploying the advantages that the old statistical system gave any government. When statistics were officially released, governments would have the benefit of seeing the figures well before the opposition parties or the press could. As a result, the government could carefully prepare its 'official' (and highly political) interpretation to accompany the release of the numbers. Because opposition parties could only see the figures after they had been released, they were at a disadvantage in the subsequent debate.

The proposed statistical legislation was not passed during Blair's first administration, but it was brought to Parliament almost ten years after the Labour party had won power. At that time, talk was growing that Blair would be handing over power to Brown. In January 2007 the government presented the Statistics and Registration Service Act to the House of Commons, with John Healey, the financial secretary to the Treasury, introducing the Bill.[20] He spoke about statistics being 'central to the

---

[19] For details of what officially constitutes an 'arm's length' body, see the 'Government Analysis Function' website, https://analysisfunction.civilservice.gov.uk/policy-store/reporting-concerns-under-the-code-of-practice-for-statistics/.

[20] For the details of the Bill, see: UK Government Legislation (2007), 'Statistics and Registration Service Act 2007': www.legislation.gov.uk/ukpga/2007/18/contents. The parliamentary discussion of the Commons is available on Hansard, https://hansard.parliament.uk/Commons/2007-01-08/debates/0701088000001/StatisticsAndRegistrationServiceBill.

business of government, but they serve us all'. He added an unjustified patriotic boast, followed by a justified admission: 'While United Kingdom statistics are widely regarded as among the best in the world, perceived levels of trust in the figures in our system are lower than we would want them to be'.

In debating the Bill, the members of Parliament on both sides complained about the 'manipulation' of statistics. Theresa Villiers, the shadow minister who was leading the Conservatives in the debate, voiced her party's support for the Bill. She said that the opposition's goal was 'to restore public trust in official figures by taking politicians out of the process of the production and release of Government statistics and removing their power to *manipulate* and spin the figures for their own short-term political ends' (emphasis added). She did not mention Raynerism, nor the problematic record of the previous Conservative administration.

That was too much for some Labour members. One Labour member remembered issuing a press release jointly with a fellow of the Royal Statistical Society 'complaining about twenty-three manipulations of the unemployment figures' that had been perpetrated by the previous government. In the course of the debate, the word 'manipulation' flowed between government and opposition speakers. In this context, the word was being used as an accusation – it was always something that 'they' did, never 'us'. All who used the word assumed it to be a self-evidently undesirable practice – a practice that needed to be stamped out by Parliament.

The House passed the Bill almost unanimously: 303 members voted in support and only 10 voted against. Not only did the Conservatives support Labour's Bill, but during the debate their official speakers pledged that any future Conservative administration would strengthen the law. The present Bill was proposing to restrict the government's right to view official statistics in advance of those statistics being released to the public, but a government would still retain an advantage. The Conservative speakers announced that their party would get rid of that advantage altogether.

Much of the Bill was concerned with creating the formal details of the new organisation: for example, specifying who should sit on its board; who should appoint the members of the board; that its chair should be non-executive and part time, in contrast to the head of assessment who would occupy an executive position, and so on. The Bill specified that the new organisation would be required to report to Parliament and how the new organisation could withdraw the title of 'official statistics' from any statistics which, in the opinion of its assessment team, had failed to meet required statistical standards.

The Bill by its emphasis and choice of language differed from the earlier consultative document, or Green Paper, and from the archived histories of the UKSA. Basically, the Bill was phrased in positive terms. One of its stated objectives, for example, was specified as 'promoting and safeguarding the production and publication of official statistics that serve the public good'.[21] The Bill was seeking to improve the standard of national statistics. Unlike the Green Paper, the Bill did not identify factors, such as meddlesome politicians, that were lowering statistical standards.

Although the word 'manipulation' featured in the debates, as politicians used it to justify the new legislation, it does not appear within the Bill itself. But, despite all the Bill's positive intentions, objectives and turns of phrase, this absent word lurks in the background. And it would continue to lurk there. The new agency might have been legally enjoined to operate neutrally, putting statistics above politics, but one thing is clear: its own creation was deeply political.

The Code of Practice

The Bill was passed in 2007, the same year as its first chair, Sir Michael Scholar, and several members of his senior team, were appointed. Early in 2008, the new body held its first official meeting where it was decided to call the new body the United Kingdom Statistics Authority. By this time Gordon Brown had taken over from Tony Blair as prime minister.

One of the new body's duties was stipulated in the Bill: to formulate a code of statistical practice which the UKSA would be obliged to keep updated. Having a code of practice would make it easier to make statistical judgements, and especially to be seen to be making them without political bias. The assessors would be able to say that a particular survey, particular research group or particular politician was failing to comply with a particular principle in the code. The accusation of bias might be reduced, but, as we will see, it would not be eliminated.

The *Code of Practice for Official Statistics* was published a year after the UKSA's inaugural meeting.[22] A revised and updated edition of the Code appeared in early 2018 with a changed title: *Code of Practice for Statistics: Ensuring Official Statistics Serve the Public.* The change in the main title

---

[21] UK Government Legislation (2007), Objective 7(1).
[22] UK Statistics Authority (2009), *Code of Practice for Official Statistics*, London: UK Statistics Authority, https://uksa.statisticsauthority.gov.uk/wp-content/uploads/2021/06/Code-of-Practice-for-Official-Statistics-ed1.0_with-cover.pdf.

was suggesting that the code covered all statistics, not just official ones. The subtitle sounded as if it had been designed with an eye to public relations rather than to improving statistical precision.[23]

Both editions followed the same format. They were not statistical documents: they contained no statistical formulae, graphs or technical formulations. No student taking a course in statistics would be likely to pass their exams merely by reading the Code. No reader will learn anything about calculating standard deviations, applying tests of probability or how to construct a representative sample of a given population. These codes are concerned with the ethical procedures that statisticians and statistical bodies should follow.

Apart from the numbers labelling each section, subsection and sub-subsection, virtually no other numbers appear. One number does appear in both editions. They both stipulate that official statistics should be released at the standard time of 9.30 am on a weekday.[24] This was part of the UKSA's attempt to restrict and standardise the government's pre-release access to data. In its foreword, the revised edition of the Code asserted as a principle that 'statistics must be equally available to all'.[25] A similar statement appeared in the first edition.

The general principles of the Code convey little, if anything, about the working life of official statisticians and why that life might expose them to demands from meddlesome politicians. In the first edition, we can read that 'at all stages in the production, management and dissemination of official statistics, the public interest should prevail over organisational, political or personal interests'.[26] The same sentiment is retained in the second edition: 'Those producing and releasing statistics should be free from conflicts of interest, including political and commercial pressures, that may influence the production, release and sharing of the statistics and data'.[27] Neither version of the Code gives an illustrative example of such untoward political pressure; nor does it say why the working life of an official statistician might be vulnerable to such pressures.

We have to look to another publication from the UKSA to discover more about the position of official statisticians who are 'cohabiting' with

[23] Office for Statistics Regulation and UK Statistics Authority (2018), *Code of Practice for Statistics: Ensuring official statistics serve the public*, https://code.statisticsauthority.gov.uk/wp-content/uploads/2018/02/Code-of-Practice-for-Statistics.pdf.
[24] *Code of Practice for Official Statistics*, (2009), p.14; *Code of Practice for Statistics* (2018), T.3.6, p. 20.
[25] *Code of Practice for Statistics* (2018), p. 4; the first *Code* contained a similar statement, p. 6.
[26] *Code of Practice for Official Statistics*, (2009), p.7.
[27] *Code of Practice for Statistics* (2018), T.1.2, p. 17.

politicians within government ministries. A UKSA document from 2010 describes the same problem but uses a more decorous metaphor than Als had.[28] Ostensibly the document is addressing the problem of ministers having pre-release access to official data, but at the same time it says something important about 'the day-to-day role of many of the senior statisticians working in the major departments of government'. In this situation, the departmental statistician is both an 'independent producer of official statistics, and departmental policy adviser'. There is a 'tension between the two roles', for, according to the document's chosen metaphor, the statistician 'wears two hats'.

The document goes further and states that only a small part of a senior statistician's job in a governmental ministry 'is devoted to the production and publication of statistics'. The other hat – the policy-advising one – is worn much more often. Ministerial statisticians, like other civil servants, have a responsibility 'which has evolved over many years, to offer confidential advice to Ministers and officials on the implications of the statistics for policy and decision-making, much as policy advisers do'. As such, statisticians might find themselves advising their ministers about how best to interpret the statistics that the department might be releasing.

The problem is not merely that this advisory hat is worn more often than the statistical one, but this role 'tends to be the more influential and respected one within the departmental hierarchy'. In short, the statisticians will have career incentives for advising ministers how best to use statistics to pursue political policies. Being acknowledged in the world of civil servants as an independent statistician, who might stand in the minister's way, pointing out that the minister really doesn't grasp the statistical evidence, is not the safest route to influence, respect and promotion – whether in Britain, Greece or elsewhere.

There is one section in the Code that might at first sight appear to be of secondary importance and is strangely placed under the broad heading of 'Trustworthiness'. In the 2018 edition a small section details the desirable structure for any organisation that produces statistics and official data: it should have a 'Chief Statistician' or 'Head of Profession for Statistics'. This is more than a bureaucratic triviality especially for a ministerial office. The chief statistician or head of profession for statistics (and the *Code*'s Glossary

---

[28] UK Statistics Authority (2010), *Pre-Release Access to Official Statistics: A review of the Statutory Arrangements,* pp. 14–15, https://uksa.statisticsauthority.gov.uk/wp-content/uploads/2015/12/images-prerelease-access-to-official-statistics-a-review-of-the-statutory-arrangements_tcm97–29772.pdf.

explains the difference between the two) should have 'sole authority for deciding on methods, standards and procedures, and on the content and timing of the release of regular and ad hoc official statistics'.[29] When statistics are released it should be under 'the guidance' of the chief statistician/head of profession for statistics.

In addition, the Code outlines a chain of communication. If a chief statistician/head of profession feels pressured, they should report misgivings to a senior statistician within the ONS, or to the UKSA's director-general for regulation, especially if they fear that the Code is being broken.[30] No junior statisticians within a ministerial department should be left unprotected, but 'roles and responsibilities of those involved in the production of statistics and data should be clearly defined'.[31]

The statisticians working in a ministerial department should be able to wear their statistical hats with more confidence. They now had a Code that told them and their political bosses that 'the Chief Statistician/Head of Profession for Statistics should challenge the inappropriate use of statistics and data and reflect upon how further misuse can be prevented'.[32] In all of this, one might hear the sound of authority draining away from ministers and flowing to statisticians. Not that this is spelled out.

Diplomatic Language to Prevent Manipulation

Both editions of the Code of Practice use a form of language that is less straightforward than it might first appear. This is certainly worth examining, especially since it reveals something about the chair of the UKSA's mode of operating that we will be exploring in later chapters. The chair is the top public representative of the agency, but not its chief statistician. So far, there have been four chairs, and although the chairs need not be trained statisticians, they must be comfortable with numbers. Each chair had prior experience of the higher echelons of the civil service, and, as such, they have known how to use what is commonly called 'diplomatic language'.

Professional diplomats are by no means the only people to speak diplomatically. Top civil servants in Britain learn to do so as a matter of habit. They will imply meaning rather than spell it out directly. One former diplomat, now a scholar of diplomacy, has written that diplomatic

---

[29] *Code of Practice for Statistics* (2018), T.2.1, p. 18. [30] Ibid., T.2.7 and T.2.8, p. 19.
[31] Ibid., T.5.2, p. 22. [32] Ibid., p. 18.

language has the tone of subdued understatement.[33] Speaking in this way enables diplomatic speakers to criticise indirectly, without the person who is being criticised taking offence and stomping off.[34] Indirect speech, filled with implications, hints and politeness, is a way to preserve the channels of communication while still expressing disagreement.[35] Earlier, we cited a statistician who said that the officials of Eurostat had 'reservations' about the Greek statistics. The writer, Reimund Mink, added that 'having reservations' was a 'technical' way for statistics officials to say that they did not believe those statistics.[36] It may have been accepted as a technical phrase, but it was also classically diplomatic: understated but clearly understood. Sometimes diplomatic language does not merely understate but its implied meanings can be at variance with the ordinary meanings of the words. Lenin reportedly claimed: 'A statesman – Bismarck if I am not mistaken – once said that to accept a thing in principle means, in the language of diplomacy, to reject it in effect'.[37]

But why does the battle against statistical manipulation require the use of diplomatic language? And what are the sorts of words to be avoided in the cause of diplomacy? We will begin with the word 'manipulation', a word which is not used in official documents by the UKSA's senior staff – just as it was not used in the Bill that created the UKSA, despite being used frequently in the debate that led to the passing of the law.

During his period of office, Michael Scholar, the UKSA's first chair, never signed his name to a public letter, written on UKSA headed notepaper, that used the term 'manipulation' as part of its statistical judgement. That may seem curious because, by his own admission, he came to the job to combat manipulation. When Scholar was approaching the end of his UKSA term of duty, he delivered the Johnian lecture at St John's College, Cambridge. He reflected on his professional life and spoke about his philosophy of 'rationality in government'. He voiced his fear that modern government was becoming less rational and more trivial,

---

[33] Stanko Nick (2001), 'Use of language in diplomacy', in Jovan Kurbalija and Hannah Slavik (eds.), *Language and Diplomacy*, Malta: Diploprojects, pp. 39–48.

[34] For discussions of the linguistics of diplomatic language, see: Biljana Scott (2013), 'Diplomacy and the unsaid', *Diplomat Magazine*, 19 August, https://diplomatmagazine.eu/2013/08/19/diplomacy-and-the-unsaid/; Biljana Scott (2018), 'Poetry and diplomacy: telling it slant', *Training Language and Culture*, 2, 51–66; Iver B. Neumann (2002), 'Returning practice to the linguistic turn: the case of diplomacy', *Millennium*, 31, 627–51; Jovan Kurbalija and Hannah Slavik (eds.) (2001), *Language and Diplomacy*, Malta: Diploprojects.

[35] Paul Chilton (1990), 'Politeness, politics and diplomacy', *Discourse & Society*, 1, 201–24.

[36] See above: Chapter 5, pp. 117–8.

[37] Quoted by Catherine Merridale (2017), *Lenin on the Train*, London: Penguin, p. 168.

with self-interested sound bites counting for more than solid evidence. This lay behind his decision to accept the opportunity to head the new Statistics Authority. The position, he said, seemed to offer:

> an unparalleled opportunity to arrest, or to push back, the mischief which I so much deplored: the manipulation of this highly important species of government information – official statistics – for political ends.[38]

But in almost four years, he did not officially identify a single piece of statistical manipulation. This should not be taken as evidence that politicians had stopped manipulating statistics; or that Scholar had failed in his purpose. Quite the opposite, it was a sign that he was succeeding.

The paradoxical situation of the UKSA is that to do its job, it must diplomatically and pragmatically avoid the phrase 'statistical manipulation', except in its positive sense when referring to the skilled handling of data.[39] But even that very specific use of the phrase seems to be in decline. The ability to 'manipulate data' is no longer specified as a necessary competence for the higher grades of statisticians in the civil service, and other words are now used to express this same meaning.[40] The word's disappearance in this context points to the onward rise of the negative sense of 'manipulation', at least in popular language.

It would seem that Scholar had found himself in the curious position of dedicating himself to combatting the manipulation of statistics by not mentioning its occurrence. It was not quite as contradictory as it might seem. The UKSA has the remit to be independent and, thus, to be without political bias. Its judgements should be entirely based on statistical judgements. To give a hypothetical example which in the course of the UKSA's history has been more than hypothetical. Let us suppose that the politicians in the government are using a particular set of statistics to argue that crime is falling and the politicians in the opposition parties are using a different set of statistics to argue that crime is rising. In these circumstances the UKSA might be called upon to judge which side is using the better statistical evidence. When the UKSA gives its judgement, it needs to stick

---

[38] Michael Scholar (2011), 'Johnian Lecture by Sir Michael Scholar at St John's College, Cambridge', UK Statistics Authority, https://uksa.statisticsauthority.gov.uk/news/johnian-lecture-by-sir-michael-scholar-at-st-johns-college-cambridge/.

[39] See above Chapter 3, especially, pp. 48–9.

[40] Until 12 November 2021, the civil service listed the ability to 'manipulate data' as one of the skills that senior statisticians should hold. The phrase is no longer used: The UK Government Analysis Function Website, 'Competency framework for the Government Statistician Group', https://analysisfunction.civilservice.gov.uk/policy-store/competency-framework-for-the-government-statistician-group-gsg/#strand-2-quality-examples.

to the statistics, and not stray into matters of politics, and certainly not into pop psychology.

The problem with the word 'manipulation' is that it directs attention to matters of motive and honesty and, therefore, goes way beyond numbers and their meanings. If the UKSA said that the government, or leader of the opposition, had 'manipulated' the crime statistics, it would be saying more than that its measure of crime was flawed. One can use flawed measures accidentally or through inadequate knowledge. But one cannot be said to 'manipulate' statistics accidentally. The word carries more than a whiff of dishonesty and intention to mislead. In consequence, once a UKSA chair or senior official starts using 'manipulation' in a negative judgement of specific official statistics, they will be seen to have passed the point of judging statistics and crossed the unwritten boundary into judging the motives of those behind the statistics.

This explains why a statistical agency like the UKSA must have a different code of conduct than a private fact-checking organisation. In the United States, the fact-checking team of the *Washington Post* was assiduous in examining and enumerating the false claims made by Donald Trump during his presidency.[41] The paper even awarded 'Pinocchios', the number of Pinocchios depending on the magnitude of the particular untruth. At the end of the year, the paper had a round-up to award the 'Pinocchio of the Year', an award that Trump dominated.[42]

It would be absolutely unthinkable for a statutory body to start awarding Pinocchios or their equivalent. No representative of the UKSA is going to write to ministers telling them how many Pinocchios each of their statistical errors merit. The job of the UKSA is not to mock or to entertain: it is to ensure high statistical standards. Any mockery or use of the m-word must be kept behind doors that are tightly closed and well soundproofed.

Using the M-word

Within the context of the UKSA, the m-word, 'manipulation', is not completely absent, for a belief in the occurrence of statistical manipulation is assumed to be a significant component of popular beliefs about statistics.

---

[41] See above, Chapter 4.
[42] For example: Glenn Kessler (2020), 'The biggest Pinocchios of 2020', *Washington Post*, 18 December, www.washingtonpost.com/politics/2020/12/18/biggest-pinocchios-2020/; Glenn Kessler and Joe Fox (2021), 'The false claims that Trump keeps repeating', *Washington Post*, 20 January, www.washingtonpost.com/graphics/politics/fact-checker-most-repeated-disinformation/.

In recent years, the UKSA has been commissioning the polling company NatCen to conduct surveys to see whether the British public trusts official statistics in general and whether it trusts the Office for National Statistics in particular. This series of surveys, entitled *Public Confidence in Official Statistics*, began in 2009 and the surveys are conducted roughly every two years. At the time of writing, the most recent survey in the series was conducted in 2021 and was published the following year.[43] The survey found that public trust in the official statistics produced by ONS remained high. Of those respondents who felt able to comment on ONS, 87 per cent said they trusted ONS statistics. Trust in the media and the government ran at considerably lower levels (23 per cent and 42 per cent respectively).

As we said earlier in this chapter, the *Economist* in the 1990s asked a small number of statisticians about trusting official British statistics. Their trust was not high and the comments of these statisticians suggested that there might be a link between a distrust of official statistics and a distrust of governments and politicians. The NatCen survey, using a wide sample of the British public rather than a small panel of international economists, finds evidence for such a link, certainly more precisely than the *Economist* did.

NatCen does more than report the levels of trust and distrust in official statistics; it explores the reasons people give for trusting or distrusting ONS statistics. The survey presents respondents with a number of different reasons from which they could select three. Those respondents who said they trusted the ONS selected most often as their reasons that the ONS 'does not have a vested interest in or manipulate the results' (64 per cent). When these same respondents were asked whether the government also did not have a vested interest in or did not manipulate the results, the rate of agreement dropped to only 23 per cent.[44]

The results get worse for government. The smaller proportion of respondents who said that they did not trust ONS statistics were asked for their reasons. The most frequently chosen reasons had nothing to do with mistrusting the ONS *per se*. These respondents said they mistrusted the statistics because the statistics had been misinterpreted by the media (48 per cent), or had been misrepresented by politicians (47 per cent), or

[43] Sarah Butt, Benjamin Swannell and Alisha Pathania (2022), *Public Confidence in Official Statistics 2021*, National Centre for Social Research, https://natcen.ac.uk/our-research/research/public-confidence-in-official-statistics/.

[44] Butt et al. (2022), pp. 18f.

that the government had a vested interest in or manipulated the results (45 per cent). That suggests that those who distrusted ONS statistics did so because they heard about the statistics from the media, politicians or the government, all of whom those respondents tended to distrust. Thus, it was not primarily the ONS that they distrusted.

The results from the survey are interesting in themselves but there is a specific point to note. The m-word has returned when the pollsters, and presumably also the UKSA, which commissioned the pollsters, are exploring the key factors that lead the public to distrust statistics. The pollsters were providing evidence that a public belief in the manipulation of statistics is related to a distrust of statistics. When it comes to the government or the media quoting statistics, then it is a matter of lies and damned lies.

Interestingly, Michael Scholar in his Johnian Lecture also used 'manipulation' when he discussed public attitudes towards statistics. He mentioned recent polls that had indicated that only one in six people in Britain thought that 'official statistics are not manipulated by ministers'. He also mentioned that the European Commission had recently conducted a survey to see how much the public in each of the twenty-seven member states trusted their government's statistics: 'The UK, I am sorry to say, came twenty-seventh, right at the bottom of the class'.[45]

There is one last thing to say about the way the UKSA operates to maintain its status as an independent body. Much of its work is reactive, rather than selecting government ministers to investigate. Politicians and members of the public are encouraged to write to the UKSA if they are concerned by the way that statistics are being used or misused, or if they believe that there are serious problems with particular statistics. If the UKSA's assessment team think that the letter writer *prima facie* has a case, they will examine the statistics and deliver a judgement. Their responses can be privately addressed to the original letter writer or their response can take the form of a public letter. If a government minister is involved, the chair of the UKSA will often write a public letter. Should the assessment team consider that a ministry's statistical team has a technical problem, the UKSA may respond by contacting the relevant statisticians and then working with them behind the scenes to remedy the problem. If that happens then neither the problem nor the solution may come to the public's attention.

Writing a public letter to a government minister can sometimes have an immediate impact as Sir David Norgrove revealed when he gave a lecture

[45] Scholar (2011).

at University College London in October 2021, during the latter part of his tenure as chair of the UKSA. In the question-and-answer session, Norgrove was asked about the effects of intervening publicly.[46] He recounted how the UKSA had experienced a number of problems with the Department of Education and its use of statistics. Behind-the-scenes contact had not resolved matters, so he wrote a public letter to the minister. Within days the minister asked to see Norgrove to tell him 'what they were doing to improve things'. The point of Norgrove's story was to show that a public letter can sometimes bring about almost immediate behind-the-scenes improvement. However, as Norgrove recounted in the same lecture and as we will be showing, a public letter does not always bring such immediate results.[47]

Occasionally it is possible to catch a glimpse of what can occur behind the scenes. In Chapter 10, we will be examining how the chair of the UKSA dropped his diplomatic politeness in order to persuade the minister of health to change his misleading statistics about how many tests for Covid had been conducted. This was not the first time that the UKSA had reacted against this minister's use of statistics. The first time was largely conducted behind closed doors. The minister, shortly after taking up his appointment, had tweeted about a 'terrific' increase of a thousand National Health Service doctors in just three months. Health groups and doctors protested that the minister's figure was misleading, because the vast majority of the thousand were students, not qualified doctors. The protestors claimed that the overall number of qualified doctors had, in fact, fallen. One of those complaining contacted the UKSA to ask the Authority whether the minister's figure was correct. The UKSA replied to him: 'We have discussed this matter with the Secretary of State's office, and they have removed the tweet'. The complainant then revealed this answer to the *Independent* newspaper which then published the story.[48] The Department of Health refused to answer queries about the vanishing tweet. Without the press story, the offending tweet would have just disappeared as if by

---

[46] For a link to the University College London podcast of the lecture, including the question-and-answer session, see: https://podcasts.apple.com/gb/podcast/policy-and-practice-covid-and-the/id1500411454?i=1000540103635.

[47] In Chapter 10, we discuss Norgrove's lecture further.

[48] For an account of the episode, see: Alex Matthews-King (2018), 'Health Secretary Matt Hancock deletes "1,000 more GPs" claim after statistics watchdog censure', *Independent*, 28 November, www.independent.co.uk/news/health/health-secretary-matt-hancock-gps-statistics-uksa-censure-false-facts-a8655961.html. See also: Michael Billig and Cristina Marinho (2023), 'Preventing the political manipulation of COVID-19 statistics: the importance of going beyond diplomatic language', *Language in Society*, 52, 733–55.

magic. One moment it was there, announcing the terrific news, and the next moment – *hey presto* – it was gone.

Because the UKSA encourages queries from public and private figures, a considerable amount of its time and effort is spent investigating and answering incoming questions. However, this mode of operating comes with a large benefit. It reinforces the image of neutrality because in the vast majority of cases the Authority is not selecting its own cases. A politician might complain to have been unfairly pursued by the Authority. However, the chair of the Authority can respond by saying that the UKSA is legally obliged to consider the cases that are brought to its attention. Neutrally, the Authority will consider cases brought by the left and by the right. What matters are not the politics of complainants nor the politics of those being complained about, but the strength of the statistics and how the statistics are being interpreted.

The use of diplomatic language is part of the Authority's *modus operandi*. Shortly after he was appointed as the third chair of the UKSA, Sir David Norgrove gave an interview to the trade magazine *Civil Service World*.[49] He outlined his strategies for dealing with ministers when their use of statistics was not up to scratch. The UKSA, he said, had no powers to censor ministers; nor did it have the legal authority to prevent them from making statistically inappropriate comments. In consequence, it was necessary to work with ministers if unsatisfactory statistics were to be changed or removed.

The use of diplomatic language is both an outcome of the Authority's function and its preferred way of fulfilling that function. For it, working quietly behind the scenes to improve the standard of statistics would be better than making a big public fuss without changing a single misplaced decimal point.

Movable Boundaries

So far, we might have given the impression that there are fixed boundaries between independent fact finders and statutory statistical agencies; and between diplomatic and non-diplomatic language. However, neither boundary is absolutely fixed, but in particular circumstances there can be

---

[49] Jim Dunton (2017), 'Sir David Norgrove interview: new chair of UK Statistics Authority on elections, the misuse of numbers and working for Margaret Thatcher', *Civil Service World*, 17 June, www.civilserviceworld.com/in-depth/article/sir-david-norgrove-interview-new-chair-of-uk-statistics-authority-on-elections-the-misuse-of-numbers-and-working-for-margaret-thatcher.

movement in one direction or another. We will start with the boundary between the UKSA and one specific fact-finding organisation. Full Fact is an independent British fact-finding organisation which was founded a year after the UKSA was established. It is devoted to checking claims by politicians, public institutions and journalists, and its board includes members from the major British political parties, both on the left and on the right.[50] It is clear from public statements that Full Fact and the UKSA have a good working relationship, sharing information about claims whose validity they are investigating. Full Fact has wider scope of facts to check than the UKSA, whose range is restricted to statistical matters.

The UKSA is obliged to report annually to Parliament. In October 2021, David Norgrove, the UKSA's chair, and Ed Humpherson, the director general for regulation, together with the national statistician Ian Diamond, appeared before the Commons Public Administration Committee to give evidence and to answer questions. Humpherson talked about the UKSA's connections with Full Fact, which he described as 'the fantastic fact-checking organisation who are close partners of ours'; he added: 'we work very closely with them'.[51]

Some of the contacts between Ed Humpherson and Will Moy, the chief executive of Full Fact, take the form of public letters. There are also behind-the-scenes meetings which their public letters allude to. The two organisations sometimes swap data. For example, in 2022 Moy wrote a public letter to Humpherson alerting him of the 'incorrect claim about the number of people in employment which has been made multiple times by the Prime Minister [Boris Johnson]'. Moy gave detailed reasons to show why Johnson's claims were incorrect and he asked Humpherson for his 'potential engagement'.[52] Two days later, Humpherson replied in a public letter, thanking Moy and giving the UKSA's support to Full Fact's analysis of the unemployment figures.[53]

It might seem curious that Full Fact should share some of its hard-earned, well-checked facts with a public authority, but there is an

---

[50] See: Full Fact, 'About us: who we are', https://fullfact.org/about/.
[51] See: Hansard, 'The Work of the UK Statistics Authority: Scrutiny Session', https://committees.parliament.uk/oralevidence/2859/pdf/.
[52] Office for Statistical Regulation (2022), 'Will Moy to Ed Humpherson, "Statements on the number of people in work"', 1 February, https://osr.statisticsauthority.gov.uk/correspondence/will-moy-to-ed-humpherson-statements-on-the-number-of-people-in-work/.
[53] Office for Statistical Regulation (2022), 'Ed Humpherson to Will Moy: "Statements on the number of people in work"', 3 February, https://osr.statisticsauthority.gov.uk/correspondence/ed-humpherson-to-will-moy-statements-on-the-number-of-people-in-work/. Humpherson sent a copy of his letter to the prime minister's director of data science.

underlying logic. As a public authority the UKSA carries national status. We will see in later chapters how the press dubs the UKSA and its chair 'the nation's watchdog for statistics'. If there is a juicy story in the offing – such as the nation's watchdog admonishing the prime minister – then it is more likely to make the pages of the British popular press than if the story were merely that an obscure, fact-checking company was doing the admonishing. Because of the close relationship between Moy and Humpherson, the former will trust the latter to give credit where credit's due. With the support of the UKSA, Full Fact's efforts will reach more people and carry more status, and both organisations, not to mention the public, will benefit from their co-operation.

A fact-checking organisation will have far less need to use diplomatic language than a public authority, for the considerations which lead the UKSA to use understatement and implied hints do not apply to Full Fact. In its reports on the validity of some of Johnson's claims, Full Fact's writers often combined forensic analysis with the informality of calling the prime minister by his first name. The UKSA in its public letters and official documents would never refer to him simply as 'Boris'. Even so, Full Fact does not award Pinocchios or their equivalent.

The boundary between diplomatic and non-diplomatic language is not absolute. In his interview with *Civil Service World*, Norgrove implied as much. Lacking the formal power to censure a minister who was misusing statistics, the Authority has to use the strategies that are open to it. If the UKSA fails to encourage the minister to change or withdraw misleading statistics, then the Authority may have to increase the directness of its language and so catch the attention of the press, which in its turn will not use the niceties of understatement.

Norgrove did not spell this out in the interview but he broadly implied it. However, in later chapters, especially Chapters 9 and 10, we will examine examples of how all this can play out in practice. We will see Norgrove corresponding with a minister. Having failed to make progress with his diplomatic hints, we will see him switching to a more direct style of language, thereby catching the attention of the popular press, who will turn the correspondence between the minister and the backroom statistician into a drama.

CHAPTER 7

Establishing a Statistical Authority in France

Social scientists should always try to avoid basing their ideas on a single case which comes from a single country. If our analysis of the United Kingdom Statistics Authority has a wider message about preventing, or at least minimising, the political manipulation of statistics, then we should look to see what happens elsewhere. So, now it is time to metaphorically cross the narrow channel of water that separates Great Britain from France.

Maybe it would be more interesting if our second country came from a land that was more physically distant from the UK, rather than one which is little more than twenty miles away at its nearest point. However, there are good reasons for looking at France's statistical authority. Like UKSA it was designed to combat the political manipulation of statistics, and, as we will see, it was partly modelled on UKSA. Although it might have similar aims to UKSA, it operates within a different political and statistical culture, and is certainly no clone.

As we look at France's Autorité de la statistique publique (Authority for Public Statistics: ASP), we will see patterns of similarity and difference between it and its older sibling across the Channel. Both authorities fight against the manipulation of statistics by avoiding the word 'manipulation' in their official documents. Our analysis of this curious feature is aided by the fact that the noun 'manipulation' is the same in both English and French, and that the verbs 'manipulate' and '*manipuler*' are virtually identical in the two languages.

There is another similarity, although it appears to be a difference. When the agencies were established, each had to fit within the structure of their country's official statistical set-up. In the case of UKSA, this meant that the new authority occupied a strange position. It was part of the Office for National Statistics (ONS) but it had to keep at arm's length from the main statistics-producing parts of the ONS, because it was the official regulator of those parts.

The French system of official statistics is structured somewhat differently. In France the nearest equivalent to the ONS is the National

Institute of Statistics and Economic Studies (L'Institut national de la statistique et des études économiques: INSEE). The National Institute is often treated as if it were the overall statistical organisation of the country, having responsibility for all French official statistics. The United Nations Statistical Division, for instance, lists it as France's overall statistical agency.[1] Officially, however, INSEE is the statistical unit of the Economics Ministry, although everyone in the French statistical world knows it is more than that. As we will see, the new authority had to keep itself separate from INSEE for a specific, bureaucratic reason. These niceties, which seemingly would only be of interest to civil servants and the occasional eccentric enthusiast for bureaucratic details, affect the ways that the agencies on both sides of the Channel go about their business of combatting political manipulation.

Before we get on to the bureaucratic and operational details, we must start with the foundation of the ASP, and why the French statistical establishment looked to take a lead from its British neighbour. In addition, we will be discussing the work of a very practical French scholar of statistics, who was to be influential in the creation of the French authority. This practical scholar saw statistical manipulation as resulting from the reality of political power in the modern state.

Establishing the Authority for Public Statistics

The founding of the French ASP resembled that of the UKSA in Britain. Both involved governments proposing laws that gave away some of their powers. In Britain, the government had been left of centre. In France the politics were different: Nicolas Sarkozy was president, heading a liberal–conservative government. His ideological leanings were to shrink the state's bureaucracies and powers. On the other hand, he recognised that his government needed good statistics – and that good statistics meant independent statistics. So, two years into Sarkozy's presidency, the Authority for Public Statistics was officially established – on 8 June 2009, to be precise.

On that day, Christine Lagarde, who was then the French minister for the economy, and who would later rise to become managing director of the International Monetary Fund and then president of the European Bank, issued a formal press release, announcing the establishment of the ASP. The new body, her press release stated, would be responsible for watching over 'the professional independence' of public statistics. The Authority had

---

[1] United Nations Statistical Division, https://unstats.un.org/unsd/dnss/docViewer.aspx?docID=579#start.

been legally instituted the previous year by article 144 of the Law on Modernising the Economy. According to Lagarde's release, that law had established 'professional independence' as a principle that would guarantee the impartiality, relevance and quality of French public statistics.[2] Thus, the whole purpose of the ASP was bound up with the notion of independence. To those in the know, statistical independence meant the fight against political manipulation.

This newly instituted Authority was in many ways similar to the UKSA and it was not chance that both organisations styled themselves as 'Authorities' – not that Lagarde's press release mentioned UKSA. Although she asserted that French statistics needed to be independent, there was an omission: her press release did not specify from whom, or from what, statistics needed to be independent. Others would not always be quite so reticent, and, as in the UK, politicians would be implicated, whether by hints or by accusation.

Today, if you go to the website of the ASP, its welcome begins with what has almost become the Authority's mantra of independence: 'The Authority for Public Statistics watches over the professional independence of the conception, production and diffusion of public statistics'. The Authority's mission statement begins with the same declaration and then goes on to say: 'This principle of independence with regard to all pressure whether coming from political, regulatory or administrative bodies, as well as from operators in the private sector, guarantees the credibility of statistics'.[3] Of the different types of pressure, note that political pressure is listed first.

Unlike UKSA, the French ASP was not legally obliged to formulate its own code of practice, but it was obliged to follow the European Statistics Code of Practice. The first edition of the European Code appeared in 2005 and the Code was revised in 2017.[4] The European Code, like the UKSA's code, deals with general principles and values rather than with the details of statistical procedure. Eurostat publishes its own code of technical

---

[2] Christine Lagarde's press release can be found on the ASP's website: www.autorite-statistique-publique.fr/communique-de-presse-relatif-a-linstallation-de-lautorite-de-la-statistique-publique-par-christine-lagarde-ministre-de-leconomie/. The 2008 Law on Modernising the Economy had established the need for an organisation like the ASP but in the following year a further decree was necessary to list the duties of the Authority.

[3] ASP, 'Présentation': www.autorite-statistique-publique.fr/presentation/missions-de-lasp/.

[4] Eurostat (2017), *European Statistics Code of Practice — revised edition*, https://ec.europa.eu/eurostat/web/products-catalogues/-/ks-02-18-142; for the first edition, see: Eurostat (2005), *European Statistics Code of Practice*, https://unstats.un.org/unsd/EconStatKB/KnowledgebaseArticle10174.aspx.

practice.[5] The European Code of principles is structured around sixteen basic principles. The first of these principles is 'Professional Independence' from which the ASP's mission statement is derived. The European Code contains some details about how independence is to be preserved and from whom it is necessary to be independent. Principle 1.6 says that the release of statistics should be 'clearly distinguished' from 'political/ policy statements'.[6]

Sometimes, members of the ASP suggest that their authority very much resembles the UKSA and the two of them differ from other European statistical organisations. In a review of the ASP's first ten years of operation, Claudine Gasnier, writing on behalf of the Authority, declared that 'the ASP has very few equivalents in Europe'.[7] According to Gasnier, most other European bodies are merely advisory, unlike the ASP and the UKSA, which possess the authority to certify the quality of statistics.

This similarity was made apparent at the very first meeting of the ASP, which was held on the same day as Lagarde issued her press release. At that meeting, Philippe Cuneo, who was to play an important role in the Authority's operations against statistical manipulation, delivered a talk which compared the new ASP with other similar organisations. He claimed that the ASP resembled the authorities of the United Kingdom and Italy because all three rested upon a tripartite system that involved producers of statistics, users of statistics and those possessing authority, with all three working together.[8] The similarities between the UKSA and the ASP were to persist. Ten years later, Dominique Bureau, who was then president of the ASP, wrote about them and how the British and French authorities differed from most other national organisations of statistics.[9]

---

[5] European Statistical System (2019), *Quality Assurance Framework of the European Statistical System*, Version 2, https://ec.europa.eu/eurostat/documents/64157/4392716/ESS-QAF-V2.0-final.pdf.

[6] The first edition of the UKSA's *Code of Practice* was published when the United Kingdom was still a member of the European Community and, therefore, needed to conform to the European Code. Both editions of the UKSA's *Code* specifically state that it is consistent with the European Code and with the *United Nations Fundamental Principles of Official Statistics*, which is a much shorter document.

[7] Claudine Gasnier (2019a), 'Ten Years in Service of the Professional Independence of Official Statistics', Colloquium, 10 ans de l'activité de l'Autorité de la statistique publique, 27 November, p. 2, www.autorite-statistique-publique.fr/wp-content/uploads/2023/08/Ten-Years-in-Service-of-the-Professional-Independence-of-Official-Statistics.pdf.

[8] A summary of the presentations given at the meeting and the decisions taken can be found on the ASP website at: www.autorite-statistique-publique.fr/event/releve-de-decisions-de-la-seance/.

[9] Dominique Bureau (2020), 'Ensuring independent quality statistics: the French Official Statistics Authority ten years after', *Courrier des statistiques*, 5 (New Series), www.insee.fr/en/information/5895237?sommaire=5894773. The English translation is on INSEE's website. We will be discussing a passage from the article later in this chapter.

The label 'Authority' was as vital for the new French organisation as it was for its older sibling. Philippe Cuneo had been a participant at a conference at which the links between older and younger sibling were apparent even before the latter's birth. After the 2008 law had been passed, but before the ASP had been formally established, the French Statistical Society (Société française de statistique), organised a seminar in Paris on the topic of 'The independence of public statistics'. The complete proceedings remain available on the ASP's website.[10]

The seminar was clearly designed to contribute to ongoing discussions about the organisation and responsibilities of the new Authority. It comprised three main talks, two round tables and an introduction. Cuneo was a participant at the first of the round tables. Two senior figures from the French Statistical Society introduced the proceedings. They expressed their admiration for the UKSA, stating that the British example had much to teach the French.[11] For the second main talk, the Society had invited representatives from the UKSA to recount the British experience. Three members of the UKSA, including the head of assessment, Richard Alldritt, and his deputy, Richard Laux, gave a talk on the independence of British statistics, specifically speaking about the creation and operation of the UK's new Authority.[12]

From our point of view, the real gem of the conference was not the contribution from the British statisticians, however interesting their reflections were. It was the first talk, which was given by a French academic, René Padieu. He spoke with insight and knowledge about politicians manipulating statistics. Best of all, he illustrated his theoretical ideas with some magnificently revealing anecdotes.[13]

Padieu: Theories and Stories

Padieu was simultaneously a statistical insider and an outsider. Only someone in an ambiguous position could have spoken about political

---

[10] ASP (2008), 'L'indépendance de la statistique publique', The Independence Seminar, organised by the French Statistical Society, 15 December, www.autorite-statistique-publique.fr/historique-des-interventions/.

[11] Avner Bar-Hen and Jean-Lous Bodin (2008), 'Avant-propos', Independence Seminar, p. 1.

[12] The English version of their talk is one of the UKSA's archived histories: Richard Laux, Richard Alldritt and Ross Young (2008), 'Independence for UK official statistics: the new UK Statistics Authority', https://uksa.statisticsauthority.gov.uk/publication/independence-for-uk-official-statistics-the-new-uk-statistics-authority/. ASP (2008) archives the French version of Laux et al.'s talk on its record of the Independence Seminar, pp. 15–28.

[13] René Padieu (2008), 'L'indépendance de la statistique publique en France', Independence Seminar, 5–14.

manipulation in the way that he did. He was an insider in that for many years he had been closely connected with the world of public statistics. He acted as inspector-general for INSEE, and he sat on a number of INSEE's important committees. These positions were honorary, and Padieu's paid employment came from being Professor of Statistics at the specialist university, the National School of Statistics and Economic Administration (NSAE) in Paris. The university is at the heart of French statistics: anyone hoping to work as a statistician in a public body needs a qualification from the National School.

Padieu was also a leading figure in the French Statistical Society. At the time of the conference, he was the Society's head of the Deontology Section – the section that was concerned with the ethical uses and abuses of statistics. Padieu, as an insider, would have known everyone of importance in the world of French social statistics. It is not surprising that he was invited to give the first of the three talks at the Society's special seminar on statistical independence.

As an academic, Padieu was outside the world of career statisticians and their relations with senior politicians. His academic standing most certainly did not depend on doing a minister's bidding within a ministry office. No governmental minister could seek his dismissal from INSEE, for the simple reason that the institution did not employ him. Nor could a minister threaten to destroy his statistical career: his career depended on his academic publications and on his status as a respected thinker at NSAE, not on his ability to work closely with ministers.

Padieu was not interested in the mathematically technical sides of statistics. His academic publications tended to discuss philosophical and moral issues, or what he called 'statistical deontology'. In one paper Padieu regretted that Anglo-Saxon statisticians tended not to use the term 'deontology', but, instead they preferred to talk about 'professional ethics'.[14] The term 'deontology' is more popular generally among intellectuals in France than in the English-speaking world. The ASP on its website claims that its mission is to oversee the good quality of statistics, ensuring that they are based on 'methodological rigour and respect for different deontological principles'. The UKSA's Code of Practice voices the same sentiment but without the words 'deontological principles'.

---

[14] René Padieu (1999), 'La déontologie statistique', *Journal de la société française de statistique*, 140, 5–21. His quote about Anglo-Saxons comes on p. 6, fn. 1. Because we are writing in English and are addressing an English-reading audience, we will not be following Padieu's lead on this matter. We prefer to write about good, ethical practices of statistics, rather than possibly perplexing our readership, and probably ourselves, by trying to write about 'deontology'.

Among Padieu's deontological interests was the problem of statistical manipulation. We have seen that official statisticians, such as those in the UKSA, tend to avoid using the word 'manipulation'; and we will see that the statisticians in the ASP also do not use *la manipulation* in their official publications. Padieu, as an insider-outsider, was under no such constraint. His 1999 deontological paper, which was published in the official journal of the French Statistical Society, openly discussed how governments use their power over ministerial statisticians. Padieu argued that the possibility of statistical manipulation was constant.[15]

Padieu cited the example of Argentina where the president had tried to tamper with the official figures for unemployment. These problems were not distant ones, he wrote, because 'near to us, the history of INSEE is a battle of fifty years to assert and preserve its independence against political power'.[16] In Padieu's view, the independence of official statisticians involves continually facing up to the danger that governments will use their powers illegitimately.

The organisers of the independence seminar would certainly have known Padieu's views when they invited him to give the opening talk. Padieu did not disappoint. Once again he voiced his fears about the political manipulation of statisticians. He backed up his theoretical concepts with more anecdotes, some of which were in the public domain. One such was a story about Valéry Giscard d'Estaing, the former president of France. When Giscard d'Estaing was minister of finance, he attempted to prevent a magazine from being able to report the rising price of beefsteak. Padieu also told some personal anecdotes. They may have been indiscrete, but in telling his stories, Padieu preserved the anonymity of the participants, although some of his audience might well have guessed who they were.

Padieu argued that public powers threaten the independence of statisticians and that the bending of statistics was 'a constant temptation for government'.[17] Throughout the various stages of statistical enquiry, there was temptation: when deciding which data to collect; when deciding how to collect the data; when deciding how to analyse the collected data; and then when deciding whether or not to publish the analysed data. There was also the temptation to present data which had been 'manipulated in an underhand way' as if it were scientific fact. Thus governments can manipulate the data by putting 'pressure on the statistician to use methods that do

---

[15] Padieu (1999), p. 8: '*d'une toujours possible divulgation de la manipulation*'.   [16] Ibid.
[17] Padieu (2008), p. 10.

not conform to the rules of the art, or to publish something other than what their inquiry has demonstrated'.[18]

Padieu had an anecdote to illustrate such pressures. A statistician whom he knew had been commissioned by the minister of education to conduct a survey into the rate of drug-taking in secondary schools. The minister found out that the statistician, as part of her representative sample of schools, had included two large Parisian lycées, which were well known for having drug-taking problems. The minister, who for political reasons did not want the survey to reveal high rates of drug-taking, removed these two schools from the sample. Encouraged by Padieu, his friend stood firm, ensuring that the minister reinstated the excluded schools.

Padieu's anecdotes give life to his theories about political power. In the previous chapter, we quoted from one of the UKSA's publications saying that statisticians working for ministers were in an awkward situation because they wear two hats – the statistical hat and the ministerial one.[19] The UKSA document gave no example how this might play out in practice. It was following the diplomatic custom of British civil servants, divulging no secrets and not using untoward words such as 'manipulation'. Above all, British civil servants take seriously the principle that what happens behind closed doors stays behind closed doors.[20]

Padieu, by contrast, was free to scatter anecdotes throughout his talk. He told how he had seen a finance minister putting pressure on a statistician from INSEE not to publish the results of a survey into the state of the economy. The minister said that he did not doubt that the results were statistically well founded, but he feared the consequences of publishing them: investment might be affected, there might be currency speculation and so on. The minister asked the statistician how 'as a loyal servant of the state and nation' he could possibly let the results appear?[21] As we saw, ministers in Greece and Argentina made similar patriotic appeals, when they sought to persuade – or to bully – their statisticians into manipulating the nation's numbers. Padieu was revealing that such incidents also occur in France.

His anecdotes share a feature with the three-stage schema that we outlined in Chapter 5. They all start with Stage 1. All seems to be proceeding well until the minister starts suggesting that the statistician should tamper with the figures or with the survey's sample. Sometimes

---

[18] Ibid., p. 7.   [19] See above p. 134.
[20] For a discussion of the differences between the language of the British civil service and the more political language of Australian and Canadian civil services, see: Dennis Grube (2013), *Prime Ministers and Rhetorical Governance*, London: Palgrave Macmillan.
[21] Padieu (2008), p. 12.

there is a second stage, but if the statistician is resolute, like Padieu's friend, then it might end there. Because such incidents take place behind closed doors, they normally remain unreported. We should be grateful when a well-placed academic becomes a witness with a story to tell.

Inspecting Ministerial Statistical Services

Three months after the independence seminar, a decree was passed, laying out the duties of the new Authority.[22] One of the key duties related directly to the problem which Georges Als, the former director of Luxembourg's statistical service, had called the problem of 'cohabitation'.[23] This is the problem of statisticians working in government ministries and being subject to pressures from the minister. In France these groups of statisticians based within ministerial offices are called Ministerial Statistical Services (Services statistiques ministériels, SSMs). Some ministries, especially the larger ministries, have their own statistical groups, while some of the smaller ones do not.

The decree declared that one of the main responsibilities of the ASP would be to inspect whether the groups of official statisticians working within ministries were functioning at acceptable standards. If the ASP decided that a group was not operating as it should be, it could recommend that the group should be closed down, merged with the statistical services of another ministry, or given another chance to redeem itself. Given the emphasis on independence in the official mission of the ASP, an important part of the inspection was whether an SSM was operating independently. This was potentially an explosive issue. A negative recommendation would be tantamount to pointing the finger at a minister for interference, or at the head of a statistical grouping for weakness, or at both simultaneously.

Previously, the ministerial organisation of statistics had been under the control of the government. Presidents and prime ministers could empower chosen ministers with statistical groups at their beck and call or punish others by taking away their statistical groupings. Now that power of decision-making was being put into the hands of an independent authority comprising statisticians. Actually, power was not being completely given away. The ASP could only recommend, not enforce its recommendation. It had to report its recommendations for reorganising SSMs to the minister

---

[22] Decree No 2009-250 of 3 March 2009.   [23] See: Chapter 6.

for finance who then had the power to decide whether or not to carry out the recommendations.

The government might not have relinquished all it powers over official statistics, but in practice it was increasing the influence of official statisticians over decisions about cohabitation. It was expected that only under exceptional circumstances would the minister for finance reject a recommendation. And then there might be a political rumpus, pitting the minister against senior statisticians.

There was a good reason why a new authority had to be created to inspect the ministerial statistical services, rather than asking INSEE to do the job. Despite its size, general scope and international reputation, INSEE was itself a ministerial statistical service, which must report to the minister of finance. If SSMs need to be regularly inspected, then this would include inspecting INSEE. It would not be appropriate, and certainly it would not look good to the outside world, if INSEE were to inspect itself.

Another duty which was assigned to the ASP was *labellisation*. This is the responsibility of granting the official label 'public statistics' to surveys or data which originate from outside the official system of public statistics – that is, from outside INSEE and other SSMs.[24] Previously this had been the responsibility of INSEE. Now the Authority had the responsibility for ensuring that the official label was only given to statistics that merited it. Since the Authority was not expected to produce its own statistics, it would not be in the embarrassing position of judging its own products.

Having taken over this work, the ASP needed to develop procedures for carrying out the necessary inspections and, most importantly, it needed to formulate criteria for establishing what should and should not qualify as official statistics. One of the key criteria concerns statistical *labellisation* itself: namely checking that the methodological procedures adequately represent the labels that are given to a survey (i.e. labels such as 'unemployment', 'violent crime', 'cost of living' etc). If methodologically the label is inappropriate – if the gap between the numbers and the labels is too large – then *labellisation* in the sense of labelling the survey as 'public statistics' can be withheld.[25]

[24] This resembles the granting or withholding of the label 'official statistics' which was a legal duty ascribed to the UKSA.

[25] On the importance of *labellisation* to the mission of the ASP, see: Claudine Gasnier (2019b), 'L'Autorité de la statistique publique', talk given to INSEE, February, https://afristat.org/wp-content/uploads/2022/03/PP05_ASP-1.pdf. For the respective roles of INSEE and the ASP in *labellisation*, see: Marc Christine and Nicole Roth (2020), 'The Label Committee: a governing body ensuring the quality of official statistics', *Courrier des Statistiques*, 5 (new series), www.insee.fr/en/information/5897304?sommaire=5894773. For INSEE's earlier involvement in *labellisation*, see:

The importance of reviewing *labellisation* and inspecting SSMs points to a difference between the French Authority and the UK Authority. Much of the UKSA's work is reactive, responding to public figures and members of the public contacting the Authority about issues relating to public statistics and their use. The ASP's mode of operation is rather different. Much of its work, such as the inspection of SSMs, is regular and can be planned in advance. Inspecting an SSM is a time-consuming task, and normally only one or two SSMs are inspected in a single year. Having inspected an SSM, the Authority is legally enjoined to write a public *Avis*, or Notice of Opinion.

A word about terminology is necessary. The phrase '*un avis*' is generally translated into English as 'an opinion'. In its official English translations the ASP follows the common translation by rendering an '*Avis*' as 'Opinion'. However, in this context the English word 'opinion', even when capitalised, fails to evoke the strength of '*Avis*' in the world of French bureaucracy. The word in its bureaucratic sense indicates something more than just an opinion in the ordinary meaning of the term; it is the official announcement of a judgement. Because of this specific meaning, we will retain the French word. By writing about 'an Avis' we will be treating the word as if it were an English, bureaucratic term, and will avoid softening its bureaucratic meaning by translating it as just 'an Opinion'.

When the ASP conducts its investigations of SSMs, it is doing much more than inspecting the findings, methodologies and interpretations of particular statistical investigations. It is assessing the way that the world of public statistics is institutionally organised, especially checking whether the statisticians enjoy sufficient independence and protection from political pressure. By contrast, the UKSA has no legal duty to report on the bureaucratic organisation of official statistics. It sticks to the statistics themselves, rather than to the organisation of the statistical services.

Each year the ASP is required to publish a report which summarises its main activities in the previous year. The first annual report of ASP, published in 2010, reviewed the activities for 2009. Section 2.3 reported on 'Professional Independence' and contained a subsection: 'Keeping a watch on independence'.[26] Here the ambiguous position of the Ministerial Statistical Services was described. The SSMs not only produced statistics,

Joël Allain. (1995), 'Le comité du label: un an et quelque', *Courrier des Statistique*, 73 (old series), 63–7.
[26] ASP, 'Annual Report, 2009', www.autorite-statistique-publique.fr/event/rapport-annuel-2009-version-francaise-et-anglaise-de-lautorite-de-la-statistique-publique/. Section 2.3 is pp. 19–21. The ASP's Annual Reports are published the following year. To avoid confusion we are identifying the

but 'they take part more broadly in steering the public policies of their ministry, and this activity can make it difficult to work impartially and independently'.[27] Here we are in the uncomfortable two-hatted territory that the UKSA recognised; the position of ministerial statisticians having to serve two masters, one statistical and the other political.[28]

As an example of the pressures that ministerial statisticians can face, the Report mentioned statisticians not being able to publish statistics in a timely manner: 'The ministerial officials to whom they report might give priority to other work, for example, or might wish to postpone publications that might not appear politically opportune to them'.[29] Of the various political threats to the independence of statistical work, the pressure to delay publication, even for reasons of political opportunism, is not necessarily the worst – delaying the numbers is not quite as bad as suppressing them altogether. Nor might it be quite as corrosive as a minister interfering in the production and analysis of statistics.

The ASP, however, did not provide an immediate solution for the problems of cohabitation. Claudine Gasnier's account of the Authority's first ten years included sections about independence that were taken word for word from the first annual Report. This included the part about statisticians being in an ambiguous position.[30] Working in ministerial departments, statisticians 'may be subject to pressures of various kinds'.[31] Gasnier gave no indication that she was quoting the words from an old report, but it reads as if she was describing the situation of 2018 – or indeed as if she were describing an enduring fact of political life.

Unlike Padieu, Gasnier does not use the word 'manipulation', but she drops some diplomatically expressed hints. She writes that since 2014 ASP has 'focused more specifically on a review of small Ministerial Statistical Services'. She gave no reasons why the small groups should be inspected first.[32] Any reader who was familiar with Padieu's talk or who had experiences that resembled his anecdotes would understand Gasnier's unspoken message: a small group of ministerial statisticians will be more vulnerable to ministerial pressure than a larger group. There is safety in numbers.

Reports by the year that is being reported, not the year of publication. The Reports are published in English as well as French; quotations are taken from the English version, unless otherwise stated.
[27] ASP, 'Annual Report, 2009', pp. 19–20.
[28] Padieu was not the only speaker at the Independence Seminar to talk about this conflict. The third speaker was the director of Eurostat, and he declared that there was 'a permanent threat of political pressure in the production of [official] statistics': Michel Glaude (2008), 'Les instituts nationaux, Eurostat et les organismes internationaux de statistique: vers une indépendance renforcée', Independence Seminar, pp. 29–39, quote p. 35.
[29] ASP, 'Annual Report, 2009', p. 20.   [30] Gasnier (2019a).   [31] Ibid., p. 3.   [32] Ibid., p. 5.

Inspecting but not Mentioning Manipulation

A key figure in the ASP's inspection of SSMs, and someone who was centrally involved in the decision to concentrate on the small ones first, was Philippe Cuneo. Formally he was a member of INSEE, where he served as director of statistical coordination. He participated in the independence conference of 2008, contributing to the round table, where he spoke about what sort of relations the about-to-be-formed Authority was likely to have with INSEE and the SSMs.[33]

Having been given special responsibility for organising and participating in the assessments of the SSMs, Cuneo regularly attended the Authority's meetings. At the ASP's first official meeting, he claimed that the UKSA and the ASP exercised greater authority than most statistical organisations.[34] At the second meeting of the ASP, held in September 2009, Cuneo spoke about the role of the Authority in determining the structures of the SSMs.[35] Judging by the official summary, this talk seems to have been somewhat bureaucratic in its approach.

In its first Annual Report, the Authority was proposing to adopt a pragmatic approach towards inspecting the SSMs. It had accepted that it was not possible 'to define an exhaustive list of approval criteria' but criteria would have to be discussed 'on a case-by-case basis'.[36] This ruled out any announcement that the ASP was specifically investigating the problem of 'statistical manipulation' or that it would be proposing a set of criteria for assessing what constituted manipulation. Whether Cuneo used the word 'manipulation' when chatting with trusted statistical colleagues behind closed doors, we cannot say; but we can say that the word was not being used in official documents.

The Authority started its inspections of SSMs with the smallest ministerial statistical group of all: the group for Fishing and Aquaculture which was part of the Directorate of Maritime Fishing and Aquaculture. The Authority decided to recommend withdrawing its status as an SSM and incorporating the group into the Ministry for Ecology and Development.

---

[33] Philippe Cuneo, Annie Fouquet, Philippe Frémeaux and Richard Laux (2008), 'Summary of the first round table: Qu'est-ce que l'indépendance? Quels enjeux? Quels problèmes?', Independence Seminar, pp. 44–8.

[34] ASP (2009a), 'Relevé de décisions de la séance du 8 juin 2009'.

[35] ASP (2009b), 'Relevé de décisions de la séance du 29 septembre 2009', www.autorite-statistique-publique.fr/event/releve-de-decisions-de-la-seance-2/.

[36] ASP, 'Annual Report, 2009', p. 27.

An Avis to this effect was duly published.[37] The ASP's October meeting for 2014 seems to have discussed at length the matter of Fishing and Aquaculture.[38] The group's director defended his statistical group and denied that their independence had been compromised. Cuneo suggested that the Fishing and Aquaculture SSM was too small to be independent.

Claudine Gasnier, in her article about the first ten years of ASP's work, gave three reasons why the ASP had recommended that the status of SSM should be removed from the Fisheries and Aquaculture statistical group.[39] She wrote: 'The absence of a critical size of the Department, which could potentially be detrimental to its independence, its efficiency and the quality of the data produced'. Note her careful, diplomatically worded language. Gasnier did not explicitly assert that the independence had been compromised, but its small size could *potentially* be detrimental to its independence. The other two reasons referred to the Department's lack of statistical publications and the fact that most of its activities were not statistical. It would not be surprising if the group's director felt attacked by the judgement and in defending his group, he was defending himself.

Cuneo was a bit more explicit at the ASP's meeting in June 2015.[40] Having discussed which ministerial department would best guarantee the independence of the Fisheries and Aquaculture statistical group, Cuneo proceeded to talk more generally about what made for a satisfactory SSM. Size, according to Cuneo, was important. He said that 'for the small SSMs, the head of the [statistical] service does not enjoy the necessary professional independence'. The public summary of the meeting does not specify what reasons Cuneo might have given for his judgement on size and independence.

Offering reasons and examples would almost certainly risk talking about what particular ministers might have done to curtail the independence of their statisticians; or how directors had failed to show sufficient resolve. Then light would have been shone into a place that the government might prefer to remain in shadow. But, a diplomatic hint here, and a mention of size there – that was enough.

[37] For the ASP's official Avis on the Fishing and Aquaculture SSM: ASP (2014a), 'L'Autorité de la statistique décide à la majorité de ne pas maintenir le statut de service statistique ministériel (SSM) au bureau des pêches maritimes et de l'aquaculture (DPMA)', 29 October, www.legifrance.gouv.fr/jorf/id/JORFTEXT000029838273.

[38] ASP (2014b), 'Relevé de décisions de la séance du 29 octobre 2014', www.autorite-statistique-publique.fr/event/releve-de-decisions-de-la-seance-22/.

[39] Gasnier (2019a), p. 5.

[40] ASP (2015), 'Relevé de décisions de la séance du 17 juin 2015', www.autorite-statistique-publique.fr/event/releve-de-decisions-de-la-seance-25/. See p. 4 for a summary of Cuneo's presentation.

The M-word Again

Something was being omitted in the assorted comments about inspecting SSMs. This omission will show that both the UKSA and the ASP, despite their different modes of operation, share common problems. The ASP omitted to say what exactly makes the smallness of a statistical grouping in a ministry so problematic. As we saw in the previous section, the first Annual Report of the Authority claimed that it was not possible to formulate a list of approved criteria, but each inspection would have to be on 'a case-by-case basis'. This is strange if size were such an important criterion. It would be easy to state that each SSM had to meet a minimum size: to stipulate, for example, that unless the group had 'x' number of senior statisticians its independence was at risk, and so it should be merged with another group to meet the minimum size.

However, no minimum size was declared: there was no proposed numerical solution to what was a problem of quality. Presumably, a group of one would be okay so long as it was the right statistician working with the right minister. But to say as much would be to expose the Authority into highlighting what sort of statistician and minister would be the 'right' ones. That would take it closer to talking about manipulation and its characteristics: for the desired characteristic would be a non-manipulative minister and an unmanipulable statistician. Neither the UKSA nor the ASP operates in a world of pure numbers. They have to be strategic in the way they interact with the world of political power. Above all, they want to avoid saying to a minister, 'You are a devious manipulator'; and they want to avoid saying to one of their own, 'You should have been far more resolute'. Appearing to talk about size, while not actually measuring that size, is a compromise.

Because acts of political manipulation tend to occur behind closed doors, there are typically no independent witnesses or objective recordings to determine who said what to whom. Even if a statistician went public and accused the politician of attempted manipulation, the politician would have ready denials, or what sometimes is called 'plausible deniability': 'just a little misunderstanding'; 'of course, I would never suggest that, I was only...', 'I was acting in the best interests of our great nation', etc and etc.[41] In later chapters, when we examine episodes of statistical

---

[41] For the way that social scientists have used the concept of 'plausible deniability', which itself originated in the world of American diplomacy, see: David Bogen and Michael Lynch (1989), 'Taking account of the hostile native: plausible deniability and the production of conventional

manipulation in detail, we will come across some pretty implausible 'plausible denials' – probably the most implausible comes in Chapter 10 when we describe how a British minister of health tried to explain away why the UKSA criticised his numbers.

Padieu recognised that a minister would normally command greater resources, including rhetorical expertise and direct political power, than would a back-room statistician.[42] On the other hand, a clash between minister and statistician need not be entirely one sided. The public are far more likely to believe the statistician than the politician. We discussed the British evidence about the public's distrust of politicians and the trust of statisticians in the previous chapter.[43] INSEE has conducted similar surveys. These surveys sampled those who had used INSEE's website, or 'Inseenautes' as the surveyors called them.[44] The overwhelming majority of the 'Inseenautes' took a positive view of INSEE and of French official statistics. In parallel with the British results, those who distrusted official statistics gave as their main reason that they distrusted politicians: 'The politicians make them [the numbers] mean whatever they want'.[45]

Occasionally, the word 'manipulation' makes an appearance in the world of French official statistics, but not in a straightforward way. One example of a statistician from INSEE using 'manipulation' occurred in January 2020. *La Dépêche du Midi*, a local newspaper in the Occitanie region, reported an interview with Gérald Péalarat, INSEE's director of projects in that region.[46] The reason for the interview was that on the following day parts of the Occitanie would be having an extra census. Péalarat was taking the opportunity to explain the reasons for the census and to urge people to take part. He said that respondents were being encouraged to provide their census information on the internet. He was lauding the advantages of filling out electronic forms rather than the

---

history in the Iran-Contra hearing', *Social Problems*, 36, 197–224; Derek Edwards and Jonathan Potter (1992), *Discursive Psychology*, London: Sage. On the way that politicians readily deny accusations, see: Peter Bull (2008), 'Slipperiness, evasion and ambiguity: equivocation and facework in non-committal political discourse', *Journal of Language and Social Psychology*, 27, 324–32; Steven Clayman and John Heritage (2002), *The News Interview*, Cambridge: Cambridge University Press; Ruth Wodak (2009), *The Discourse of Politics in Action*, Basingstoke: Palgrave Macmillan.

[42] Padieu (1999).   [43] See above, pp. 139–40.

[44] INSEE (2021), 'Image de l'Insee et de ses indicateurs auprès des Inseenautes: résultats de l'enquête menée en 2020', 15 March, www.insee.fr/fr/information/5232245.

[45] Ibid. See: Figure 6.

[46] Gérald Camier (2020), 'Toulouse 3e ville de France, c'est pour quand?', *La Dépêche du Midi*, 15 January.

traditional paper ones. Among the advantages were 'less losses and less manipulations'.[47]

It was a strange thing to say, and it was not entirely clear what Péalarat meant. Who previously had been causing the losses and manipulations? Surely it could not have been the respondents: if they had lost their paper forms, then it was the duty of census agents to supply new ones. And what does it mean to say that the respondents were *manipulating* the census? Was Péalarat hinting that the census agents may have used their own biases to guide respondents to particular answers or to register those answers in distorted ways? This had happened in an earlier age of censuses. In the nineteenth century, as we mentioned in Chapter 2, British census enumerators made sure that 'prostitution' was not an acceptable answer to a question on employment. Whatever he meant, Péalarat was talking as if 'manipulation' had been a problem in the past, but now, with electronic censuses, the problem was solved.

In the larger scheme of things, Péalarat's throwaway remark to a friendly provincial journalist was hardly big news, although it might cast a light on the assumptions and choice of words by a middle-ranking official statistician. On the other hand, it is a matter of political and statistical significance when a very senior figure in the world of French statistics uses the word 'manipulation' in an official document. When this happens, we should assume that the word has been deliberately chosen, not just slipped out carelessly. In 2020 Dominique Bureau, who as president of the ASP held the top position in the Authority, published an article in INSEE's annual journal *Courrier des statistiques*.[48] In his piece the ASP's president looked back over the first ten years of the Authority's life.

It had been, according to Bureau, a difficult period with a number of public controversies, which mostly occurred before his presidency. Soon after it had been established, the Authority found itself involved in what Bureau described as a 'fierce' public controversy. This centred on the statistical claims that the minister of the interior was making. In France, this is a senior ministerial post and it is the equivalent of a ministry for home affairs whose primary responsibilities cover policing, social order and public protection. In 2011, the minister was quoting INSEE's figures about educational achievement. He was claiming that they provided the evidence to show how poorly the children of immigrant parents were performing at school. We will be looking at his use of the statistics in the next section. But, first, we should note what Bureau said about the public outcry.

[47] Camier (2020).   [48] Bureau (2020), see above, fn. 9.

Bureau wrote that ASP had been founded at a time when trust in official statistics was at a low point in France. More people were doubting the validity of official statistics than ever before. This had come to a head with the minister of the interior's controversial remarks about children of immigrant parents. The minster's critics, according to Bureau, were calling into question 'the way in which the phenomena were being measured, with the recurring suspicion that the figures were being *manipulated*' (emphasis added).[49]

Rather like the UKSA's commissioned surveys into public attitudes about statistics, Bureau was attributing the belief in statistical manipulation to others. He was not directly voicing the belief himself, but he was saying that this was a serious situation. And then he went a bit further. Regarding the public belief in manipulation, he wrote that 'the lack of professional independence' that was associated 'with the production of figures provided to the public' in this matter 'appeared to be untenable'.

However, Bureau did not say, or hint, that the lack of professional independence was all in the public mind. Moreover, he wrote that the consequence of the controversy was the establishment of an SSM 'with all the necessary guarantees of independence' in the Ministry of the Interior. This went a long way to reassuring the public that the statistics were reliable and not being manipulated.[50] Bureau was too experienced a public servant to identify the minister of the interior, or any other minister for that matter, as a manipulator of statistics. But he knew how to hint without directly uttering.

It is the details of the episode, however, that are particularly revealing. They show how the ASP was developing its strategies for dealing with intense public controversies, while appearing not to take sides. At the same time it was learning how to resist manipulative ministers. This required strategic thinking combined with firmness, and the lead was not always coming from the top.

Direct Action Behind the Scenes

René Padieu wrote that the conflict between statisticians and ministers is an instance of a more general clash: that between knowledge (*connaissance*)

---

[49] Ibid.
[50] Bureau was referring to the 2014 Avis which recommended that the Ministry of the Interior should have its own SSM. For the Avis, see: www.autorite-statistique-publique.fr/lautorite-de-la-statistique-publique-donne-un-avis-favorable-a-linscription-du-service-statistique-ministeriel-de-la-securite-interieure/.

and power (*pouvoir*).[51] These words of Padieu attribute power to the politicians and knowledge to the statisticians. He assumes that knowledge is at a disadvantage when it is pitted against those who enjoy political power. But official statisticians, especially if they have a legal authority to back them, do have powers of their own – and these powers can be exercised carefully and strategically.

What should the Authority do if a senior politician, especially a government minister, persists in misquoting statistics and making false statistical claims? In the United Kingdom the usual procedure is clear. Typically, another politician will write a public letter to the Authority and ask whether the UKSA can check the figures that are being quoted by the government, or by any public figure. If UKSA thinks that the letter writer has made a reasonable case, then it will look into the matter and deliver a judgement which may or may not be published.

The French statistical authority, unlike the UKSA, may spend much of its time and efforts in making regular inspections. However, the ASP and INSEE are aware that they face damage to their reputations for impartiality, if they spontaneously join public controversies about the statistical claims that politicians might be making. On the other hand, their reputations for serving the public can be damaged if they do not comment on controversies about statistics. Thus statistical controversies set both organisations a dilemma: to speak out or not to speak out, that is the question.

The ASP's solution is to operate behind the scenes while encouraging other statistical institutions, most notably INSEE, to provide the public with relevant statistical information. The ASP did not formulate this general procedure in advance of any actual controversy. The procedure arose from necessity, when it and INSEE found themselves being drawn into the highly public controversy that Claude Guéant, the minister of the interior, provoked.

In the summer of 2011, Guéant announced that two-thirds of the children who left school without qualifications came from immigrant families. Guéant, a close ally of President Sarkozy and generally recognised to be on the political right, claimed that he was taking the figures from surveys that INSEE had conducted in 1995 and 2005. Guéant's claims were widely reported in the French media.[52] The media also reported that

---

[51] Padieu (1999), pp. 8–9.
[52] For press accounts of the episode, see: *Le Point* (2011), 'L'Insee corrige les chiffres de Guéant sur les enfants d'immigrés et l'échec scolaire', 27 June, www.lepoint.fr/societe/l-insee-corrige-les-chiffres-de-gueant-sur-les-enfants-d-immigres-et-l-echec-scolaire-27-06-2011-1346533_23.php#11; *L'Humanité* (2011), 'L'Insee s'inscrit en faux contre Claude Guéant', 28 June, www.humanite.fr/linsee-sinscrit-en-faux-contre-claude-gueant; *Figaro* (2011), 'Immigration/Insee: Guéant contredit', 27 June, www.lefigaro

Guéant's numerical claims provoked the fury of political opponents who held that the minister was deliberately misquoting INSEE's statistics.

Guéant was not helping his own case by appearing to use the 'two-thirds' ratio to describe two very different things. On 25 May, while speaking on the radio station Europe 1, Guéant claimed that 'two-thirds of school failures' came from 'the children of immigrants'. A few days later in the National Assembly, Guéant claimed that two-thirds of children with immigrant parents left school without a diploma.[53] It is as if Guéant had little grasp of statistics and was unaware that the percentage of unqualified school leavers coming from immigrant families is numerically very different from the percentage of immigrant children leaving school without qualifications.

Here would seem to be a public controversy in which either the statistical Authority or INSEE, or possibly both, might justifiably explain to the public why the two numbers are very different and what might be the most accurate figure. Both organisations, however, seemed reluctant to enter the fray. The French press carried stories that INSEE had been approached to comment on whether the minister was using the statistics correctly. The director general of INSEE was quoted as saying that it was not INSEE's job to comment on the interpretation of its statistics.[54]

But something changed quickly. The declaration of INSEE's director general did not reflect the views of the statisticians who were working at INSEE. Their trade unions issued a statement which criticised the director general and suggested that his position broke the European Code of statistical practice.[55] The Code asserted that statistical authorities should publicly comment if public statistics were being abused or misapplied. The professional statisticians of INSEE would have been aware that their director general was trying to make a distinction between the numbers and their interpretation. In practice such a distinction is hard, if not impossible, to maintain clearly.

INSEE's professional statisticians would have been well aware that the minister was statistically in the wrong. INSEE had reported that

.fr/flash-actu/2011/06/27/97001-20110627FILWWW00611-immigrationinsee-gueant-contredit.php; *Le Monde* (2011), 'Echec scolaire et immigration: la direction de l'Insee corrige Guéant', 27 June, www .lemonde.fr/politique/article/2011/06/27/echec-scolaire-et-immigration-la-direction-de-l-insee-corrige-gueant_1541697_823448.html; Cédric Mathiot (2011), 'Immigration et échec scolaire: Guéant enfin corrigé par l'Insee', *Libération*, 28 June, www.liberation.fr/france/2011/06/28/immigration-et-echec-scolaire-gueant-enfin-corrige-par-l-insee_745612/.
[53] *Le Monde* (2011), 27 June.   [54] *Libération* (2011), 28 June.
[55] *L'Humanité* (2011), 28 June.

proportionally two-thirds more children from immigrant families left school without qualifications than did children from non-immigrant families. But it would be an error to interpret this as suggesting that two-thirds of the total number of non-qualified school-leavers came from immigrant families because proportionally there were far fewer students from immigrant families than from non-immigrant families. Similarly, it would be a mistake to assume that the figure implied that two-thirds of school leavers from immigrant families left without qualifications. Neither claim was supported by the numbers.

Facing opposition from their statisticians, the management of INSEE relented and they took what was then an unusual step. They issued a press release, which re-presented the original statistics and emphasised what the figures were measuring and what they were not measuring.[56] The press release also included a new calculation: the proportion of children from immigrant families who left school without qualifications. The figure was 16 per cent, not the 66 per cent, or two-thirds, that Guéant was claiming. However, the press release did not mention Guéant. Nor did it link the statistics to the controversy created by Guéant. By not doing so, INSEE could maintain the fiction that it was not entering into the public controversy. It was merely presenting some old numbers and a new calculation.

The press is not obliged to maintain polite fictions in the way that public servants are – especially if politeness would come at the expense of a good story. The next day, the broadsheets, both from the left and the right, carried the story of INSEE and the minister's figures. There were headlines that presented the story as INSEE 'correcting' the minister.[57] A correction implies that an error has been made, and, thus, the headlines were implying that the minister's well-publicised claims were erroneous. *L'Humanité*, a left-wing paper, rhetorically went a step further.[58] It used the verb *démentir* as well as *corriger* (to correct). Literally, *démentir* means to 'de-lie', to remove a deliberate untruth, and it can also be used to mean 'to refute'. In this sense, it conveys a stronger condemnation than *corriger*, because an error, which is being corrected, might have been made in good faith. Whatever the reasons for the minister's statistical claims, the papers from the right and left were siding with INSEE, backing it against the minister. To use Padieu's expression, they were backing knowledge over power.

But what was the ASP doing during this public brouhaha? It might have been keeping a low public profile but it was acting behind the scenes. This

---

[56] For INSEE's press release, see the report in *Le Figaro* (2011), 27 June.
[57] *Libération* (2011), June 28; *Le Monde* (2011); *Figaro* (2011).   [58] *L'Humanité* (2011).

became clear years later. The ASP's Annual Report for 2019, looking back over the first ten years of the Authority's existence, described what the ASP did.[59] Basically, it encouraged INSEE to distribute the details of the 1995 and 2005 studies to journalists, so that the press would have the relevant numbers at their disposal. The Report said that it was the duty of the ASP to remain in contact with INSEE and the other statistical services to 'ensure that the facts are established'.

That was not all the president of the ASP did, for he took what the 2019 Report called 'direct action'.[60] Sometimes the phrase 'direct action' refers to street demonstrations or forceful public protests, especially by those far removed from the corridors of power. The ASP's direct action was almost the complete opposite: it was action performed by a high-ranking bureaucrat in the corridors of bureaucracy. In this instance, the president of the ASP wrote directly and privately to the minister of the interior, informing him what 'could be deduced' from INSEE's figures. The president also stressed 'at the same time the discrepancy between the estimate made by the minister and the orders of magnitude obtained from the statistics disseminated'.[61] Thus, the ASP was discretely correcting the minister's errors, well away from the prying eyes of the press.

There we see what would become the basic *modus operandi* for dealing with political controversies about statistics. There is a division of labour. INSEE and other ministerial producers of statistics will clarify the relevant statistics and their meaning. The statistical Authority will continue to do what it did in 2011, namely operating behind the scenes, thereby taking direct action to confront *pouvoir* with *connaissance*.

Discovering How to Oppose Political Manipulation

The effect of the ASP's behind-the-scenes action seems to have been mixed. On 7 July, Guéant was speaking on the French radio station RTL and he took the opportunity to deliver his latest thoughts on statistics and the educational failures of children from immigrant families. He was telling the nation that the scholastic failures of immigrant children were a condemnation of France's policy of assimilation. It was important, he also said, to accept that one can say whatever one wants about statistics that

---

[59] ASP, 'Annual Report, 2019', see particularly pp. 53–4.   [60] Ibid., p. 54.
[61] Ibid. The same sentence appears in Dominique Bureau's 2020 article.

have been published – a jibe against INSEE's statisticians.[62] However, he did not repeat the 'two-thirds' figures which he had been vociferously promoting. Perhaps he had not liked the press reports that the statistical authorities had corrected him and did not wish to repeat the experience.

The procedures of 2011, with their division of labour between INSEE and the ASP, have solidified in the course of other controversies. Over the years the ASP has encouraged INSEE to use social media to raise its profile, and, most importantly, to combat the sorts of rumours that proliferate on social networks.[63] To this day, INSEE's website retains the words that its director used when launching the Institute's blog. It was important, he said, for INSEE to use 'the new channel of communication to exercise its mission … to highlight the lessons that can be drawn from the use of statistics and from [knowing] their limits, to publicise the work of the Institute and … to fight against the spread of false or misleading information'.[64]

As the director's words indicate, INSEE's blogs are much more than the presentation of numbers. They can include methodological arguments about the strengths and weaknesses of different measures, and discussions about the inferences that can and cannot be drawn from particular data sets. In this respect, INSEE's blogs resemble the intermittent blogs that the UKSA publishes – for example, the UKSA's blog about the different ways of measuring poverty.[65] One of INSEE's blogs concerned the difficulty of interpreting figures for crime and delinquency.[66] This issue lies at the heart of the following chapter, which discusses the case of another minister of the interior and his highly controversial statistical claims.

When Guéant's successor makes his statistical faux pas, INSEE and the ASP will have their plans of action at the ready; and so will the statistical trade unions. Knowledge, to use Padieu's phrase, need not be powerless, especially when it has strategies. We briefly mentioned one outcome of the

---

[62] *Agence France Presse* (2011), 'Echec scolaire/immigration: "on fait dire ce que l'on veut" aux chiffres (Guéant)', 8 July.

[63] The ASP declared that it 'approves of the introduction of a "blog" by INSEE to combat the spread of false or misleading information', ASP, 'Annual Report, 2019', p. 9.

[64] Jean-Luc Tavernier, 'Pourquoi un blog?' INSEE, 20 January, https://blog.insee.fr/pourquoi-un-blog/.

[65] Elise Baseley (2020), 'The trouble with measuring poverty', UKSA, 27 July, https://osr.statisticsauthority.gov.uk/blog/the-trouble-with-measuring-poverty/.

[66] Christine Gonzalez-Demichel (2020), 'Délinquance enregistrée par la police et la gendarmerie et enquête statistique de victimation: deux outils indissociables pour mesurer une même réalité', INSEE blog, 9 December, https://blog.insee.fr/delinquance-enregistree-par-la-police-et-la-gendarmerie-et-enquete-statistique-de-victimation-deux-outils-indissociables-pour-mesurer-une-meme-realite/.

controversy with Guéant: his ministry was granted a statistical group. At first sight, it would seem that Guéant was being rewarded for his poor statistics – he was granted a statistical group to command and to flaunt. But the statisticians of the ASP are simultaneously gaining power – the power to inspect the minister's statistical group, and thereby the potential power to control the minister. A future head of statistics in the Ministry of the Interior would hint that this is why the statistics group was established.[67] We will be hearing from her again. In matters of strategic thinking not all is necessarily quite as it seems.

---

[67] Christine Gonzalez-Demichel (2022), 'Le Service statistique ministériel de la sécurité intérieure (SSMSI)', talk given to CNIS (Le Conseil national de l'information statistique), 17 March, www .cnis.fr/wp-content/uploads/2022/03/SSMSI_pour-bureau-CNIS_17032022_diffusion.pdf.

CHAPTER 8

Gérald Darmanin
Populism against Statistics

In democracies, statistical authorities like the United Kingdom Statistical Authority (UKSA) and the Authority for Public Statistics in France (ASP) face a common problem: their legal powers to combat manipulation are limited. Both the UKSA and the ASP can withhold the title of 'official statistics' from a body of data that the authority finds to be methodologically flawed. And they can check whether official statistics are released fairly and equally, without the government having privileged access to the data in advance of the public and politicians from other parties. In France, the ASP can also make recommendations about the organisation of statistical departments within government ministries. But even this legal responsibility does not confer direct power. The Authority must report its recommendations to the government which technically has the power to accept or reject those recommendations.

What the authorities cannot do is, perhaps, as significant as what they can do. They cannot silence politicians who are determined to manipulate statistics for their own political advantage. Even if the statistical authority has officially criticised a body of statistics as being methodological unsound, it cannot prevent a politician talking about the data as if it were methodologically rigorous. Statistical authorities like the ASP and the UKSA have no powers to discipline a politician who is determined to use poor data for their own advantage or who is deliberately determined to misinterpret good data. Nor can they actually prevent ministers from peeking at the data before they should. When there is a direct clash between a powerful, manipulative politician and a senior statistician who is trying to prevent statistical manipulation, even in a democracy it can be the statistician who ends up in the dock, facing the criminal charges.[1]

In this chapter, we will present the case history of a French politician who has been determined to resist the statistical authorities of France.

---

[1] See Chapter 5 for the cases of Becquava in Argentina and Georgiou in Greece.

Gérald Darmanin is a senior French politician, who, at the time of writing, is the French minister of the interior, thereby heading the ministry responsible for order, police and the protection of French citizenry. There is much that could be written about Darmanin, but we focus on his awkward relations with the French statistical authority. In the following chapter, we will be telling the story of Boris Johnson's possibly even more fractious relations with the United Kingdom Statistical Authority.

In examining Darmanin's clashes with the ASP, we will be observing something that we touched on in the previous chapter. We recounted how a previous French minister of the interior, Claude Guéant, tried to assert his right to say exactly what he wanted about published statistics, regardless of what the statistical authorities said about the meaning of the numbers. We will see Darmanin continuing with this battle and trying to devalue the authority of the Statistical Authority. It will become apparent that statistical issues do not necessarily stand on their own, but they can become entangled with a politician's ideology, strategy and personal failings.

The examples will show something that we have already mentioned: if the authorities are to protect the integrity of official statistics, then they need to act strategically. Just publishing a statistical rebuttal of a minister's comments can sometimes be insufficient: how the rebuttal is made and how it is communicated can be as important as its statistical content. At times, the authorities and manipulative politicians might seem to be locked in a contest for reputation or what ancient rhetoricians called 'ethos'.[2] This contest may appear to be a zero-sum contest with only one possible winner. The politicians may believe that a victory for the statistical authority will be at the expense of their own reputation. So, politicians might try to protect their own reputation by undermining that of the authority. We will see how the authorities try to strategically avoid this zero-sum mentality.

As we have already seen, the French and British statistical authorities almost never use the word 'manipulation'. They try to act as if the politician, who may be twisting the numbers or using them in misleading ways, is operating in good faith. It is as if the politician is guilty of little more than a bit of statistical naivety. This polite fiction allows the

---

[2] For accounts of the ancient rhetorical concept of 'ethos' and its relevance for understanding political discourse today, see: Kristine Bruss and Richard Graff (2005), 'Style, persuasion, and character in Aristotle's "Rhetoric"', *Advances in the History of Rhetoric*, 8, 39–72; Dale L. Sullivan (1993), 'The ethos of epideictic encounter', *Philosophy and Rhetoric*, 26, 113–33; James Wynn (2023), 'Exploring expert appeals to ethos with statistical corpus analysis', in Randy A. Harris, and Jeanne D. Fahnestock (eds.), *Routledge Handbook of Persuasive Language*, New York: Routledge, pp. 60–77.

authority to impose their statistical judgement without suggesting that they are exposing the politician as having intentionally misled the public.

A Preliminary Episode

To begin with: a prelude before the big, public clash. This was an episode when the ASP acted politely and strategically in an early dispute with Darmanin. In March 2019, when he was minister of action and public accounts in President Macron's government, Darmanin broke the official European Statistics Code of Practice. He divulged on radio details of the national accounts for the previous year before those figures had been officially released. The president of the ASP, Dominique Bureau, contacted the minister's chief of staff for a behind-the-scenes resolution.[3] Matters were quickly smoothed over. In a magazine interview, Bureau described the breach as an accident, and added 'one hopes that there will be no more accidents'.[4]

The president of the ASP was clearly being diplomatic, but we do not know whether he had noted down Darmanin as an awkward customer – the sort of politician who will push to gain every advantage that he can. Perhaps Bureau privately passed on this information to his successor. Nevertheless, we do know what happened when Darmanin tried to commit a similar offence after he had been promoted to be minister for the interior, and the Authority had a new president. Darmanin asked his ministerial statisticians to give him advance notice of some crime statistics that they were compiling. Far from being overawed by their ministerial boss, the statisticians told him that they could not fulfil his request because it contravened European regulations and the minister would have to wait for the numbers like everyone else. The statisticians then informed the ASP of Darmanin's request.

The Authority's new president, Mireille Erlbaum, did more than back the statisticians with behind-the-scenes support. In the ASP's next Annual Report, she publicly described the incident and, significantly, she did not call it an accident. She also underlined her support for the ministerial statisticians.[5] By then, as we will see, the Authority had good reason to

---

[3] ASP, 'Annual Report, 2019', p. 33: www.autorite-statistique-publique.fr/event/rapport-annuel-2019-version-anglaise-de-lautorite-de-la-statistique-publique/.
[4] Grégoire Normand (2019), 'La bataille complexe de l'indépendance des statistiques publiques', *La Tribune*, 29 November.
[5] ASP, 'Annual Report, 2022', p. 29: www.autorite-statistique-publique.fr/event/rapport-annuel-2022-version-anglaise-de-lautorite-de-la-statistique-publique/.

suspect that Darmanin was not the type of politician to maintain polite fictions. The public persona that he was projecting throughout the media was not that of a diplomatic insider.

Gérald Darmanin: Ambitious Minister

It is a fact of democratic life that politicians will tend to cite advantageous statistics and ignore disadvantageous ones. We will see plenty more examples of this when looking at Darmanin and Johnson, both of whom are right-wingers. So is Donald Trump, whose pragmatic approach to numbers was discussed earlier. No one should think that we are dealing with an exclusively right-wing vice. Left-wing politicians are also likely to use statistics pragmatically, with accuracy and methodological precision being distant runners-up, except, of course, when they are highlighting the statistical deficits of opponents.[6]

In the case of Darmanin, there is, however, something else. A central element of his politics and his strategic planning involves downgrading statistics. Darmanin is not at present an internationally known political figure but, having been appointed by President Emmanuel Macron as the minister of the interior in 2020, he has become very much a senior, and highly controversial, figure in French politics. Moreover, he has presidential ambitions and in the not-too-distant future, he might possibly succeed in becoming internationally known.

Macron had been a member of the Socialist Party, but in 2016 he founded a new party, En Marche, with the aim of advocating a new sort of politics which would draw supporters from all the old parties. So successful was this strategy that in the following year Macron was elected president of France. He was re-elected in 2022 with his party having changed its name rather than its overall strategy. After a further name change, Macron's party, now called Renaissance, continues to claim to be politically situated above the conventional left–right distinctions.

Unlike Macron and many in his government, Darmanin came from a background in right-wing politics. He was a member of the conservative Gaullist party, the Union for a Popular Movement (UMP) and a great admirer of its leader Nicolas Sarkozy, who was president of France between 2007 and 2012, during which time the ASP was established. Standing as a member of the UMP, Darmanin was elected in 2014 as mayor of

---

[6] This is something that Joel Best strongly emphasises, arguing that the left and the right are both likely to misuse statistics: Joel Best (2004), *More Damned Lies and Statistics*, Berkeley: University of California Press.

Tourcoing, a small town in the unfashionable part of northern France. He presented himself as a man of the people, having himself been born in the area to working-class, immigrant parents. As a hard-working, ambitious politician from a humble, non-metropolitan background, Darmanin caught the eye of Sarkozy.

This information sounds as if it forms the background for a discussion of Darmanin and his statistical views. However, in this matter, the background is very much part of the foreground. For Darmanin, Tourcoing is much more than the place where he established himself politically before he became a national politician. The town provided him with a rhetorical image which he would use to counter the very notion of statistical thinking.

When Macron promoted Darmanin to be minister of the interior, there was concern, both within and outside the government. Some feared that his promotion signified a shift too far to the right. Darmanin had been adopting some of the language used by Marine Le Pen, the leader of the far-right party Rassemblement national (National Rally), which appeared to be growing in popularity. As we will see, there would be public controversy about Darmanin using one of Le Pen's words in particular.

In the summer of 2023, Darmanin, backed by his mentor Sarkozy, seemed to be organising his strategy for a bid to succeed Macron whose presidency would end in 2027. Sarkozy publicised the idea when he launched his book *The Time of Conflicts* in August 2023.[7] In this book Sarkozy argued that Marine Le Pen would win the next presidential election unless she was faced by someone like Darmanin who would be able to attract votes from centrists and the right.

Sarkozy's book was launched just days before Darmanin had organised a large gathering of more than 400 right-wing supporters to be held in his home territory of Tourcoing. The aim was to discuss France's political future and especially the next presidential election. Before, during and after the rally Darmanin repeated Sarkozy's point that only a candidate from the right could defeat Le Pen. Many observers thought that it could not have been a coincidence that the two events – the book launch and the Tourcoing rally – occurred so close together. The ex-presidential mentor and his pupil seemed to have deliberately coordinated their efforts to promote the latter as a credible future president.[8]

---

[7] Nicolas Sarkozy (2023), *Le temps des combats*, Paris: Fayard.
[8] See for example, the report in *Figaro* (2023), 'L'offensive Darmanin crée des remous', 25 August. See also: Tadhg Pidgeon (2023), 'French Minister Darmanin eyes up 2027 presidential run,' *Brussels Signal*, 15 August.

Darmanin was careful not to declare himself to be aiming for the presidency, but he hinted none too subtly that he might be just the person for the job. He told *Le Figaro* that the presidential candidate would need to be someone who could talk the language of ordinary working people, and not use complicated words that went over their heads.[9] He summed up the ideal candidate with what the paper called his 'mantra'. Darmanin said 'we must not put our future in the hands of technicians who use words that the French never understand'. Instead 'one must talk with the heart, not with statistics'.

And there it is: statistics, or rather the dismissal of statistics, right at the centre of Darmanin's politics, ideology and strategy.

A Statistical and Semantic Controversy

The French statistical authority had developed its procedures for dealing with public controversies in 2011 when dealing with one that involved Sarkozy's minister of the interior, Claude Guéant, and his statistically misleading claims about the educational failures of immigrant children.[10] Ten years later, there would be another public outcry in France, involving another minister of the interior and another president. Again the theme of immigration was involved, as Darmanin implicitly linked immigrants and their children with violent crime.

Much was to hinge on a politically controversial word that Darmanin used to describe what was happening to France: *l'ensauvagement* of France or turning France into a savage country. In French politics, the word *ensauvagement* has been associated with the extreme right and its claims that immigrants, particularly those from Africa, were bringing violence, drug-taking and other 'savage' behaviour into France. Marine Le Pen, the leader of Rassemblement national, which was formerly called Front national, had been using the word for a number of years.[11] The term

---

[9] Tristan Quinault-Maupoil (2023), 'Les nouvelles ambitions de Gérald Darmanin', *Figaro*, 14 August; see also the extensive interview with Darmanin in the local newspaper, *La Voix du Nord*, coinciding with his Tourcoing rally: Julien Lécuyer and Sébastien Leroy (2023) 'Gérald Darmanin, ministre de l'intérieur "Il faut s'occuper de la marmite sociale qui bout"', *La Voix du Nord*, 25 August, www.lavoixdunord.fr/1365331/article/2023-08-24/exclusif-gerald-darmanin-je-me-sens-legitime-pour-dire-qu-il-faut-s-occuper-de.

[10] See above, pp. 162–7.

[11] On Le Pen's adoption of the phrase *l'ensauvagement de la vie quotidienne* (making everyday life savage), see for instance the report in *Le Monde*: Franck Johannès (2020), 'Marine Le Pen met l'immigration au cœur de sa campagne des municipals', *Le Monde*, 7 March, www.lemonde.fr/politique/article/2020/03/07/a-marseille-marine-le-pen-met-l-immigration-au-c-ur-de-sa-campagne_6032144_823448.html.

'*l'ensauvagement*', however, has a much longer history and it has been claimed that not all its uses have been racist or even negative. In the nineteenth century the word was sometimes used to argue in favour of a utopian wildness. It has been pointed out that the word, even in this sense, was much favoured by French fascists.[12] Today the word is largely confined to the far right accusing their enemies of turning France into a lawless, dangerous and savage place.[13]

In the hands of Le Pen and Darmanin the word contains a statistical aspect, for the idea of *ensauvagement* implies that the nation, or some of parts of the nation, are becoming more savage, more lawless. In a characteristic tweet, Le Pen wrote: 'Delinquency, the making of savagery [*ensauvagement*] of our country, is a drama, and a drama that increases'.[14] As the so-called drama of savagery increases, then it should be reflected in the statistical evidence for crimes, such as knife crime, drug-dealing and sexual violence.

Before Darmanin had become the minister for the interior he had been using the sort of anti-immigrant language normally associated with the extreme right. It has been said that he had a political reason for turning to a more extreme way of talking: in his home territory he was competing for votes with Le Pen's party. The opinion polls for the municipal elections had been showing that in Tourcoing Le Pen's party was over six points ahead of Macron's.[15] In any case, such language fitted his image as a rough-and-ready right-winger who had worked his way from unprivileged, immigrant parents.[16] He was now competing with the far right for the support of hard-line, anti-immigrant voters. Because his own parents were Muslim immigrants, he seemed to be protected from charges of racism. His own background seemed to make the semantics of *ensauvagement* and other such terminology more acceptable, but not respectable: he still sounded like a tough populist.

---

[12] See, for example, the report in *L'Humanité* of Darmanin's use of '*ensauvagement*': 'Salade sécuritaire à la niçoise', *L'Humanité* (2020), 27 July.

[13] For a short account of the ideological history of the word, see: Sébastien Dalgalarrondo and Tristan Fournier (2020), 'A propos d'ensauvagement: pour une sociologie modeste', *AOC*, 11 November, https://aoc.media/opinion/2020/11/10/a-propos-densauvagement-pour-une-sociologie-modeste/.

[14] Marine Le Pen @MLP_officiel (2021), 'La délinquance, l'ensauvagement dans notre pays, est un drame, et un drame qui augmente', (X, formerly Twitter), 10 November, https://twitter.com/MLP_officiel/status/1458514046416822275.

[15] *La Voix du Nord* (2019), 'Gérald Darmanin a un toupet monstre', 5 July.

[16] On Darmanin's background, politics and ambitions, see: Nicholas Vinocur (2017), 'Gérald Darmanin, France's new (and improved) Sarkozy', *Politico*, 2 August, www.politico.eu/article/gerald-darmanin-emmanuel-macron-france-francois-fillon-france-new-and-improved-nicolas-sarkozy/.

When Darmanin was promoted to his high position of state, some wondered whether he would start toning down his rhetoric. They did not have to wonder for long. He had become minister on 6 July 2020, and less than three weeks later *Le Figaro* carried an exclusive interview with him. Darmanin took the opportunity to show that he was not softening his politics. He told the paper that 'we must stop *l'ensauvagement* of a part of society'.[17] Darmanin would have guessed that the word would provoke uproar. *Le Figaro*, sensing a good story, put his use of the word into the headline of their article.

Within days, journalists and distinguished French academics were giving their reactions, mostly claiming that *ensauvagement* carried a colonial history and a present association with racism.[18] Even the *New York Times* got in on the act. Several months after the interview, it reported the story of Darmanin's use of the word and it quoted distinguished French historians and social scientists.[19] One French expert on black history told the paper that *ensauvagement* is 'coded language to mean young, violent youths of sub-Saharan or North African origin'.

Some members of the government, such as the justice minister and the minister for ecological transition, made statements saying that they would not personally use the word *ensauvagement*. The arguments rumbled on, and after about three months INSEE published a blog about crime and delinquency. Rather like INSEE's earlier reactions to Guéant, this blog was not presented as if it were an answer to Darmanin, nor an intervention in the debate about *ensauvagement*. The fiction was maintained that, at this moment of intense public controversy, INSEE just happened to be discussing methodological issues about the calculation of the crime rate, and how to interpret figures that might at first sight appear to show a rise in crime, especially violent and sexual crime.[20]

---

[17] Arthur Berdah, Jean Chichizola, Christophe Cornevin and Albert Zennou (2020), 'Darmanin: "il faut stopper l'ensauvagement d'une partie de la société"; Dans un entretien au *Figaro*, le ministre de l'Intérieur s'inquiète de la fragmentation de la République' , *Le Figaro*, 23 July.

[18] Barbara Pompili (2020), 'Barbara Pompili critique l'emploi du mot "ensauvagement" par Gérald Darmanin', *Le Nouvel Obs*, 27 July; Sébastien Crépel (2020), 'Sauvagerie', *L'Humanité*, July 27; Camille Vigogne (2020), 'Wahnich: "Historiquement parlant, ensauvagement n'est pas un mot d'extrême droite"', *L'Express*, 27 July.

[19] Norimitsu Onishi and Constant Méheut (2020), '"Ensauvagement": the weight of a word makes a deep impact in France', *New York Times*, 6 September, www.nytimes.com/2020/09/04/world/europe/france-ensauvagement-far-right-racism.html.

[20] Christine Gonzalez-Demichel (2020), 'Délinquance enregistrée par la police et la gendarmerie et enquête statistique de victimation: deux outils indissociables pour mesurer une même réalité', INSEE blog, https://blog.insee.fr/delinquance-enregistree-par-la-police-et-la-gendarmerie-et-enquete-statistique-de-victimation-deux-outils-indissociables-pour-mesurer-une-meme-realite/.

The blog's author, Christine Gonzalez-Demichel, began by stating that measuring crimes that affect victims is a 'delicate enterprise, subject to numerous debates'. It could have easily been the bland opening sentence of a first-year textbook about the methodology of criminology. Much of the blog cautions against measuring crime rates by using the number of crimes recorded by the police. The problem with using the police figures is that the police may not record all reported crimes, especially if they consider the offence to be comparatively trivial or if they believe that they have little reasonable chance of finding the perpetrator of the crime. Just as importantly, victims may not report all offences to the police.

The blog emphasised that it was important to try to obtain reliable evidence for crime rates and to chart changes over time. The author did not directly state that *ensauvagement*, and whether it was happening, was an empirical matter. But she did state that it was indispensable to conduct statistical inquiries of '*victimation* whose principle subject is the victim'. That is why INSEE has conducted regular household surveys, asking the members of a large sample of families whether they had been victims of crime and, if so, what sort of crime.

These measures of *victimation* – or the creation of victims of crime – have, so Gonzalez-Demichel claimed, more accurately measured the number of victims of criminality than do the police figures, which are patchy at best.[21] The first part of the blog justifies putting the study of victims at the heart of studying rates of crime. However, it contains little to link the methodology of *victimation* with the semantics of *ensauvagement*. Nevertheless, slowly and inexorably the author was moving in a direction that would draw the two themes together.

In the context of her blog, this meant paying particular attention to violent sexual crimes committed against women. Some of the recent figures from both the police data and the household victim survey had indicated a rise in violent sexual crimes. There were, nevertheless, good reasons why a rise in the number of sexual crimes reported to the police, or to the researchers of the household surveys, might not indicate a rise in the actual number of sexual crimes committed. More women might today be reporting sexual crimes that previously they would not have reported.

---

[21] The problem is by no means confined to France. The United Kingdom Statistics Authority advises politicians and others that if they want to talk about the rise and fall of crime rates, they should use figures derived from the crime survey conducted by the Office for National Statistics, rather than using figures based on police reports. See, for instance, the letter from Sir David Norgrove, UKSA chair, to the Labour Party leader, Sir Keir Starmer, 17 May, 2021, https://uksa.statisticsauthority .gov.uk/correspondence/letter-from-sir-david-norgrove-to-sir-keir-starmer-crime-statistics/.

The author gave several reasons for this. There were the revelations of the Harvey Weinstein case in October 2017, in which the famous Hollywood film producer was accused of sexually assaulting, even raping, women working in the film industry at lower levels than himself. The scandal was followed by the '#MeToo' movement' of women reporting similar sexual assaults. The result of this was, according to Gonzalez-Demichel, that victims are now 'potentially better aware' of different forms of sexual assault, and improved training may have made police officers, social workers and prosecutors more attentive to victims. Consequently a rise in the number of victims reporting sexual offences to the police should be expected; and fewer victims would be embarrassed to recount their experiences to interviewers for INSEE's official surveys.[22]

This meant that 'a rigorous measurement of any societal phenomenon' cannot be straightforward. Here, the unspoken, indeed unspeakable, implication of the blog was becoming apparent. Rising totals of violent sexual crime do not necessarily indicate that society, or at least part of society, is becoming more savage. The numbers might be indicating quite the opposite: a society that is no longer accepting the routine sexual violence which men, especially men with power, have for years committed against women, as well as the violent crimes that 'straight' men have committed against sexual minorities. As always, the numbers are insufficient in themselves: they need to be understood. And some interpretations can be more plausible and some less so.

Darmanin is unlikely to have been worried about INSEE's blog. He was a young politician, clearly on his way up. He had shown that he was not abashed about using *ensauvagement*. As he said, 'personally, I use the word *ensauvagement* and I repeat it'.[23] The word was bringing him publicity. Left-wing intellectuals, his colleague in the justice department and some newspaper critics might have dissociated themselves from the word and the reality of *ensauvagement*, but others did not.

There was some evidence to suggest that the public at large did not wish to prevent the word from being used. In early September of that year, *Figaro* published the results of a public opinion poll about the word *ensauvagement*. The paper interviewed the director of the company that

---

[22] The #MeToo movement has had a global impact on women's readiness to report rape and other sexual assaults. For its effect on women's perspectives in a very different culture to France, see: Rahul Sambaraju (2020), '"I would have taken this to my grave, like most women": reporting sexual harassment during the #MeToo movement in India', *Journal of Social Issues*, 76, 603–31.

[23] Darmanin quoted in the *New York Times* (2020), 6 September.

conducted the poll.[24] According to the director, the results indicated that seven out of ten French people thought that the word *ensauvagement* was justifiable; a majority of that 70 per cent believed that there had recently been *ensauvagement* in France. At the time of INSEE's blog, French semantics seemed to be heading in Darmanin's direction.

Savagery, Statistics and Methodological Notes

Darmanin is the sort of ambitious politician who cannot keep out of the headlines for long. Having prompted INSEE to publish its blog about measuring crime, it would surely be just a matter of time before he would raise another big issue to provoke the statisticians. When it came, the issue was about statistics in general, rather than about specific statistics and their interpretation.

In May 2021, almost a year after his appointment, Darmanin gave a wide-ranging interview to the magazine *L'Express*. He talked about his early political life, when he was still mayor of unfashionable Tourcoing. He outlined his fears for France and cited statistics to back up his views about the collapse of society.[25] In this interview he did not use *ensauvagement*, but he was describing what in the past he had called the *ensauvagement* of parts of France. He said that France was being attacked from all sides, with threats coming from Islamism, communitarianism, immigration, declining parental authority and, of course, a rise in violent crime.

Darmanin said that he would use 'the truth of numbers' to illustrate the sharp decline of French morality. He quoted figures from the annual crime surveys of *victimation* that the INSEE blog had discussed. These surveys were conducted by INSEE with the cooperation of other organisations including some based within his own ministry.[26] Darmanin did not mention INSEE's blog. Instead, he made boldly confident claims about the central issue about which Gonzalez-Demichel had urged caution: why there had been a rise in the figures for sexual violence. Darmanin asserted that 'if one takes the period 2017–2019, leaving aside 2020 which was a

---

[24] Paul Sugy (2020), 'Insécurité: sept français sur dix jugent qu'il y a un "ensauvagement de la société"', *Le Figaro Vox*, 7 September, https://www.lefigaro.fr/vox/politique/insecurite-sept-francais-sur-dix-jugent-qu-il-y-a-un-ensauvagement-de-la-societe-20200907.

[25] Étienne Girard and Éric Mandonnet (2021), 'Grand entretien; Gérald Darmanin: "L'Etat est attaqué de toutes parts"', *L'Express*, 18 May.

[26] SSMSI (2018), 'Rapport d'enquête cadre de vie et sécurité: Victimation, délinquance et sentiment d'insécurité', Ministry of Internal Security, www.interieur.gouv.fr/Interstats/L-enquete-Cadre-de-vie-et-securite-CVS/Rapport-d-enquete-Cadre-de-vie-et-securite-2018. The research is based on an annual survey of 20,000 to 25,000 'ordinary' families, see Methodological Note, p. 209.

somewhat particular year because of Covid', then there was a rise in 'personal violence, sexual, conjugal and familial violence'. Sexual violence, he said, had risen by 35 per cent since 2017. The minister declared this to be 'a durable trend' ('*c'est une tendance durable*').

Darmanin offered no reason why the pattern observed during the brief period between 2017 and 2019 should be taken to be durable. Nor did he say why he was only including surveys conducted since 2017 – after all, the delinquency and *victimation* surveys had a much longer history. The fact that he only cited the surveys from 2017 onward suggests that possibly he was more methodologically aware than he was admitting in the interview, or possibly that he was being briefed by statistically aware advisors in his ministry.

There were sound methodological reasons for not directly comparing the post-2017 finding about sexual violence with the pre-2017 ones. The published reports of the delinquency and *victimation* surveys contain a 'Methodological Note'. In the years which Darmanin was quoting, the Methodological Notes specified that comparisons of sexual violence could not be made with earlier years because the researchers had altered their questions in 2017. Because of changing sexual attitudes, it was now possible to ask questions that could not have been asked previously. In addition, what was now being called a sexual assault would not necessarily have been recognised as one in earlier years.

When social attitudes change, researchers often face a dilemma: whether to change their questions in long-running surveys. They can be damned if they change their questions to keep up with the times, and they can be damned if they don't change them. When researchers change the questions, this often means that they can no longer make comparisons across time and therefore cannot discover durable trends, at least not immediately. Having changed the questions because the old ones have become dated, they must now use their new questions for a sufficiently long period before they can start discerning trends across time. Three years would normally be counted as too short a period to make a confident judgement about a durable trend. This basic problem affects measures of all social phenomena that change over time, not just measures of sexual violence.[27]

---

[27] It has been argued that many economists persist in using outdated measures. Most economists measure gross domestic product in standard ways that permit researchers to observe long-term trends. However, these trends are often inaccurate, because capital has changed, becoming internationalised and moved transnationally. See: Daniel Mügge and Lukas Linsi (2020), 'The national accounting paradox: how statistical norms corrode international economic data', *European Journal of International Relations*, 27, 403–27.

In the present case, matters were complicated by the nature of the changing social mores. INSEE's blog was not the only discussion of the effects of the #MeToo movement on crime figures. The blog writer was drawing on the Methodological Notes of the *victimation* surveys. The Note for the 2018 survey discussed why the questions about sexual violence had been changed. It said that the publicity from the Harvey Weinstein scandal and the ensuing #MeToo movement had 'freed the words' of sexual victims, and this was leading to more women reporting sexual crimes.[28] According to the data in the report, even in the age of #MeToo, a majority of the female respondents said that if they were raped or abused, they would not go to the police.[29] The statisticians in Darmanin's ministry were reporting that victims of sexual crimes are less likely to report crimes than victims of other crimes: only one in ten survivors of domestic physical or sexual violence report the crime, as compared with nine in ten victims of car theft.[30]

Darmanin did not discuss these methodological matters with *L'Express*. His style was to make sweeping declarations, not methodological caveats. There was, however, something else that caught the attention of official statisticians, even more than his improbable confidence in being able to spot a three-year, durable trend.

The Home Town Boy and the Pork Butcher

In the *Express* interview, Darmanin made a highly provocative statement about statistics. Having quoted his 'figures of truth' about the rising rate of

[28] The difficulty of explaining figures for sex crimes has been known for a comparatively long time. In his classic paper about corruption of measures for evaluating social policies, Donald Campbell discussed evidence indicating a drop in sex crimes in Denmark. He warned against claiming without further evidence that this drop was the result of easing the laws against pornography: it might just as easily have been caused by an increasing reluctance of victims to report sex crimes to the police. See: Donald T. Campbell (1979), 'Assessing the impact of planned social change', *Evaluation and Program Planning*, 2, 67–90.

[29] SSMSI (2018), 'Rapport d'enquête cadre de vie et sécurité', especially pp. 134 and 210–1. SSMSI (2019), 'Rapport d'enquête cadre de vie et sécurité: Victimation, délinquance et sentiment d'insécurité', pp. 146 and 229–31, www.interieur.gouv.fr/Interstats/L-enquete-Cadre-de-vie-et-securite-CVS/Rapport-d-enquete-Cadre-de-vie-et-securite-2019. The INSEE crime reports use the phrase 'liberation of the word' (*la libération de la parole*) to describe the rise of women reporting sexual violence following the #MeToo movement. In his *Express* interview Darmanin uses the same phrase when speaking of the increase of violent crimes, not just sexual ones, but he does not connect the phrase with the possibility that the statistical increase in violent crime may not be due to a rise of crimes committed.

[30] Christine Gonzalez-Demichel and Maud Guillonneau (2021), 'Improving how to measure crime and monitor criminal justice to address security challenges', *Security & Society*, INSEE *Références*, 9 December, www.insee.fr/en/statistiques/6439714?sommaire=6439743.

violent crime, he then appeared to question the value of statistics in general. He told *L'Express* that although he liked the inquiries into *victimation*, 'I prefer the good sense of the pork butcher of Tourcoing'.[31] It was not the first time that he had openly expressed his support for Tourcoing's butchers.[32]

It is at this point that Darmanin did something that was not entirely obvious. He combined his various political and statistical themes, but the interconnections are not easy to disentangle for he left much unspoken, including his controversial word about savagery. This seemingly plain-speaking politician may have been presenting himself as a man of the people, but, as we unpack his densely packed words, we will see that he was speaking in a less than straightforward way.

Linguists have often argued that those who hear the utterances of a speaker will assume, all other things being equal, that the speaker's successive utterances are relevant to each other, unless the speaker gives a sign that they are switching to another topic. This assumption is often called by linguists 'the maxim of relevance'. This means that hearers will try to make sense of a speaker's successive utterances by interpreting them to be relevant to each other, and this may mean filling in unspoken gaps.[33] Politicians can sometimes take advantage of their audiences by exploiting the maxim of relevance. They imply that their statements are relevant one to each other, but without actually saying so and then denying later that this is what they meant.[34] Darmanin's statements about liking *victimation* research but preferring the good sense of the Tourcoing pork butcher are clearly linked. Darmanin was making clear his preference for the pork butcher over the *victimation* research.

What comes next in the interview is presented as if it is relevant to the pork butcher utterance without Darmanin specifying that it is. At first sight, it would seem to be a non sequitur. He asserts that the minister of justice had good reason for saying what he did. He does not state what the

---

[31] Girard and Mandonnet (2021), *L'Express*, 18 May. Darmanin's words were: '*J'aime beaucoup les enquêtes de victimation et les experts médiatiques, mais je préfère le bon sens du boucher-charcutier de Tourcoing.*'

[32] *La Voix du Nord* had reported that Darmanin agreed to promote the foods and crafts of Tourcoing. The first group to receive his very public demonstration of support were Tourcoing's butchers: *La Voix du Nord* (2019), 'Quand Gérald Darmanin joue au garçon boucher', 1 June.

[33] See for example: Dan Sperber and Deirdre Wilson (1995), *Relevance*, Oxford: Blackwell; Louis de Saussure (2013), 'Background relevance', *Journal of Pragmatics*, 59, pp. 178–89. The idea of 'the maxim of relevance' comes from the classic chapter: H. P. Grice (1975), 'Logic and conversation', in P. Cole and J. Morgan (eds.), *Syntax and Semantics*, vol. 3, New York: Academic Press, pp. 41–58.

[34] Agung Budi Kurniawan and Lilia Indriani (2023), 'Flouting relevance maxim benefits of Hillary Clinton's President candidate debate on 2016', *Journal of Pragmatics Research*, 5, 135–52.

minister said or why this might be relevant to what he, Darmanin, has just said about the pork butcher of Tourcoing. Readers of the interview, as well as the interviewer, must assume that Darmanin is referring to the minister of justice saying that he would not use the word *ensauvagement*, which Darmanin has also not just used.

Darmanin does, however, say something more about the minister of justice. He says that the minister, like himself, faces reality. He states that one must not 'deny the real', for the political extremes make progress when the men of politics (sic: *les hommes politiques*) deny the real. Unpacking the tightly packed allusions in these few utterances, we have Darmanin referring to, but not actually uttering, the word *ensauvagement*. Given that Darmanin has been talking of the rise in violent crime, and done so without using *ensauvagement*, then he is implying that what he has been describing about the breakdown in France is 'the real'. Thus, the real is what he has in the past called *ensauvagement*, but he is implying that it is not necessary to use that word in order to speak about this so-called reality of modern France.

But there is something else that we have not explicated. Why, from talking about crime using the figures of truth, should he suddenly say that he prefers 'the good sense of the pork butcher of Tourcoing'? What is the connection here that he is suggesting rather than stating? First, he is implying that these pork butchers face up to reality: their words and actions do not deny the real. And then there is another unspoken implication: the pork butchers face up to reality better than the statisticians do – and that is why he prefers their good sense to the statistics. The pork butchers publish no methodological notes; they are straight speakers with good sense.

In talking like this, Darmanin was exemplifying what has become the mantra which he hopes will lead him to the presidency. As he told *Le Figaro* in 2023, we need to talk in ways that the French people understand – with the heart, not with statistics.[35] Nevertheless, he was not rejecting statistics altogether. He was suggesting that he will cite the statistics when he believes that the numbers are the figures of truth. But if the numbers do not match his version of the real, then the figures of truth will be less than the truth. Would the pork butchers of Tourcoing – those exemplars of good sense – claim that something was true just because some statisticians have produced some numbers? In Darmanin's universe,

[35] See above, p. 174.

their sense of what is real is more firmly based than that. And so is his own, at least in his own political imagination.

The left-wing papers who reported the *Express* interview portrayed Darmanin as downgrading statistics. Centrist and right-wing papers, such as *Le Monde* and *Le Figaro* did not carry a story about the interview. The story in *La Libération* was headlined 'Darmanin, the butcher of INSEE'.[36] According to the paper, 'feeling more than the facts' and 'approximation more than the precision of numbers' were the options that Darmanin had chosen. The story in *L'Humanité* was similar: Darmanin preferring intuition to 'the real'.[37] Both papers were turning Darmanin's own words against himself.

Official French statisticians saw Darmanin's preference for the pork butcher of Tourcoing as a deliberate slight on their profession. The various trade unions representing INSEE's statisticians published a leaflet, just as they had ten years earlier when another minister of the interior had used poor statistics to proclaim the educational failures of immigrant children. The new trade union leaflet was headed: 'Our work does not deny reality; it describes it … including that of the pork butcher of Tourcoing!'[38]

As in the previous episode, the trade unions wanted the French Statistics Authority to act. And, as before, the ASP's mode of action was very much behind the scenes. The Annual Report of the ASP for 2021 contained a short description of the way that the ASP reacted to Darmanin's comments about victim surveys and the butcher of Tourcoing, rather than to his use of the *victimation* statistics. The president of the ASP sent a message to the minister's chief of staff. Also the head of the ministry of interior security's statistical services (SSMSI) met with the minister's deputy chief of staff to discuss the issues. Following the Guéant controversy, the ASP had granted his ministry the right to have its own statistical group. Ten years later the group was able to take advantage of the ASP's strategic thinking. The ASP was able to communicate directly with Darmanin's chief of statistics, who could pass on statistical messages to the minister. And who was Darmanin's chief of statistics? It was Christine Gonzalez-Demichel.

We do not know what was said in these private meetings. However, we do know that the director general of INSEE issued a response to Darmanin

---

[36] Simon Blin (2021), 'Darmanin, le boucher de l'Insee', *Libération*, 19 May, www.liberation.fr/idees-et-debats/opinions/darmanin-le-boucher-de-linsee-20210519_7U42F54O7FH6PKMXVKY3K7QNKM/.

[37] *L'Humanité* (2021), 'Insécurité: Darmanin préfère l'intuition au reel', 21 May.

[38] *Nos travaux ne nient pas le réel, ils le décrivent… y compris celui du boucher-charcutier de Tourcoing!* Published by trade unions CGT, FO and SUD de l'INSEE (2021), 20 May.

on social media – a response that is no longer available in INSEE's archive of social media publications.[39] Basically the minister was met by the same double act that had met Guéant: INSEE dealing publicly on social networks with the specific statistics, and the ASP acting behind the scenes to defend the value of statistics. Now the authority was in an even stronger position than before: it had positioned one of its own behind the scenes, heading up statistics in his own ministry.

There is little evidence that the private meetings had any effect on changing Darmanin's ideological priorities: he *knew* that France was being threatened by a rise in violent savagery whatever the statisticians might say. He would pick the numbers that backed this knowledge. And if the numbers failed to work, he always had the butchers of his local town to tell him what was really happening.

Butchers, Hairdressers and the Denial of *Victimation*

We still have not got to the unspoken force of Darmanin's position about the statistics of *victimation*. Something glaringly obvious is hiding in plain sight – something that gives Darmanin personal and political reasons for avoiding the logic of his own ministry's studies about the victims of violent sexual crimes. We will approach the matter cautiously.

One of the most interesting reactions to the *Express* interview came from the magazine *20 Minutes* which asked a small number of Tourcoing's butchers whether they thought that violent crime had increased in recent years.[40] The magazine's respondents all said that they thought that France was becoming a more dangerous place; violent and sexual crimes were more common than they had been when they were young; there was less discipline today, and the punishment of offenders was far too lenient. None of the butchers cited any statistics to support these views. Their 'knowledge' came from elsewhere, but not necessarily from personal experience. One of the butchers said that he had worked in Tourcoing for more than thirty years and never had a problem. Nevertheless, he was convinced that crime was rising and the young were becoming more

---

[39] ASP, 'Annual Report, 2021', www.autorite-statistique-publique.fr/event/rapport-annuel-2021-version-anglaise-de-lautorite-de-la-statistique-publique/. See particularly the section on public controversies, pp. 32–3.

[40] Thibaut Chevillard (2021), '"Délinquance: Je ne sais pas si j'ai le regard qu'il faut..." comme Darmanin, on a demandé l'avis des bouchers-charcutiers de Tourcoing', *20 Minutes*, 19 May, www.20minutes.fr/societe/3045383-20210519-delinquance-sais-si-regard-faut-comme-darmanin-demande-avis-bouchers-charcutiers-tourcoing.

violent. Like the other respondents, he looked back to the days of his youth, when he and his friends respected the police and their own misdemeanours were minor.

However, it is not the sources of their beliefs that is the obvious, missing feature in Darmanin's depiction of the butchers' good sense. The missing feature is also reflected in the *20 Minutes* depiction of Tourcoing's butchers. They are all assumed to be men, and this is something so obvious that it seems to escape specific comment. Of the various trades to be found in Tourcoing, Darmanin chooses the good sense of a typically masculine one. Linguistically his pork butcher is a man – Darmanin refers to *le boucher*, not *la bouchère*. He doesn't select the good sense of the female hairdresser – *la coiffeuse*. Nor does *20 Minutes* counterbalance its emblematic handful of male butchers with some of Tourcoing's female tradespeople.

In itself, this is not what gives Darmanin's downgrading of *victimation* its hidden meaning and its forcefulness. But it belongs to a specific context of masculinity which has specific personal meaning for Darmanin. Before Macron promoted Darmanin to the position of minister of the interior, the president said that he spoke to Darmanin 'man to man' (*d'homme à l'homme*, or literally 'from man to man') about a legal matter that involved Tourcoing's former mayor.[41]

Darmanin was being accused of raping a woman in Tourcoing. In 2009, when he was involved in local politics, but before he had become the town's mayor, a woman had sought his help. According to her, Darmanin agreed to help on condition that she had sex with him. Neither disputes that sex took place, but Darmanin, unlike the woman, claimed it was consensual. After a series of trials, Darmanin was eventually acquitted. Rape, of course, can be legally difficult to prove, especially if the case hinges upon one person's word against another's. The rates of conviction tend to be low compared with estimations of the frequency of the crime.

However, there was also the enduring evidence of text messages. These show that Darmanin continued to contact the woman, asking to see her again and take her for a drink. The woman's replies indicate that she did not welcome his messages and that she wanted nothing more to do with

---

[41] The man-to-man discussion was widely reported by the French press. For examples, see: *L'Humanité* (2020), 'Macron refuse tout nouveau chemin', 15 July; Frantz Durupt (2020), 'Les quatre épines dans le pied du Président', *Libération*, 15 July; *Figaro* (2020), 'Darmanin: 167 parlementaires de la majorité défendent la présomption d'innocence du ministre de l'Intérieur', 15 July.

him: 'Don't contact me again!!!!'.[42] At the minimum Darmanin's messages reveal an exercise of power, which, to change Macron's revealing phrase, flows from man to woman. Also, there was another vulnerable woman from Tourcoing, who complained that Darmanin had forced her to have sex with him against her wishes.[43] The second complainant did not specifically use the word 'rape', as if not all the acts of powerful men who pressure women for sex were tantamount to rape.

The *victimation* surveys explicitly put the position of the victim at the centre of their inquiries into crime. Darmanin gave a different account of the events than the two Tourcoing women did. Had the women been answering a *victimation* survey, their accounts methodologically would have not been challenged. If they said they had been sexually abused, forced or raped, that is how their responses would have been recorded. It is a tenet of these surveys that this method produces a more accurate survey of sexual crimes than do police records. It is not a perfect method; the statisticians do not claim that it is. When measuring complex social phenomena there are seldom perfect measures, but statisticians make advances by improving their measures and by understanding their limitations.

One problem for Darmanin was the involvement of his own ministry in the *victimation* surveys for sexual crime. The INSEE blog, written by his own head of statistics, stated clearly that the ministry of the interior was committed to providing the financial and human resources to ensure that the annual *victimation* surveys would continue.[44] Accordingly, Darmanin was finding himself in a position that ought to have been awkward for him. As we have seen, he possibly knows some of the methodological issues associated with the surveys and the information that they provide. He has little to gain, either personally or politically, from pursuing the *victimation* route too strongly. He cannot proclaim as a matter of principle that victims' claims must be at the centre of any investigation of sexual crimes.

---

[42] *Mediapart* gained access to some of the text messages and estimated that Darmanin sent the woman about forty messages. Antton Rouget et Marine Turchi (2021), 'Enquête pour viol: Gérald Darmanin face à ses contradictions', *Mediapart*, 26 January, www.mediapart.fr/journal/france/260121/enquete-pour-viol-gerald-darmanin-face-ses-contradictions. See also: Morgane Giuliani (2021), 'Gérald Darmanin accusé de viol: des SMS insistants du ministre à sa victime présumée révélés', *Marie Claire*, www.marieclaire.fr/gerald-darmanin-accuse-de-viol-des-sms-insistants-du-ministre-a-sa-victime-presumee-reveles,1369607.asp.

[43] For example, see: *Figaro* (2018), 'Affaire Darmanin: la seconde plaignante s'est "sentie obligée" d'avoir un rapport sexuel', 25 February, www.lefigaro.fr/flash-actu/2018/02/25/97001-20180225FILWWW00142-affaire-darmanin-la-seconde-plaignante-s-est-sentie-obligee-d-avoir-un-rapport-sexuel.php.

[44] Gonzalez-Demichel (2020), INSEE blog.

On the other hand, Darmanin cannot dissociate himself from the *victimation* surveys. After all, he has promised his president that he has no legal problem, and as a matter of policy his ministry supports the surveys. So, Darmanin uses the numbers from the *victimation* surveys to imply that France is becoming savage, while ignoring the different interpretation of those numbers that the survey researchers give, including his own head of statistics. In the ideological story that Darmanin tells, the *ensauvagement* is happening because of the savage actions of others: he is not part of his own story about French savagery. Although he says that he likes the *victimation* surveys, he immediately switches to saying that he prefers his Tourcoing pork butchers.

The French annual surveys on crime and delinquency suggest that what is recognised to be sexual assault or even rape might be in the process of historical change, as more women object to the sort of men's behaviour that previously they believed that they had to accept without complaint. During periods of such change, there will be differences of opinion about what constitutes a sexual assault. This prompts a question about who might be thought to have the best sense for judging what is, or is not, a sexual assault. The question could be phrased as if it were part of a survey about French public attitudes, to be administered during Darmanin's tenure as minister of the interior:

On the issue of what is, or is not, a sexual assault, whose good sense would you most trust?

(a)   Tourcoing's pork butchers
(b)   the president of France
(c)   the minister of the interior
(d)   none of the above.

CHAPTER 9

Boris Johnson
Untruthful Words and Numbers

Time for another biographical chapter – a chapter focusing upon a senior political figure. In the previous chapter we looked at Gérald Darmanin and his relations with the French Statistical Authority. Much earlier we had a chapter about Donald Trump and his record of manipulating numbers. Now we examine Boris Johnson, a man who was prime minister of Britain for three years, before his party got fed up with his weakness for untruth. While he was still prime minister, one former cabinet colleague said on the radio that Johnson was 'probably the best liar we've had as prime minister' because 'he knows a hundred ways to lie'.[1] Among those hundred, more than a few involved numbers.

There are similarities and differences between our three biographical personalities. All are populists, breaking with the conventions of politics and seeking to relate directly to the people. Darmanin is a populist who actually came from the people, while Johnson and Trump have privileged backgrounds. Unlike Trump, Johnson scatters posh words and literary references as he voices his populism in the accent of an upper-class Briton. Shortly after Johnson became prime minister, the American president offered his congratulations and said that 'they call him "Britain Trump"'.[2] Trump is unlikely to have grasped that those in Britain who claimed that Johnson was following in the president's footsteps were probably criticising, not praising, the incoming prime minister.

---

[1] Rory Stewart on *Good Morning Britain*, 27 Jan 2021, www.youtube.com/watch?v=E3-6nXSKmN4. Stewart had made similar accusation when reviewing a book that was favourable to Johnson: Rory Stewart (2020), 'Review: Tom Bower: "Boris Johnson, the gambler"', *Times Literary Supplement*, 6 December. See also: Sarah Lyall (2022), 'Johnson's lies worked for years, until they didn't', *New York Times*, 8 July, www.nytimes.com/2022/07/08/world/europe/boris-johnson-lies-britain-parliament.html.

[2] For Trump's comments on 'Britain Trump', see the *BBC News* report (2019), 23 July, www.bbc.co.uk/news/av/world-us-canada-49090804.

Johnson's working career has been framed by untruth. He was a journalist before becoming a politician. Initially, he worked for *The Times*, before he was dismissed for inventing quotations to embellish a story.[3] Having turned to politics, he represented the Conservatives in Parliament and rose to be a member of the shadow cabinet. In 2004 this became the second job that he lost for reasons of dishonesty. His party leader had asked him privately whether, as being reported in the press, he was having an affair with a journalist. In characteristic style, Johnson replied that the rumours were 'complete balderdash' and 'an inverted pyramid of piffle'.[4] The rumours turned out not to be piffle pyramids, and Johnson had to leave the shadow cabinet.

Despite having been dismissed twice for lying, Johnson was elected mayor of London in 2008 and re-elected in 2012.[5] His past record did not prevent him from rising to foreign secretary and then in 2019 to becoming prime minister. He won a general election in the same year, and looked set to remain in power for a good number of years. However, dishonesty once again led to his downfall. Members of his own party, not to mention the public at large, objected when he kept emphatically denying that he had broken the Covid laws that forbade social gatherings, despite accumulating police and photographic evidence to the contrary.[6]

Such is the power of Johnson as a celebrity that there have already been more biographies of him than might have been expected of someone who was only prime minister for three years.[7] Although we have described the present chapter as being biographical, that is not strictly accurate, especially when compared with the full-scale biographies. We are not offering a complete account of Johnson's life, any more than we provided full

---

[3] For accounts of the episode see: Peter Oborne (2021), *The Assault on Truth*, London: Simon and Schuster, pp. 53f.

[4] Anthony Seldon and Raymund Newell (2023), *Johnson at 10*, London: Atlantic Books, pp. 29f; Oborne (2021), pp. 53f.

[5] Oborne (2021) writes that 'Johnson's earlier misdemeanours' did not stop him becoming mayor of London or prime minister, p. 137.

[6] For detailed, critical accounts of Johnson's premiership, see: Andrew Blick and Peter Hennessy (2022), *The Bonfire of the Decencies*, London: Haus Publishing; Seldon and Newell (2023). Both books, especially Blick and Hennessy, detail how Johnson's regime systematically broke constitutional rules of the United Kingdom, and thereby threatened the constitution itself.

[7] Among the personal and political biographies of Johnson, see: Tom Bowyer (2020), *Boris Johnson: the gambler*, London: Penguin; Andrew Gimson (2023), *Boris Johnson: the Rise and Fall of a Troublemaker at Number 10*, London: Simon & Schuster; Nigel Cawthorne (2018), *Blond Ambition*, Northampton: Endeavour Press.

accounts of Darmanin and Trump. Our biographical chapters have a restricted aim: to focus on statistical misdemeanours.[8]

With Johnson, even within the restricted area of statistics, we will have an extra focus: his long-standing squabbles with the UK Statistics Authority. Most obviously, this provides further evidence of the hundreds of ways that numbers can be abused and misused. We will see that Johnson does not confine himself to a single mode of manipulation. There is another point: over the years, Johnson has objected again and again when the UKSA has tried to point out the errors of his statistical ways. As time passed, the Authority seemed to grow more tactically aware, and, in its battles with Johnson, its chairs became more experienced at resisting the political entertainer when opposing his manipulation of numbers in the eyes of the public.

In many respects the UKSA and Johnson were engaged in a competition for the public's trust or what in the previous chapter we called the battle for 'ethos'.[9] There will be examples when Johnson attempted to dismiss and devalue the UK Statistics Authority. We will also see the UKSA's largely successful efforts to counter those efforts and to maintain its national reputation with the public who know little about the technicalities of statistics, but who feel they have good reason to distrust politicians. This includes a politician like Johnson who appears to have a switch marked 'amusing charm' that he turns on and turns off.

Boris Johnson: Crime on London's Public Transport

Our story starts in 2011 when Johnson's popularity as mayor of London was at its height. There were two episodes in which Johnson clashed with Sir Michael Scholar, who was the first chair of the UKSA. On one side of these clashes stood an instantly recognisable politician, with an engaging sense of humour and distinctively ruffled, blond hair. On the other side was the little-known chair of a recently established, obscure statistical agency. The big political celebrity was seeking to squash the backroom geek who had dared to criticise him.

---

[8] For a detailed account of Johnson's failure to tell the truth as prime minister, see particularly Oborne (2021). See also: Jamie Grierson (2021), 'Lies, damned lies: the full list of accusations against Boris Johnson', *Guardian*, 10 December, www.theguardian.com/politics/2021/dec/10/lies-accusations-boris-johnson-full-list-dishonesty-christmas-party. In compiling his list of Johnson's lies, Grierson includes an example which we discuss in the next chapter: the claim to have built forty 'new' hospitals, most of which were not new.
[9] See Chapter 8, fn. 2.

The first part of this statistical story concerned figures for crimes committed on London's system of public transport. Scholar took it upon himself to write spontaneously to Johnson in complaint. For a number of years, Transport for London had been publishing quarterly statistics and an annual report about the number of crimes committed on their bus, underground and overground rail services.[10] These statistics are based on incidents which have been recorded by the Metropolitan Police and the British Transport Police.

Like practically all social measures, the figures are by no means perfect, and the quarterly and annual reports readily admitted their methodological faults. The levels of crime tended to be underestimated because the data rested on police reports. Not all crimes are reported to the police and the police do not record all the crimes that are reported to them. As we saw in the previous chapter, the French estimations of crime based on police reports also tended to underestimate the number of crimes committed. The crime figures for London transport, however, contained one set of figures that routinely overestimated crimes committed on London's buses. This figure was based on electronically scanning police reports for the words 'bus, bus stop, bus station and other transport related words somewhere in the electronic case file'. The result was that crimes committed at or near bus stops were included in the figures for crimes committed *on* buses.[11]

Neither the actual statistics about crime on London's buses and trains, nor the methods for assessing those rates of crime, were the reason that Scholar wrote to the mayor. After all, the reports had correctly described methodological limitations. It was the way that Johnson released the statistical news to the public that disturbed Scholar, although the figures for London's crimes, as regional figures, fell outside the UKSA's official remit for national statistics. In February 2011 the mayor and his office had issued a press release, announcing that crime on London transport had fallen substantially. This prompted Scholar to take action, and that meant writing a public letter, which he did on 16 March.

---

[10] Transport for London annual reports – *Transport for London Crime and Anti-Social Behaviour Annual Bulletins*, are available on: https://tfl.gov.uk/corporate/publications-and-reports/crime-and-incident-bulletins. The annual reports are based on the financial year from 30 March to the following 1 April rather than the calendar year.

[11] Transport for London, *Transport for London Crime and Anti-Social Behaviour Quarterly Statistics Bulletin, Quarter 3 (1 October – 31 December) 2010/11*, https://content.tfl.gov.uk/crime-and-anti-social-behaviour-statistics-bulletin-q3.pdf. The report comments on the difficulty of relying on police reports of crime because the figures exclude 'crimes that have not been reported to the police or those that the police decide not to record', p. 3.

London Transport and London's mayor had no legal obligation to follow the UKSA's Code of Practice. Scholar began his letter by referring to Johnson's press release, which in Scholar's words had been issued as part of a 'media event to publicise the success of your policies, sometime ahead of their normal release date in Transport for London's regular quarterly statistical bulletin'. The 'normal release date' would have been after 30 March when the period of data collection for the quarter finished. Scholar was writing two weeks before this and before the figures for the whole quarter could possibly have been calculated.

Scholar stressed that this advance release of information clearly conflicted with the Code of Practice. Quoting from the Code, Scholar wrote:

> Statistical reports should be published "separately from any other statement or comment about the figures"; that "no statement or comment – based on prior knowledge – is issued to the Press or published ahead of the publication of the statistics"; and that "no indication of the substance of a statistical report is made public or given to the media prior" to publication.[12]

In his letter, Scholar recognised that Transport for London's statistics were not classed as official statistics and so need not conform to the Code. He suggested, however, that 'statistics of such importance' should be treated 'with the same care and propriety as is now required by law for the most significant official statistics'. He would be writing to the home secretary, Theresa May, to recommend that London's transport statistics should be reclassified as official statistics. Scholar wrote at the end of his letter to Johnson that he would be sending a copy of the letter to Full Fact, 'the organisation which drew my attention to your Press Release'. For its part, Full Fact welcomed Scholar's letter to Johnson.[13]

We can see how Scholar's letter reflects the difference between the UKSA's field of operation and that of the Authority for Public Statistics (ASP) in France. It is very much part of ASP's official duties to inspect how public statistics are produced and which ministry should be officially responsible for producing which types of statistics. Had the ASP decided that the statistics for crime on buses and trains in Paris should be the responsibility of statisticians working within the ministry of inland

---

[12] UK Statistics Authority (2011), 'Sir Michael Scholar; Statistics on crime across the London Network', 16 March, https://osr.statisticsauthority.gov.uk/correspondence/statistics-on-crime-across-the-london-transport-network/.

[13] Full Fact (2011), 'Mayor's transport crime briefing risks "damaging public trust" in statistics, watchdog warns', 16 March, https://fullfact.org/news/mayors-transport-crime-briefing-risks-damaging-public-trust-statistics-watchdog-warns/. In Chapter 6, we discussed the UKSA's close cooperation with Full Fact.

security, rather than the responsibility of the mayor of Paris, it would have issued an official Avis to that effect. Then, the government would be expected to follow this advice. In Britain on this sort of matter, the UKSA carries far less authority. It is expected to concentrate on statistical practices rather than the organisational arrangements for producing statistics.

Scholar wrote to the home secretary on the same day that he wrote to Johnson. He suggested that there might be advantages in treating figures for crime in London as national, rather than regional, statistics and, if they were national, they would be subject to meeting the standards of the Code of Practice.[14] May replied, expressing a distinct lack of enthusiasm for Scholar's proposal, and saying that it was 'an issue for the mayor of London to consider'.[15] Scholar appeared to let the matter drop; in point of fact, he could do little else.

When May wrote her reply, she would have already consulted Johnson to find out his reaction to Scholar's proposal. Johnson was not someone who liked powers being taken from him or, indeed, anyone telling him what he could or could not do.[16] He waited until 8 April before replying to Scholar – a delay sufficiently long to demonstrate that he was not jumping to oblige Scholar. His reply was, in essence, to state that your authority does not cover me, nor should it: 'I see no good reason to change current arrangements'.[17]

Johnson's letter contains a couple of turns of phrase that show his attitude. He wrote that he was 'naturally very keen that good news about improvements in safety and crime reduction are brought to Londoners' attention'. Was it not just as important, and perhaps even more important, for Londoners to hear about bad news? Good and bad news might be equally important for ordinary citizens, but promoting the former was more important than promoting the latter for a mayor, who would soon be facing re-election. Johnson also wrote that he was satisfied that the good news was based 'on the principles of statistical relevance, integrity and

[14] For Scholar's letter to Teresa May, see: https://osr.statisticsauthority.gov.uk/correspondence/official-statistics-transport-for-london/.

[15] For May's reply, see: https://osr.statisticsauthority.gov.uk/correspondence/official-statistics-transport-for-london-3/.

[16] Seldon and Newell (2023) claim that deep-seated flaws in Johnson's character account for his continual belief that rules do not apply to him.

[17] Boris Johnson's letter to Sir Michael Scholar, sent 8 April 2011. UK Statistical Authority: https://osr.statisticsauthority.gov.uk/correspondence/official-statistics-transport-for-london-4/.

quality'. He asserted, rather than justified, this statement, thereby demonstrating no evidence of his ability to assess statistical quality.

Then there is Johnson's irritated comment: 'it would have been helpful had you approached me first about your concerns about statistical standards for London before publicly releasing your letter'. Note the ambiguity in the word 'helpful'. Johnson does not say how it would have been helpful, nor who would have been helped. Of course, it would have been politically helpful for Johnson if their correspondence had taken place privately. Or not at all.

In his letter, Scholar mentioned the bad statistical practice of not separating persuasion from information. When a politician does both together, they are likely to be partial in their choice of statistics to mention and those to overlook. We can see this in Johnson's use of Transport for London crime statistics. As part of his campaign for re-election, Johnson published a booklet *Fighting Crime in London.*[18] It had much of the style and presentation of an official document, with footnotes supposedly supporting statistically based statements. The inside cover bore the Conservative Party's symbol without identifying the Party as the document's publisher. The cover included a roundel with the slogan 'Better off with Boris'.

Johnson's booklet used statistics to substantiate his claim that the lives of Londoners had greatly improved during his mayoralty. An instance was crime on London's buses and trains. Johnson wrote that if you compared his mayoralty with that of his Labour predecessor, then 'robbery on public transport is down 46.5 per cent; crime on buses has fallen by 30 per cent and crime on the Tube has fallen by 20 per cent'. There is a footnote at the bottom of the page that seems to provide the source for these figures. The relevant footnote does not cite Transport for London's quarterly reports on transport crime, or its annual bulletins. It cites the mayor's own press release: 'GLA Press Release, Mayor highlights drop in crime across public transport network, 21 February 2011'.[19]

A campaigning document or a politician's press release are not neutral sources of information. This is why the Code of Practice insists on separating the publication of new statistics, such as the 46.5 per cent drop in robbery on London's transport, from political documents. Johnson in *Fighting Crime in London* has political reasons for wanting to take the

---

[18] Boris Johnson (2012), *Fighting Crime in London*, Conservative Party, www.london.gov.uk/sites/default/files/Boris-Johnson-2012-Crime-Manifesto.pdf.
[19] Ibid., p. 11.

credit for this unpublished drop. Predictably, he does not mention other figures that indicate that the fall in transport crime had already started in his predecessor's reign. Transport for London's bulletin about transport crime during the last three months of 2007, when Ken Livingstone was still mayor, mentioned that there had been a large drop in crime on buses from the previous year. The bulletin offered an explanation: 'these reductions in crime have been driven by a range of initiatives undertaken by TfL [Transport for London] in partnership with the police forces in London'.[20]

We do not want to go into these statistical details or to decide whether TfL or Johnson had the better explanation for the fall in crime on London's transport system. During the 2012 election campaign for mayor, both Johnson and his left-wing opponent, Livingstone, made different claims about the rates of crime in London. Full Fact has examined the numbers cited by both candidates. It found that both candidates measured percentage rises and falls in crime differently and they took different time periods for their measurements. Each selected the time periods and ways of slicing up the numbers to suit their own purposes. Here is an object lesson. Neither left nor right has a monopoly on using statistics selectively; and when they disagree there isn't necessarily one who is absolutely right (and telling the truth) and the other who is absolutely wrong (and telling lies).[21]

This does not make a statistical authority redundant, for it is their task to point out the limitations of statistical claims and to say when partiality crosses over into bad statistical practice. We should note that Johnson, in his reply to Scholar, did not appear to be bothered in the least that he might have infringed some basic principles of the Code of Practice. In his 'Better off with Boris' booklet he infringed them again. The act of validating claims by referring to one's own press release is the act of a politician who wishes to control the public's knowledge of statistics. He does not direct his readers to the statistical reports where they might find and assess the numbers for themselves. By self-citing his own press release, Johnson was insulating his readers from the data. This is exactly the sort of action that the statistical Code of Practice was designed to prevent.

Underlying this first clash between Scholar and Johnson was something more fundamental than an argument about a press release or how to

---

[20] Transport for London, *Crime and Anti-Social Behaviour Quarterly Statistics Bulletin*, Quarter 3 (1 October–31 December 2007/8), https://tfl.gov.uk/corporate/publications-and-reports/crime-and-incident-bulletins, see p. 4.

[21] *Full Fact* (2012) 'What is Boris Johnson's record on crime?', 18 April, https://fullfact.org/news/london-2012-what-boris-johnsons-record-crime/.

measure what happens on London's buses. In his 2011 Johnian lecture at Cambridge University, Michael Scholar outlined his vision for rational politics. Citizens, he argued, should be encouraged to assess statistical evidence for themselves, free from political manipulation.[22] The clash with Johnson was a confrontation between Scholar's vision of statistics and the actions of a politician who self-interestedly seeks to control the statistical information that the public receives.

Boris Johnson and the UKSA: Rates of Reoffending

The second clash between Boris Johnson and the UKSA differs from the first, both in terms of Johnson's statistical offence and Scholar's strategy to expose that offence. The topic again was crime. This time they clashed over claims that Johnson was making about the rates of reoffending shown by young offenders in the Heron unit which was situated within Greater London.

In May 2011, Johnson wrote an article for his old newspaper, the right-wing *Daily Telegraph*. This was the newspaper that had employed Johnson after he had been sacked by *The Times*. In his article Johnson wrote about the importance of doing more than just locking up young offenders in secure institutions: they should be re-educated to stop them from reoffending once they were released.[23] Johnson was claiming that the Heron unit, for which his deputy Kit Malthouse had responsibility, had spectacularly low rates of reoffending, far below the national average. It was, Johnson said, setting an example that the whole prison system would do well to follow.[24]

Scholar had his doubts about the statistical basis for Johnson's claims, but he did not write another public letter to Johnson. Nor did he write a few months later when Johnson wrote a second article boasting about Heron's successes. This article appeared in the popular right-wing

---

[22] See Chapter 6, pp. 136–7: UK Statistics Authority (2011), 'Johnian Lecture by Sir Michael Scholar at St John's College, Cambridge', 10 September, https://uksa.statisticsauthority.gov.uk/news/johnian-lecture-by-sir-michael-scholar-at-st-johns-college-cambridge/.

[23] Boris Johnson (2011), 'Why I agree with Ken Clarke – we shouldn't just lock them up; Prison sentences are a vital deterrent, but we need to teach offenders that crime doesn't pay', *Telegraph*, 23 May.

[24] Kit Malthouse was a loyal supporter of Johnson, and followed him into the House of Common in 2015. Johnson made Malthouse minister of state for crime and policing and then promoted him to the cabinet in 2022. When Johnson was removed from the premiership, Malthouse lost his ministerial post.

newspaper the *Sun*.[25] In September Johnson wrote yet another article for the *Telegraph*, again praising Heron and exulting in its successes.[26] This now prompted Scholar to write a public letter disputing Johnson's statistics.

Scholar had learned a lesson from his first letter to Johnson. The mayor had seemed to have little interest in good statistical practice. So long as the statistics were politically advantageous to him, little else seemed to matter. If Scholar wrote to Johnson about the weakness of the statistical evidence for Heron's supposed successes, then the mayor would probably be just as dismissive as he had been previously. So, when Scholar wrote, his letter was not addressed to Johnson. He sent it to Keith Vaz, a Labour member of Parliament who chaired Parliament's Home Affairs Committee. A month earlier, Johnson and his deputy Malthouse had appeared before Vaz's Committee to give evidence about the summer's rioting in London. True to form, Johnson had used the occasion to promote the Heron unit: 'We cut reoffending rates in that wing from 80% to 19%' and that was, he declared, a model that 'should be replicated around the country'.[27]

Scholar began his letter to Vaz by explaining that he was writing to him because of the political and media interest shown in the comment by the mayor 'during recent oral evidence to your Committee'.[28] Scholar had found his way to bypass Johnson, although he sent him a copy of the letter. The real substance of Scholar's letter came in its attached notes. The first notes listed the occasions when Johnson had made statistical claims for the achievements of the Heron unit (although the earliest article in the *Telegraph* was omitted). These were followed by notes undermining Johnson's claims.

Scholar stressed that Heron's rate of reoffending had not been published nor had it been properly validated. The figure had been taken from 'internal, unpublished, management information', which contained the caveat that the data was based on 'anecdotal information and does not

[25] Boris Johnson (2011), 'No rehab, no release: soft is the perfect way to enjoy French cheese, but not how we should approach punishing criminals', *Sun*, 20 June. Johnson claimed that the Heron wing, which he opened at Feltham Young Offenders Institution, had halved national youth reoffending rates.
[26] Boris Johnson (2011), 'Britain should bang up the trouble-makers, but let's turn them round, too', *Telegraph*, 19 September, www.telegraph.co.uk/politics/0/britain-should-bang-trouble-makers-turn-round/.
[27] For a full account of the evidence given by Johnson and Malthouse, see the Parliamentary record: https://publications.parliament.uk/pa/cm201012/cmselect/cmhaff/uc1456-i/uc145601.htm.
[28] For Scholar's letter to Keith Vaz: UK Statistics Authority (2011), 'Statistics on juvenile offending', 21 October, https://osr.statisticsauthority.gov.uk/correspondence/statistics-on-juvenile-re-offending/.

represent a re-conviction rate and should not be used publicly'. The attached notes also pointed out that the national figures, with which Johnson was comparing the Heron figures, were based on rates of reoffending within a year of release. However, the Heron figures seemed to be based on reoffending within a much shorter time period and so would predictably have a lower percentage of reoffenders. The claimed rate of reoffending for the Heron unit 'is therefore likely to be an underestimate of reoffending, and is not comparable with the national figure' – a comparison that Johnson was making again and again.

The Effect of Scholar's Second Letter

Scholar had judged his strategy well. The second letter received extensive media coverage, largely focussing on the weakness of Johnson's claims. *BBC News* quoted the civil servant who had devised and run the Heron project, saying that the mayor's claims were 'complete nonsense'.[29] *BBC News* also quoted Vaz, who stated that he was 'very concerned by allegations that the mayor of London may have misled' his committee.

Of all the press coverage of Scholar's letter, the *Telegraph's* was the most revealing. Here was a newspaper that might have been expected to back Johnson. Throughout his political career Johnson has maintained close personal and professional ties with the *Telegraph*.[30] It was in the *Telegraph* that Johnson had written about the Heron unit shortly before Scholar's letter, not to mention his earlier piece for the paper. So, the *Telegraph* might have taken Scholar's criticism of Johnson as a criticism of itself for publishing his poor statistical claims. Moreover, Johnson was an old favourite of *Telegraph* readers.[31] For many years, he had a weekly column in the paper, writing amusing little stories about EU regulations – that the EU was about to ban bendy bananas or standardise the size of coffins. Many of Johnson's readers appear to have taken these products of his literary imagination as if they were literal truths.[32]

[29] BBC News (2011), 'Boris Johnson's use of reoffending data criticised', 21 October, www.bbc.co .uk/news/uk-england-london-15410654.
[30] See Sebastian Payne (2022), *The Fall of Boris Johnson*, London: Macmillan, especially the introductory chapter 'Drinks at the Garrick Club'.
[31] When Johnson became prime minister, the *Telegraph* established a Boris Johnson Archive, on the grounds that 'Boris Johnson has taken on many topics in his regular *Telegraph* column which readers have loved over the years'. *Telegraph* (2019), 'The Boris Johnson archive', www.telegraph.co .uk/boris-johnson-archive/.
[32] Blick and Hennessy (2022) suggest that Johnson used his weekly column in the *Telegraph* 'to ascend to new levels of historical hyperbole', p. 26. See also Oborne (2021) for Johnson's 'gonzo journalism'.

So, the *Telegraph* might well have chosen to defend one of its own against an official of the state. But it didn't. It published an account of Scholar's letter on 22 October written by its correspondent Andy Bloxham.[33] Media analysts often emphasise the importance of headlines. Not only is the headline designed to attract the interest of readers, but it tells readers what sort of story they can expect to find in the main body of the article.[34] The *Telegraph's* headline was: 'Boris Johnson rebuked over use of dodgy statistics'. The subheading identified who was doing the rebuking and what the statistics were: 'Boris Johnson, the Mayor of London, has been rebuked by the head of Britain's statistics watchdog for repeatedly using questionable figures to overstate his claims of cutting reoffending rates'.

The statistics are described as 'dodgy' and 'questionable', with no qualification that might express doubt, such as '*apparently* dodgy' or '*seemingly* questionable'.[35] Similarly, 'rebuked' is unqualified, without anything to suggest that Johnson might have been *wrongly*, *unfairly* or *controversially* rebuked. Neither the headline nor the subheading mention that it was the *Telegraph* that had published the dodgy statistics. While Johnson is depicted as 'repeatedly' using dodgy figures, as if he were a serial offender, his rebuker is accorded full rank and status: 'Sir Michael Scholar' – 'the head of Britain's statistics watchdog'. There is nothing here that questions his expertise, integrity and, above all, his national status.

Scholar's strategy had paid off. In this very public battle for ethos, round two went to Scholar and to the institution that he represented.

Johnson Attacking Scholar's Ethos

If there was one thing that Boris Johnson disliked more than being criticised, it was not being the centre of attention. By addressing his letter to Labour's Keith Vaz, Scholar had slighted him. The mayor did not take long to hit back with an ill-tempered attack on Scholar's standing. Johnson

---

[33] Andy Bloxham (2011), 'Boris Johnson, the Mayor of London, has been rebuked by the head of Britain's statistics watchdog for repeatedly using questionable figures to overstate his claims of cutting reoffending rates', *Telegraph*, 21 October, www.telegraph.co.uk/news/politics/8842121/Boris-Johnson-rebuked-over-use-of-dodgy-statistics.html.

[34] See for example: John E. Richardson (2007), *Analysing Newspapers*, London: Red Globe Press; Roger Fowler (1991), *Language in the News*, London: Routledge; Daniel Dor (2003), 'On newspaper headlines as relevance optimisers', *Journal of Pragmatics*, 35, 695–721.

[35] On the linguistics of hedging and qualifying, see: Ken Hyland (1998), *Hedging in Scientific Research Articles*, Amsterdam: John Benjamins; Ken Hyland (2009), *Academic Discourse*, London: Continuum.

did not write a public letter: he could hardly reply to a letter that was pointedly not addressed to him. It came in the London Assembly on 16 November, as the mayor faced his weekly question time from the elected members.[36]

A senior member of the Labour group was quizzing Johnson about the Heron unit and the statistics for reoffending that Johnson had given the Parliamentary committee. It is clear from the transcript that Johnson was getting increasingly tetchy. Johnson never enjoyed being forced to admit that he might have made a mistake. Under pressure, his typical reaction has been to deflect criticism by attacking the critic. He was true to character in the London Assembly.

The Labour member said that she would ask her final question. She brought up the Statistics Authority and its Code of Practice. She asked the mayor whether would he voluntarily sign up to the Code. Repeatedly Johnson interrupted as she was asking her question. One of his interruptions was to say: 'There is this guy called Scholar who writes me letters who appears to be some sort of Labour stooge'. Note: Johnson does not identify Scholar by his position or title – he is 'this guy'. Note also 'this guy' is someone 'who writes me letters'. Scholar had only written Johnson one public letter. He is someone who isn't writing Johnson letters.

Johnson is rhetorically stripping Scholar of his ethos, particularly his independence of judgement and statistical expertise. After calling Scholar a Labour stooge, Johnson then refers to the Authority but without uttering its name and being deliberately disrespectful: 'I am not impressed by the conduct of that particular body and its chief, if I may say so, disrespectfully'. Then he turns on his questioner: 'Nor am I impressed, frankly, by your whole line of questioning which I think is petty, political and mindboggleingly [sic] trivial by comparison with what we are trying to do'.[37]

In short, Johnson was irritated by the questioning: it was petty, when compared with the marvellous success of his policy. Not only had Johnson attacked the reputation of the UKSA's chair, but he was refusing to discuss the statistical points that he had raised. The statistics were trivial. No wonder Johnson did not want to be constrained by a code of good statistical practice. He was demonstrating that he backed his own judgement over that of experts. It could have been Darmanin talking, except

---

[36] For the transcript of the Mayor of London's Question Time, 16 November 2011: www.london.gov .uk/about-us/londonassembly/meetings/documents/b5701/Minutes%20-%20Appendix%202% 20-%20Transcript%20of%20Question%20and%20Answer%20Session%20with%20the% 20Mayor%20Wednesday%2016-Nov-20.pdf?T=9.

[37] Mayor of London's Question Time, 16 November 2011, pp. 4–5.

that Johnson was backing himself rather than the good sense of a butcher, baker or candlemaker.

Johnson's outburst did not produce a victory. The great and the good, even in his own Conservative Party, did not come to his rescue. By and large the national press ignored the outburst. Of Britain's national news-papers, only the *Guardian* carried the story and, as to be expected, it was critical of the mayor.[38]

Nevertheless, a month later the 'Labour stooge' accusation surfaced in the House of Commons. Scholar's term of office was coming to a close, and the House needed to officially endorse Andrew Dilnot as his succes-sor.[39] It was an occasion in which political divisions seemed to have been put aside. Speakers from the main parties paid tribute to the achievements of the UKSA's first chair and praised the qualities of his proposed successor.

But politics is seldom completely absent from the business of the House of Commons. After a leading Conservative, Jesse Norman, had praised the UKSA and its incoming chair, a Labour member asked him whether he supported the mayor of London calling Scholar 'a Labour stooge'. Norman replied: 'I certainly do not share that view and I am not sure that the mayor would share that view if he had further time to reflect on it'.[40] Of course, Johnson had already sufficient time to reflect on what he had said a month ago. True to character, he had not retracted his statement.

If Jesse Norman's comment is the coda to Johnson's outburst, then the coda has its own coda. This came after Johnson had scaled the heights of national politics. Norman had become one of his big supporters and, in return, Johnson rewarded him with a ministerial post and a seat in the cabinet. When Johnson's ethos started crumbling, principally owing to his belief that the laws of the land did not apply to him and his continual untruthfulness, Norman was one of his first ministers to resign. He wrote an excoriating public letter to Johnson, accusing him of presiding over

---

[38] Hélène Mulholland (2011), 'Boris Johnson says UK Statistics Authority chair is "Labour stooge"', *Guardian*, 16 November, www.theguardian.com/politics/2011/nov/16/boris-johnson-statistics-authority-labour-stooge. The previous week, the *Guardian* had published an article criticising Johnson on the reoffending rates at Heron: Dave Hill (2011), 'Boris Johnson was "aware" of problems with youth re-offending unit claims', *Guardian*, 9 November, www.theguardian.com/politics/davehillblog/2011/nov/09/boris-johnosn-heron-unit-overclaiming.

[39] See Hansard: https://publications.parliament.uk/pa/cm201011/cmhansrd/cm111213/debtext/111213-0002.htm.

[40] See Hansard: https://publications.parliament.uk/pa/cm201011/cmhansrd/cm111213/debtext/111213-0001.htm.

'a culture of casual law-breaking at 10 Downing Street'.[41] Some observers have claimed that Norman's resignation was the decisive catalyst that led to further resignations and then to fellow Conservative members of Parliament removing Johnson from office.[42]

As for the UKSA, the Authority and its successive chairs would keep their public reputation as the nation's independent inspectors of official statistics. Johnson's ethos, by contrast, would be shattered beyond repair.

Johnson: Attacking Once Again

There was to be another episode in which Boris Johnson would face criticism from the UKSA and then attempt to undermine the reputation of its chair. This occurred in the aftermath of Britain's 2016 referendum to leave the European Union. Johnson played a major role in the Brexit campaign, touring the country in the campaign bus, which was emblazoned with the slogan: 'We send the EU £350 million a week – let's fund our NHS [National Health Service] instead'.

Andrew Dilnot, as chair of the UKSA, wrote a public letter criticising the slogan. He had followed the usual procedure of reacting only after the UKSA had been approached. In March 2016, when the Brexit campaign was in full sway, a Liberal Democrat MP wrote to him publicly requesting the UKSA to judge whether the slogan was statistically justified. Dilnot replied, saying that 'the £350 million figure' appeared to be a 'gross figure' which did not take into account 'the rebate or other flows from the EU to the UK public sector'.[43] The slogan was misleading, he concluded, because it implied that Britain actually sent the EU £350 million each week. If Britain left the EU, it would not have this extra £350 million to divert each week into the National Health Service.

The figure '£350 million' is at the centre of our episode. Statistics can be rhetorical in two senses. First, there is the obvious sense that politicians and others use numbers to make rhetorical claims, thereby mixing numbers and words. Second, some numbers have their own rhetorical

---

[41] Jesse Norman (2022), 'My letter of no confidence in Boris Johnson', 6 June, www.jessenorman .com/2022/06/letter-to-the-prime-minister.html.

[42] Blick and Hennessy (2022), pp. 20f. See also: Payne (2022), pp. 133f.

[43] Andrew Dilnot (2016), 'Letter to Norman Lamb, MP', 21 April, https://osr.statisticsauthority.gov .uk/wp-content/uploads/2016/04/Letter-from-Sir-Andrew-Dilnot-to-Norman-Lamb-MP-210416 .pdf. Dilnot appended to his letter a statistical note about the different ways of assessing the UK's contribution to the EU. The speed of Dilnot's reply suggests that the note had already been prepared in case the UKSA was approached to adjudicate on the issue.

meaning, such as some big rounded numbers which can have an almost semi-magical meaning.[44] In the context of Brexit, '£350 million' had become a symbolic number, a numerical metonym that represents to some the benefits of leaving the European Union, but that also conveys to others the dodgy statistical claims of the Brexit campaign. It is an example of a number with a life of its own.[45] Georgina Sturge, the House of Commons Library statistician, says in her book *Bad Data* that some numbers continue to live on as 'zombie numbers' after they have statistically died. She writes that the '£350 million' claim was 'demonstrably false', having been statistically refuted as Britain's weekly saving from leaving the EU, but still it continued to haunt political discourse like a zombie.[46]

The success of the Brexit campaign brought in a new prime minister, Theresa May, with the Conservatives remaining in power. May appointed Johnson as her foreign secretary. From the outset there were tensions between the two, especially as May struggled to get a bill through Parliament to legalise the exit from the EU. To many political observers, it looked as if Johnson was plotting to replace May with himself. He was certainly promoting himself as a politician with a grand view of Britain's future.

In September 2017 Johnson expressed his big vision in a 4,000-word article for the *Telegraph*.[47] The media coverage of this article would mostly focus on the short paragraph with the familiar zombie of '£350 million'. Johnson wrote that when Britain had settled its accounts 'we will take back control of roughly £350 million per week' and it would be good 'if a lot of that money went on the NHS'. The political editor of the *Telegraph* wrote a piece to accompany Johnson's article. His commentary was headlined: 'Exclusive: Boris Johnson – Yes, we WILL take back £350m from EU for NHS.'[48] According to the political editor, Johnson 'restates the key demand of the Leave campaign – that £350m a week currently sent to Brussels should be redirected to fund the NHS'.

---

[44] For details: Michael Billig (2021), 'Uses of precise numbers and semi-magical round numbers in political discourse about Covid-19: examples from the government of the United Kingdom', *Discourse and Society*, 32, 542–58.

[45] For an excellent discussion of the idea that certain numbers have lives of their own, see: Brendan T. Lawson (2023), *The life of a Number*, Bristol: Bristol University Press.

[46] Georgina Sturge (2022), *Bad Data*, London: Bridge Street Press, pp. 97f.

[47] Boris Johnson (2017), 'My vision for a bold, thriving Britain enabled by Brexit', *Telegraph*, 15 September, www.telegraph.co.uk/politics/0/boris-johnson-vision-for-brexit-bold-thriving-britain/.

[48] Gordon Rayner (2017), 'Exclusive: Boris Johnson – Yes, we WILL take back £350m from EU for NHS', *Telegraph*, 15 September, www.telegraph.co.uk/news/2017/09/15/exclusive-boris-johnson-yes-will-take-back-350m-eu-nhs/.

Johnson's article caught the attention of David Norgrove who had recently been appointed the UKSA's chair. He took the initiative of writing publicly to Johnson, expressing his disappointment that the foreign secretary was ignoring the letter that his predecessor Andrew Dilnot had written about £350 million being a gross figure and that the actual sum that Britain sent to the EU was much lower. Norgrove stated that Johnson's comments were 'a clear misuse of official statistics'.

Johnson replied fiercely and lengthily, calling Norgrove's letter 'a wilful distortion of the text of my article' and 'a complete misrepresentation of what I said'.[49] What was this 'complete misrepresentation'? According to Johnson: 'You say that I claim that there would be £350 million that "might be available for extra public spending" when we leave the EU'. But, he claimed: 'I in fact said: "Once we have settled our accounts we will take back control of roughly £350m per week"; and much of that money could be spent on the NHS'. It's hard to see a substantial difference between what he actually wrote and what Norgrove said he wrote. Certainly, the political editor of the *Telegraph* was attributing to Johnson the views that Johnson was telling Norgrove he wasn't saying.

In his *Telegraph* article Johnson had used the rhetorically charged number '£350 million'. He could have used a different number. In an interview that Johnson gave to the *Guardian* not long afterwards, he claimed that there was an error in the slogan on the side of the Brexit bus. Johnson, who hates to admit an error, was teasing the paper. His error: 'We grossly underestimated the sum'.[50] Johnson said that after the Brexit transition period, Britain's weekly benefit would have risen to £438 million.

Johnson, in the *Telegraph* piece, had not written about taking control of '£438 million'. Although that number might be higher, and therefore more conducive to his overall argument, it lacked the rhetorical symbolism of '£350 million'. A politician who was more concerned with statistical accuracy than with statistical rhetoric might not have persisted with '£350 million' if he genuinely believed it to be a gross underestimation. However, the figure '£350 million' was not a purely economic projection: it was a symbolic figure with its own political meaning. Norgrove had

[49] *Evening Standard* (2017), 17 September, published Norgrove's and Johnson's letters in full: www .standard.co.uk/news/politics/boris-johnson-hits-back-at-claims-nhs-brexit-pledge-was-clear-misuse-of-figures-in-scathing-letter-a3636856.html.
[50] Anushka Asthana and Heather Stewart (2018), 'Leave campaign's £350m claim was too low, says Boris Johnson', *Guardian*, 15 January, www.theguardian.com/politics/2018/jan/15/leave-campaigns-350m-claim-was-too-low-says-boris-johnson.

suspected that supporters of Brexit had reasons for keeping the number alive in public debate, regardless of whether it was accurate or not.[51]

Norgrove had risked provoking Johnson's followers by writing directly to Johnson without being requested to do so. The *Daily Express*, which supported Johnson devotedly, published a story which contained more than a hint of threat. The headline was unambiguous: "'Complete misrepresentation!' Boris Johnson slams watchdog chief over £350m NHS row'. According to the paper, 'The UK's chief number cruncher Sir David Norgrove is under pressure to resign'. The paper identified Norgrove's offence: he had criticised the foreign secretary for pointing out 'that the UK pays around £350 million a week to the EU'.[52] Johnson in his reply to Norgrove seemed to be denying that he had written this.[53]

The *Express* quoted 'senior' Conservatives calling for Norgrove's resignation. One member of Parliament accused Norgrove of 'playing politics'. The phrase is generally used as criticism: the person said to be 'playing politics' is being criticised for treating politics as if it were a game of strategy and advantage.[54] Using the phrase to describe someone like the UKSA's chair is doubly derogatory: the person in question should not be acting politically, let alone 'playing' politics.

When a regulator chooses to criticise a politician publicly, then that politician, especially if thin skinned, may suspect that the regulator has an

---

[51] Norgrove said as much in his interview with *Civil Service World*, which we discussed in Chapter 6. He said that "the controversy about the number was helpful to their [the Brexiteers'] cause because it kept people discussing it, and most people don't see a big difference between £350m and – say – £100m because [either way] it's a lot": Jim Dunton (2017), 'Sir David Norgrove interview: new chair of UK Statistics Authority on elections, the misuse of numbers and working for Margaret Thatcher', *Civil Service World*, 17 June, www.civilserviceworld.com/in-depth/article/sir-david-norgrove-interview-new-chair-of-uk-statistics-authority-on-elections-the-misuse-of-numbers-and-working-for-margaret-thatcher.

[52] David Maddox (2017), "'Complete misrepresentation!' Boris Johnson slams watchdog chief over £350m NHS row', *Daily Express*, 18 September, www.express.co.uk/news/politics/855710/Brexit-news-NHS-Boris-Johnson-Foreign-Secretary-Sir-David-Norgrove.

[53] Andrew Blick and Peter Hennessy, in their 2019 report on the threats posed to the British constitution by recent governments, discuss the exchange of letters between Norgrove and Johnson under the heading of 'A tendency towards misinformation'. It is clear that they attribute the misinformation in the episode to Johnson and the information to Norgrove. Andrew Blick and Peter Hennessy (2019), *Good Chaps No More? Safeguarding the Constitution in Stressful Times*, Report of The Constitution Society, pp. 15f, https://consoc.org.uk/wp-content/uploads/2019/11/FINAL-Blick-Hennessy-Good-Chaps-No-More.pdf.

[54] The OED defines 'to play politics' as 'to act on an issue for personal or political gain rather than from principle; to take part in politics for amusement or as a competitive activity': www.oed.com/view/Entry/145475#eid30110137. For an analysis of the way that the media often frames politics as if it were a game, see: Toril Aalberg, Jesper Strömbäck and Claes H. de Vreese (2011), 'The framing of politics as strategy and game: a review of concepts, operationalizations and key findings', *Journalism*, 13, 162–78.

ulterior motive: they are trying to do me down, they are anti-Brexit, they are a Labour stooge, and so on. But if a public figure, who may themselves be a politician, officially asks the British statistical regulator a statistical question, then the regulator can be seen to be fulfilling their statutory and professional duties by attempting to answer that query to the best of their abilities. To an extent, this protects chairs of the UKSA from accusations of bias and playing politics.

Johnson's supporters did not pursue their campaign to force the UKSA's chair to resign. Nor did other right-wing newspapers join the *Express* in their campaign. The *Telegraph* was a notable absentee. Henceforward, Norgrove would be more circumspect in his dealings with Johnson, especially after the latter had become prime minister. As Norgrove settled into his post, he was to act more strategically and to better effect.

To mark the third anniversary of Britain leaving the EU, the *Observer* newspaper commissioned Opinium to conduct a survey into British attitudes towards Brexit. Only 9 per cent of the population thought that Brexit had made a good impact on the NHS, as compared with 46 per cent who claimed it had made a bad impact.[55] The zombie number of '£350 million' might have continued on its haunting ways, but its ghostly wail was becoming fainter.

Why We're Writing and What You're Doing

Johnson's premiership kept the UKSA busy: there was no shortage of statistical claims for it to assess. We will discuss three such claims and each concerned an important issue: poverty, employment and crime. How the UKSA reacted was not necessarily straightforward. None involved its chair taking the initiative and writing directly to Johnson. There were other roundabout channels of communication. We will take the three examples in chronological order.

Poverty: Action behind the Scenes

On 29 June 2021, a public letter was sent from the UKSA to 10 Downing Street about the claims that the prime minister had been making for about a year. He had been claiming that his government had succeeded in

[55] Toby Helm (2023), 'Brexit has completely failed for UK, say clear majority of Britons – poll', *Observer*, 30 December, www.theguardian.com/politics/2023/dec/30/britons-brexit-bad-uk-poll-eu-finances-nhs.

reducing the number of children living in poverty. The letter was not sent from David Norgrove to Boris Johnson. It was from one backstage person to another: from Ed Humpherson, the UKSA's director general for regulation and senior statistician, to Laura Gilbert, the prime minister's director of data science. The letter followed unsuccessful behind-the-scenes attempts to resolve what the UKSA was seeing as a continuing problem.[56]

Humpherson wrote that 'a number of concerns have been raised to us' concerning the prime minister's use of statistics on child poverty during prime minister's questions in Parliament. This is the weekly set-piece drama in which the prime minister faces questioning from both friendly and hostile members. It is an occasion for loud cheering and booing as the prime minister seeks to delight his supporters by scoring points off opponents. Rhetorical display rather than forensic analysis is its order of the day.[57]

Whenever the prime minister had made questionable claims about the statistics for child poverty, then, as Humpherson wrote, 'we have brought this to the attention of the briefing team in No. 10'. He was now writing publicly to Gilbert, the senior data analyst in the briefing team, because the prime minister had recently said that there were 'fewer households now with children in poverty than 10 years ago'. Again concerns had been raised: who had raised these concerns Humpherson did not say.

The problem was that there were different ways of measuring poverty, and Humpherson was recommending that the briefing team should read the UKSA's review and blog on the subject.[58] It would be helpful, he wrote, that, when the prime minister cites figures for child poverty, he were clear about which 'measure is being referred to, particularly where other measures present a different trend'. The UKSA blog to which he referred had said that there were no right and wrong ways to measure poverty, but some measures consistently produce higher figures than others. Some of the measures are based on indicators for relative poverty,

[56] Office for Statistical Regulation (2021), 'Ed Humpherson to Laura Gilbert: Use of official statistics on child poverty in Prime Minister's Questions', 29 June, https://osr.statisticsauthority.gov.uk/correspondence/ed-humpherson-to-laura-gilbert-use-of-official-statistics-on-child-poverty-in-prime-ministers-questions/.

[57] For comparative linguistic analyses of question times in various European parliaments: Cornelia Illie (ed.) (2010), *European Parliaments under Scrutiny*, Amsterdam/Philadelphia: John Benjamins.

[58] The review which Humpherson cited in his letter to Gilbert was: UK Statistic Authority (2021), 'Review of income-based poverty statistics', 19 May, https://osr.statisticsauthority.gov.uk/publication/review-of-income-based-poverty-statistics/. The blog he recommended was: Elise Baseley (2020), 'The trouble with measuring poverty', UK Statistics Authority, 27 July, https://osr.statisticsauthority.gov.uk/blog/the-trouble-with-measuring-poverty/.

in which poverty is defined in terms of comparisons with levels of finance throughout the population; other measures are based on absolute poverty which defines and measures poverty in terms of poor people's absolute lack of spending power.

Generally, measures of relative poverty produce higher percentage rates of poverty than those of absolute poverty, but this is not always the case.[59] Even though there was not a single correct way of defining poverty and then measuring it, the UKSA blog emphasised that one thing was completely unacceptable: alternating between different measures, in order to select at any given moment the most politically advantageous set of figures.[60]

By writing publicly to Gilbert, Humpherson was moving from a behind-the-scenes strategy that had not worked. Previously, we discussed how statisticians working for ministers are said to 'wear two hats': they have their statistical hat and they have their supporting-the-minister hat.[61] Statisticians who are preparing the prime minister for the weekly bout of questioning will be likely to have the prime-ministerial hat firmly planted on their heads. The job of the briefing team is to supply their boss with numbers that will trip up opponents and raise cheers from supporters in the rhetorical jousting match.

For someone like Gilbert, a gentle behind-the-scenes word from Humpherson will be nothing compared with the dramatic immediacy of the occasion. Even if Gilbert passed on the statistical message to her boss, it would be unlikely to emerge at the top of his priorities when he stepped into the Parliamentary arena. By sending a friendly but public letter, Humpherson was raising the stakes a little bit higher. If his message were ignored, and the statistical errors persisted, Humpherson could always raise the stakes further by calling on the UKSA's chair to write directly to the prime minister.

Crime: UKSA's Usual Procedure

From his days as mayor of London, Johnson had a fractious relationship with the UKSA, particularly about crime statistics. Together with his deputy, Kit Malthouse, Johnson had sought to boast about the wonder properties of the Heron young offenders unit. The UKSA had firmly

---

[59] For a clear description of the statistical advantages and disadvantages of measuring poverty in absolute or relative terms, see Sturge (2022), pp. 77ff.

[60] Baseley (2020). The issue is basically the same as that discussed in Chapter 4 about Trump and the different measures for unemployment produced by the Bureau for Labor Statistics.

[61] See above, Chapter 6.

confronted the boasting with the details of statistical evidence. Neither Johnson nor Malthouse had enjoyed the experience or valued being corrected.

Malthouse, the devoted disciple, followed Johnson into Parliament and had been appointed minister of state for crime and policing. In May 2012, Malthouse wrote to David Norgrove, the chair of the UKSA, complaining about Keith Starmer, the leader of the Labour party, who had quoted police figures as evidence that crime was rising. Malthouse was claiming that Starmer should have quoted the Office for National Statistics (ONS) survey which was more accurate and which was not showing a rise in crime. Malthouse's style was revealing, as if he had a past injury: 'I request that you investigate the Leader of the Labour Party's claims and issue the necessary censure should you decide that his comments were misleading'.[62] The UKSA did look into the matter, and Norgrove did write to Starmer, telling him that he had not quoted the best statistics. Needless to say, the UKSA's chair did not censure him.[63] After all, his job requires that he does not appear to be in the business of censuring.

Norgrove would be writing another public letter about crime, this time commenting on the prime minister's misuse of crime statistics. A leading Liberal Democrat member of Parliament had written to the UKSA about the prime minister and home secretary claiming that crime had dropped by 14 per cent in the previous year. The MP claimed that the claim contradicted the figures produced by the Office for National Statistics. It would only be true, he continued, if you excluded the figures for fraud and computer crime, but these figures should not be excluded if you are talking about an *overall* drop in crime.[64]

We could call the prime minister's error the 'metonymic error' because it takes a part for the whole.[65] Metonymy can be an effective way to use language figuratively – for instance, 'hired hands' as a way of alluding to

---

[62] UK Statistics Authority (2021), 'Kit Malthouse to Sir David Norgrove – Crime statistics', 2 May, https://uksa.statisticsauthority.gov.uk/correspondence/kit-malthouse-to-sir-david-norgrove-crime-statistics/.

[63] UK Statistics Authority (2021), 'Letter from Sir David Norgrove to Sir Keir Starmer – Crime Statistics', 17 May, https://uksa.statisticsauthority.gov.uk/correspondence/letter-from-sir-david-norgrove-to-sir-keir-starmer-crime-statistics/.

[64] UK Statistics Authority (2022), 'Alistair Carmichael MP to Sir David Norgrove – Use of official crime statistics by Prime Minister, Home Secretary and Home Office', 3 February, https://uksa .statisticsauthority.gov.uk/correspondence/alistair-carmichael-mp-to-sir-david-norgrove-use-of-official-crime-statistics-by-prime-minister-home-secretary-and-home-office/.

[65] Michael Billig and Cristina Marinho (2020), 'Metonymy, myth and politicians doing things with words: examples from the Portuguese celebration of April 25', *Pratiques Psychologiques*, 26, 265–78. Linguists tend to treat metonymy as a sort of figurative language which has more forms than just

employed workers, but no one thinks that only the workers' hands are hired. Metonymy becomes an error when the part is literally held to indicate the whole. This is what happens when some crimes such as burglary and violence are taken to indicate all crimes, while other crimes such as white-collar crime and computer fraud are removed from the total number of crimes as if they are not 'proper' crimes.

Norgrove replied by agreeing that the crime rate dropped only if fraud and computer crime were excluded. He wrote that if fraud and computer crime were included, as they should be, then the figures showed that crime had risen, not fallen, by 14 per cent. In consequence, the prime minister and home secretary had been using statistics 'in a misleading way'. Norgrove said that he would be contacting their offices about this.[66]

The following day most of the British press reported Norgrove's letter, and this included the right-wing press. The *Telegraph's* coverage was headlined: 'Boris Johnson and Priti Patel "misled" public over 14 per cent fall in crime'. It began: 'UK statistics authority ruled figures were presented in "misleading" way, as total crime had actually risen by 14 per cent'.[67] The *Daily Mail* in its online edition was equally damning: its headline declared 'another disaster for Boris'. The 'statistics watchdog' had blasted the PM and home secretary for claiming that crime had fallen by 14 per cent when it 'in fact has RISEN [sic] by 14 per cent'.[68]

No longer were the *Telegraph* and the *Mail* writing about Norgrove's failings, even urging him to resign. His ethos and that of the UKSA had been restored. Once again, stories about the national watchdog protecting the public from misleading politicians and their misleading statistics were too good to resist.

---

taking the part as if it were the whole: Jeannette Littlemore (2015), *Metonymy*, Cambridge: Cambridge University Press.

[66] UK Statistics Authority (2022), 'Response from Sir David Norgrove to Alistair Carmichael MP – Use of official crime statistics by Prime Minister, Home Secretary and Home Office', 3 February https://uksa.statisticsauthority.gov.uk/correspondence/response-from-sir-david-norgrove-to-alistair-carmichael-mp-misuse-of-official-crime-statistics-by-prime-minister-home-secretary-and-home-office/.

[67] Charles Hymas (2022), 'Boris Johnson and Priti Patel "misled" public over 14 per cent fall in crime', *Telegraph*, 3 February, /www.telegraph.co.uk/politics/2022/02/03/boris-johnson-priti-patel-misled-public-14-per-cent-fall-crime/.

[68] Katie Feehan (2022), 'ANOTHER disaster for Boris: Stats watchdog blasts PM Johnson and Priti Patel for claiming crime has fallen by 14 per cent when it has in fact RISEN by 14 per cent', *MailOnline*, 3 February, www.dailymail.co.uk/news/article-10473803/Watchdog-blasts-Johnson-Patel-claiming-crime-fallen-14-fact-RISEN.html, emphases in the original.

Employment Figures: Fact-Finding and the UKSA

The letter that Norgrove wrote to correct Johnson's claims about crimes would not be the only one that he would write that month about the prime minister's errors. It was part of a new sequence of letters, which also involved another from Humpherson to Gilbert. However, the sequence starts with a letter from Full Fact, the independent fact-checking agency. This letter tells us much about the status of the UKSA and ultimately why this status is so vital for combatting statistical manipulation.

In January 2021, Will Moy, the chief executive of Full Fact, publicly contacted Humpherson: 'I write to make you aware of an incorrect claim about the number of people in employment which has been made multiple times by the Prime Minister (and repeated by others) and ask for your potential engagement around it'.[69] Moy's letter was detailed but his basic charge was simple. Johnson and other ministers were regularly claiming that there were now more people in employment than there had been at the start of the Covid pandemic. Full Fact had already pointed out this would only be true if you omitted the self-employed, many of whom had become unemployed during the past year.[70] Once again, the prime minister was speaking of the part as if it were the whole: the number of people on a payroll was standing for the total number of employed people.

Humpherson thanked Moy for his letter and told him that he was writing to Downing Street's director of data science.[71] In his letter to Laura Gilbert, Humpherson told her that he had been contacted by Full Fact. It seems that Humpherson had previously spoken to Gilbert about this same issue and that she had assured him that the briefing team took care to give the prime minister accurate numbers. Humpherson also said in his letter that things had seemed to be improving but recently errors had been returning.[72] The behind-the-scenes strategy had been effective, but only temporarily.

[69] UK Statistics Authority (2022), 'Will Moy to Ed Humpherson: Statements on the number of people in work', 1 February, https://osr.statisticsauthority.gov.uk/correspondence/will-moy-to-ed-humpherson-statements-on-the-number-of-people-in-work/.

[70] Full Fact (2021), 'Numbers "in work" not yet back to pre-pandemic levels', 25 November, https://fullfact.org/economy/employment-november-2021/.

[71] UK Statistics Authority (2022), 'Ed Humpherson to Will Moy: Statements on the number of people in work', 1 February, https://osr.statisticsauthority.gov.uk/correspondence/ed-humpherson-to-will-moy-statements-on-the-number-of-people-in-work/.

[72] UK Statistics Authority (2022), 'Ed Humpherson to Laura Gilbert: Statements on the number of people in work', 1 February, https://osr.statisticsauthority.gov.uk/correspondence/ed-humpherson-to-laura-gilbert-statements-on-the-number-of-people-in-work/.

Three weeks later Norgrove was writing a public letter to Johnson about employment figures. The previous day, in Parliament Johnson had reverted to claiming that employment rates were now higher than before Covid. Norgrove told the prime minister that he had been using the data selectively and in a way that was 'likely to give a misleading impression'.[73] Behind-the-scenes was not working, and now the head of the UKSA was communicating directly with the head of the government.

We might speculate why the gently-gently strategy had slipped up. Perhaps Gilbert had briefed Johnson but the difference between 'employed' and 'on a payroll' slipped his mind in the excitement of achieving a rhetorical victory. Or perhaps the briefing from Gilbert and her team had concentrated on achieving those rhetorical victories. We do not know. But the question 'Why did Johnson make his metonymic error again?' may not be the most important one if we want to understand how to combat statistical manipulation. There is a less obvious question, but one that we can answer. Why did the CEO of Full Fact write to Ed Humpherson in the first place?

Ethos and Combatting Manipulation

At first glance, there would appear to be little for Full Fact, or any other independent fact-checker, to gain by sharing its prize findings with the UKSA. A fact-checking business depends on obtaining contracts if it is to flourish. Why would Full Fact want to pass on some of its best data to the UKSA, who might then be seen to take the credit? The letter from the chair of the UKSA about the Johnson's employment claims was reported in national newspapers, but Full Fact's earlier exposure had not been.

Nevertheless, when Humpherson sent his letter to Johnson about employment, Full Fact declared unambiguously that 'we welcome today's intervention from the Office for Statistics Regulation'.[74] The reason was simple. Full Fact has never considered that the exposure of statistical errors was a sufficient end in itself. Its website asserts: 'We can't fight bad information through fact checking alone'. The bad information needs to

[73] UK Statistics Authority (2022), 'Sir David Norgrove to the Prime Minister – Employment statistics', 24 February, https://uksa.statisticsauthority.gov.uk/correspondence/sir-david-norgrove-to-prime-minister-employment-statistics/.

[74] Full Fact (2022), 'Statistics watchdog challenges government's "disappointing" false employment claims', 1 February, https://fullfact.org/blog/2022/feb/osr-government-employment-claims/.

be officially corrected or withdrawn. To achieve this, Full Fact needs to act with others, especially with regulators.[75]

As we have said, the UKSA and Full Fact have cooperated closely over a number of years.[76] Because UKSA is a legally constituted regulator, it carries a greater public ethos than an independent fact-checking company. This is seen in the newspaper headlines about 'the statistics watchdog' rebuking the prime minister. The regulatory body is presumed to be acting neutrally and protecting the nation. In France, the ASP bears a similar status. When Darmanin broke the embargo on the early release of official statistics, he was challenged by the ASP. Unlike Johnson facing a similar objection from the UKSA, Darmanin did not react with bluster and aggression. He did something that Johnson rarely did – he apologised.[77]

This would not be possible without a political culture in which regulatory bodies carry national status. In Britain there are numerous regulatory bodies, such as the Electoral Commission, the National Audit Office, the Committee on Standards in Public Life, the Infrastructure and Projects Authority, and so on. During the premiership of Johnson, many of these regulatory bodies found themselves being ignored or worse, but the system survived the attack.[78] The situation is very different in the United States, where there is no accepted statistical authority nor an established culture of regulatory bodies. American fact-checking teams work independently and without regulatory authority. For them, fact-checking is an end in itself. As we saw in Chapter 4, the more that the *Washington Post* exposed Trump's untruthfulness, the more untruthful he became, and the more he attacked the newspaper for its 'phoney' reporting.

In the United Kingdom and in France, the public and politicians are largely willing to accept the reputation of the statistical authorities. For their part, the statistical regulators must be strategic in the way they expose statistical error, even to the extent of engaging in polite fictions. Most importantly, the regulators seem most successfully to oppose the political manipulation of statistics when they act as if there is no statistical manipulation to speak of.

---

[75] Full Fact, 'After we fact check', https://fullfact.org/about/interventions/. Full Fact discusses how fact-checking can make an impact; one way is to work with 'another actor that can influence the claimant, such as a regulator'.

[76] See Chapter 6.

[77] ASP, 'Annual Report, 2021', p. 32, www.autorite-statistique-publique.fr/event/rapport-annuel-2021-version-anglaise-de-lautorite-de-la-statistique-publique/.

[78] Blick and Hennessy (2022), especially pp. 45ff.

This chapter has been based around the doings of a single politician. It might be expected that once he fell from grace, his influence would be over and a greater sense of truthfulness would immediately return to British politics. However, it has not worked out like that. Some observers argue that Johnson's assault on the British constitution has left a deep mark, with the political culture now more favourable to dishonesty and manipulation and less capable of regulating itself.[79]

When Rishi Sunak, Johnson's former chancellor of the exchequer, became prime minister he pledged that his government would be committed to honesty. Nevertheless, some things had not changed. The UKSA's chair still got practice in writing public letters advising the prime minister not to mislead the public with his statistics.[80] And the media remained primed to report such letters with their familiar 'watchdog rebukes prime minister' format.[81] A change of personnel does not necessitate a change of political culture, nor an end to the battle for ethos.

---

[79] Ibid., pp. 92ff.

[80] See, for example: UK Statistics Authority (2024), 'Response from Sir Robert Chote to Alistair Carmichael MP – Asylum backlog figures', 18 January, https://uksa.statisticsauthority.gov.uk/correspondence/response-from-sir-robert-chote-to-alistair-carmichael-mp-asylum-backlog-figures/.

[81] See for instance: BBC News (2024), 'Rishi Sunak rebuked by stats watchdog over asylum backlog claim', 18 January, www.bbc.co.uk/news/uk-politics-68017887; George Parker and Lucy Fisher (2024), 'Rishi Sunak rapped by UK statistics watchdog over asylum backlog claim', *Financial Times*, 18 January; Geraldine Scott (2024), 'PM's asylum claim "misled"', *Times*, 19 January; Kate Devlin (2024), 'Watchdog censures Sunak for asylum backlog claims', *Independent*, 19 January.

CHAPTER 10

How a Manipulated Covid Target Was Exposed

Boris Johnson's fractious responses to the UKSA have put in place the background scenery for another statistical drama, which happened during Johnson's premiership and which we recount here. It features a clash between his health minister and the chair of the UKSA. The devil is in the detail, especially when we observe a politician manipulating numbers, and when we see his efforts starting to fall apart in the face of increasing pressure from the Authority.

Sometimes you have to dig down deep into a single incident to understand what is going on. In this instance, we will see what happens when the UKSA's favoured, softly-softly diplomacy meets a ministerial brick wall. It's certainly not the end of the story. But to appreciate what comes next, you have to look closely at the words in the exchange between the chair and the minister – this includes the words that they use and, just as importantly, those that they do not.

Politicians and Their Hunger for Advantageous Categories

Our chosen example occurred in the summer of 2020, during the early months of the Covid-19 pandemic. It is centred around a public exchange of letters between Matt Hancock, the minister of health, and Sir David Norgrove, the chair of the UKSA. The issue focussed on a matter of great importance: the number of people who had been tested for Covid-19 in the United Kingdom. At the time, there was no vaccine against the highly infectious disease, and testing seemed to be the only way of controlling its spread. For political reasons the government wanted to claim as high a figure as possible, but the Statistics Authority thought the government was claiming a number that was higher than was legitimate. Like many statistical disputes, this one concerned the meaning of words. The question was: what legitimately counted as a test that had been administered?

We have already had occasion to quote Ian Hacking's apt saying that 'counting is hungry for categories'.[1] When politics are involved, there can be a double hunger. First, there is the metaphorical hunger for categories that Ian Hacking was alluding to: all statistics must be measures of something and that something has to be labelled. In the case of politically controversial numbers, there can be another hunger that is slightly less metaphorical: that of politicians to have numbers that will bring them political advantage. Sometimes they hunger for higher numbers and some-times for lower ones. Whichever it is, this hunger opens the way to manipulating not just the numbers that are being counted, but also the labels that are chosen to describe those numbers. In the previous chapter, we saw Boris Johnson's government satisfying their hunger for low crime rate figures by contracting the label of 'crime' so that it excluded computer crime and other white-collar crime. By using these contracted figures, the government trumpeted its triumph of reducing 'crime'.[2]

If there is a double hunger, then there is also a double process of counting, one numerical and the other linguistic. In order to count instances, you have to determine what should count as an instance of what you are counting numerically. The skilled manipulator of statistics might manipulate the use of the category, and so appear to be counting instances of one thing, when they are actually excluding instances of that thing, as in the example of 'computer crime'. If politicians want higher numbers of a particular category, then they might be counting instances, which properly speaking should not be counted as instances. The result is that the category will be expanded and used in a deliberately misleading manner. That happened in the case of the health minister and the apparently high numbers of administered Covid tests.

Something similar had happened in a previous incident involving Johnson and the same minister. In 2019, shortly after he became prime minister, Johnson announced his government's commitment to building forty new hospitals within the next ten years. The promise was included in the Conservatives' election manifesto of December that year.[3] Matt

---

[1] Ian Hacking (1982), 'Biopower and the avalanche of printed numbers', *Humanities in Society*, 5, 279–95.
[2] See above, pp. 209–11.
[3] The Conservative Party 2019 Manifesto is no longer available on the Conservative Party website. But see BBC News, 24 November, 2019: www.bbc.co.uk/news/election-2019-50524262. Also see: Heather Stewart, Jamie Grierson, Hilary Osborne, Richard Partington and Fiona Harvey (2019), 'Conservative party manifesto: what it says and what it means', *Guardian*, 25 November, www.theguardian.com/politics/2019/nov/24/conservative-manifesto-the-key-points-policies-boris-johnson.

Hancock, as minister of health, issued an official document making the same commitment, and he personally endorsed that commitment in the document's foreword.[4]

So far so good – there is nothing wrong with a government having an ambitious plan, even one that experts doubt can be achieved within the announced timescale. All governments do this sort of thing. But what came next exploited the gap between the two sorts of counting. When it was becoming clear that the plan was unlikely to be achieved, the Department of Health published a fourteen-page document which it distributed to the communication teams of hospital trusts. The publication told the teams how to talk to the media about building new hospitals and building new parts of hospitals.[5] Not long before this publication was issued, Matt Hancock had resigned his post in disgrace, for reasons that we will return to later in this chapter. However, the document must have been planned and largely written while he was still the minister.

Part of the instructions concerned what constituted a 'new hospital'. Among the projects that 'must always be referred to as a new hospital' were the following: 'a major new clinical building on an existing site or a new wing of an existing hospital' and 'a major refurbishment and alteration of all but building frame or main structure'.[6] Critics were not slow to point out that new refurbishments or new buildings in existing hospitals did not constitute new hospitals. When the government published its plans for the forty 'new hospitals', the critics made it clear that a large majority of the forty were not new hospitals, but were new buildings and refurbishments within existing ones.[7]

---

[4] Department of Health and Social Care (2019), 'Health Infrastructure Plan', 30 September, https://assets.publishing.service.gov.uk/media/5d933a4de5274a2fb969d767/health-infrastructure-plan.
In his foreword, Hancock wrote: 'We're giving the green light to more than 40 new hospital projects across the country, six getting the go-ahead immediately, and over 30 that could be built over the next decade'. He described the plan as 'the biggest, boldest, hospital building programme in a generation', p. 4.

[5] Department of Health and Social Care (2021), 'New hospital programme communications playbook', August   https://nursingnotes.co.uk/wp-content/uploads/2021/08/NHP-Communications-Playbook-_August-2021_-Redacted.pdf.

[6] Ibid., p. 12.

[7] See, for example: David Parsley (2021), 'NHS trusts ordered to call hospital refurbs "new hospitals" as Government scrambles to hit 2030 build target', *Independent*, 26 August, https://inews.co.uk/news/government-orders-nhs-trusts-to-call-hospital-refurbs-new-hospitals-as-it-scrambles-to-hit-2030-build-target-1169978; Toby Helm (2022), 'Boris Johnson faces investigation into claims over 40 "new" hospitals', *Guardian*, 2 July, www.theguardian.com/politics/2022/jul/02/boris-johnson-faces-investigation-into-claims-over-40-new-hospitals; David Oliver (2023), 'The "40" new hospitals' pledge was always a mirage', *British Medical Journal*, 381, p. 1259; Hannah Smith (2022), 'Is the government going to build 48 new hospitals by 2030?', Full Fact, 4 July, https://fullfact.org/health/48-new-hospitals/.

The devious and self-interested manipulation of language is apparent. The concept of 'a new hospital', or 'a new house', is not a technical concept. It is a part of everyday understanding. We all know that adding an extension to an existing house – perhaps a new kitchen or a new garage – is not the same as building a new house. You don't need to consult a dictionary, or a statistical authority, to know that something deliberately misleading was going on. Numbers of 'new hospitals' were being artificially boosted.[8] Thus, categories of ordinary language were being stretched to mislead, just as the government, when it wanted lower numbers, contracted the category of 'crime'.[9]

This should be borne in mind when we deal with the example of Hancock and the Covid tests. The numbers of tests are much larger than forty, and the statistics are more complex. Yet basically there was a similar strategy of manipulating numbers by manipulating the words that describe those numbers, and then numerically counting the instances of those misleadingly labelled categories.

The Incident

The Covid pandemic turned Matt Hancock from a minor politician into a major, national figure, at least before he disappeared in disgrace. When Johnson became prime minister, he inherited Hancock as minister of health. Johnson did not remove him from his position, although he removed many of the ministers from the previous administration. This was not because Hancock appeared to have outstanding ministerial talents. For Johnson, the major criterion for being retained was not talent and certainly not a commitment to truthfulness: it was political loyalty to him.[10] Hancock must have given the impression that he would faithfully serve his leader. If the prime minister said that old hospitals were new hospitals, then the minister would say 'yes, yes'.

---

[8] Even after he left the government, Hancock continued to deny that there was anything wrong in describing refurbishments as 'new hospitals'. See his interview on BBC TV *Newscast* (2022), 14 July, www.bbc.co.uk/sounds/play/pocmowto.

[9] According to one political observer, whose political outlook was not unsympathetic to the Conservatives, when Johnson and Hancock campaigned in 2019 on the promise that the Conservatives would build forty new hospitals, they 'were lying, pure and simple': Peter Oborne (2021), *The Assault on Truth*, London: Simon and Schuster, p. 14.

[10] See, for instance: Anthony Seldon and Raymund Newell (2023), *Johnson at 10*, London: Atlantic Books; Simon Kuper (2022), *Chums: How a Tiny Caste of Oxford Tories Took over the Whole UK*, London: Profile Books.

It seems that Hancock was not a particularly proficient minister. As the pandemic developed, it is said that he tried to give the impression that he was on top of everything but his fellow ministers, and especially their leader, could tell that he was struggling. Why didn't the prime minister get rid of him? According to some insiders, if things went badly for Johnson, he wanted to have someone around whom he could blame and then sack.[11] When Johnson gave evidence to the Covid Inquiry after he had fallen from power, he denied this.[12] However, as we know, Johnson should not be taken as a reliable witness of his own actions and motives.

So, there was Hancock, insecure and at risk, but giving nightly briefings to the nation about Covid. He was hungry for big successes. In the early stages of the pandemic, medical scientists and the government agreed that widespread testing held the key to containing the disease. If those who had contracted Covid could be identified by means of tests, then they could be isolated and the transmission of the disease could be slowed. On 2 April 2020, at a press briefing Hancock announced his plan to increase national testing to 100,000 tests a day by the end of the month.[13] He indicated that this was an ambitious plan and that, if he succeeded, then he, together with the government, would have achieved something extraordinary.[14]

On 1 May, Hancock announced that he had accomplished his 'incredible achievement'. The previous day, the target of 100,000 tests a day had been met, as 122,347 tests had been administered. Hancock gloried in his achievement: 'I knew it was an audacious goal but we needed an audacious goal', because setting 'ambitious goals in a national crisis has a galvanising effect on everyone involved'. He declared it a national triumph.[15]

---

[11] Seldon and Newell (2023), pp. 208f.

[12] Toby Helm (2023), 'Former UK health secretary Matt Hancock's early Covid warnings were ignored by No 10, say allies', *Observer*, 26 November, www.theguardian.com/uk-news/2023/nov/25/former-uk-health-secretary-matt-hancocks-early-covid-warnings-were-ignored-by-no-10-say-allies. See also: Nick Triggle (2023), 'Covid inquiry hears Matt Hancock wanted to decide who lived and died', BBC News, 2 November, www.bbc.co.uk/news/health-67297446.

[13] For Hancock's actual words, see: BBC News (2020), 'Coronavirus: Matt Hancock sets aim of 100,000 tests a day by end of April', April 2, www.bbc.co.uk/news/uk-52140376.

[14] For detailed analyses of the language used by Hancock: Michael Billig (2021), 'Uses of precise numbers and semi-magical round numbers in political discourse about Covid-19: examples from the government of the United Kingdom', *Discourse & Society*, 32, 542–58; Michael Billig and Cristina Marinho (2023), 'Preventing the political manipulation of COVID-19 statistics: the importance of going beyond diplomatic language', *Language in Society*, 52, 733–55; Cristina Marinho and Michael Billig (2024), 'How can governments be prevented from manipulating statistics about COVID-19? An example from UK politics', in Cornelia Ilie (ed.), *Manufacturing Dissent*, Amsterdam: John Benjamins, pp. 186–214.

[15] Heather Stewart and Denis Campbell (2020), 'Hancock says UK hit 100,000 tests amid claims tally is artificially boosted', *Guardian*, 1 May, www.theguardian.com/world/2020/may/01/ministers-accused-of-changing-covid-19-test-tally-to-hit-100000-goal.

There is always someone determined to dampen every great achievement, whether it is building forty new hospitals, reducing crime or administering 100,000 Covid tests a day. On the same day that Hancock made his announcement, Full Fact, the independent fact-checking organisation, cast doubt on Hancock's numbers. The organisation questioned whether 122,347 people had actually been tested, as the minister was claiming.[16]

According to the fact-checkers, the Department of Health had altered its definition of administered tests. It now included tests which had been subcontracted to independent organisations; and if a test had been sent to a patient to test themselves at home, then, as soon as the test was dispatched, it was counted as a test that had been administered and analysed. Some of these home tests were not received back and some failed to be analysed. Nevertheless, they were counted in with the actually administered and analysed tests. By Full Fact's estimation, only 81,978 of the 122,347 of the tests on 30 April could be said to have been fully processed. By stretching the definition of 'an administered test' to include all tests that had been sent out, regardless of whether they had been used, returned or analysed, Hancock could claim to have met his great target.

There was also the problem that the target figure was only reached on one day. Does one day provide sufficient evidence to say that the target was being reached 'daily'? That would stretch the meaning of the ordinary word 'daily'. Again this was as much a semantic problem as a numerical one. You don't have to be an expert mathematician or an accomplished linguist to suspect a misleading, self-interested use of words.

Maybe the problem was worse than semantic. Could it be that analysing the tests administered in the health centres had been slowed down earlier in the week, so that a bigger number – a target-busting number – could be recorded on the final day? What happened immediately after the target-busting day provides some circumstantial evidence. If the target-busting day was followed by further days with more than 100,000 recorded tests, then Hancock's claims would be supported. In the following days, however, the numbers slipped backed to around 80,000 per day.[17]

---

[16] Pippa Allen-Kinross (2020), 'Has the government really hit 100,000 tests a day, and what happens next?', Full Fact, 1 May, https://fullfact.org/health/coronavirus-100k-tests/. For a broader Full Fact investigation into the government's testing figures and its targets, see: Leo Benedictus (2020), 'Did the government meet its Covid-19 test targets?', Full Fact, 10 July, https://fullfact.org/health/six-test-targets/.

[17] Kate Ng (2020), 'Coronavirus daily tests fall to 76,496 just two days after 100,000 target met', *The Independent*, 3 May, www.independent.co.uk/news/uk/home-news/coronavirus-uk-testing-rate-daily-target-falls-hancock-a9496656.html; Sarah Marsh and Diane Taylor (2020), 'Ministers under fire as Covid-19 testing drops back below 100,000 daily target', *Guardian*, 4 May, www

We do not know for certain whether the testing and analysing procedures had been deliberately manipulated to produce a surge on the final day of April. It is, however, hard for ministers and prime ministers who gain a reputation for manipulating statistics to escape suspicion when politically desirable figures seem to pop up handily at precisely the most convenient moment. This does suggest something else as well. The manipulation of statistics may sometimes require more than the manipulation of words and how the numbers are counted: it may sometimes involve manipulating *when* the numbers are to be counted.

We have had occasion in earlier chapters to mention Campbell's law. Donald Campbell had said that measures become corrupted when they are used to evaluate targets.[18] The evidence from Full Fact seemed to suggest that Hancock only met his self-defined target because he had evaluated his own performance by using a corrupted measure. Thus, it would seem to be a candidate for Campbell's law. However, what happened with Hancock is somewhat different. Campbell was analysing the corruption of measures, not the corruption of people. For him, people might be doing good things for the right reasons: namely, seeking to put policies into action, measuring the effects of the policies, and assigning real rewards and sanctions on the basis of scientific evaluations. The problem for Campbell was that doing good things can lead to measures ceasing to measure satisfactorily what they were designed to measure, because of the actions of those being measured. Consequently, the measures can become corrupted by circumstances.

Manipulation refers something a bit different. To suggest that a politician has manipulated a measure does not imply that something well meant has turned out to have unforeseen effects. It implies the sort of deliberate deviousness that Full Fact seemed to have uncovered. Hancock, having set his own target, appeared to have given himself the maximum chance of success by manipulating the measure so that it was designed to record extra numbers. In this case, the measure had not been corrupted by good intentions or unforeseen circumstances. Hancock's chosen measure had never been innocent.

Facing Parliament and the Press

Prima facie, this would seem to be a case for the UKSA to investigate, but the Authority followed its usual practice and waited to be asked. Political

.theguardian.com/world/2020/may/03/ministers-under-fire-as-covid-19-testing-drops-back-below-100000-daily-target.
[18] See Chapters 2 and 5.

pressure was building on Hancock. The deputy leader of the Labour Party tweeted that if Hancock had failed to meet his target, he should have admitted it and not sought 'to fudge the figures'. The acting leader of the Liberal Democrats said Hancock had played 'fast and loose with the truth' and the government had decided to 'massage the metrics'. The national press, especially left-wing papers, were reporting these accusations.[19] *The Guardian* said that Hancock was being accused of 'artificially inflating the number of coronavirus tests' and that he was claiming 'his self-imposed' target as a 'national achievement'.[20] The fiercest response came in the headline of the *Mirror*: 'Matt Hancock shamelessly fiddled figures to reach coronavirus tests target'. It reported that Hancock 'brazenly added 40,000 tests "in the post" to 80,000 really taking place'.[21]

When the minister of health answered questions in the House of Commons on 5 May he faced similar accusations, especially from Labour's new health spokesperson, Dr Rosena Allin-Khan.[22] She used the m-word, claiming that the 'testing figures are now being manipulated'. If she had said that Hancock had manipulated the figures, she would have almost certainly been called to order by the Speaker on the grounds that members of Parliament are not permitted to accuse each other of lying.[23] Sometimes the offence of calling a member a liar is seen to be worse than the offence of a member actually lying.[24]

Hancock was clearly riled. He said that he objected to Allin-Khan's tone, without saying what he didn't like about it. He would not have taken kindly to hearing his great achievement dismissed as being 'manipulated'. Nor would he have appreciated some of the newspaper coverage of the debate. Dr Allin-Khan was combining her political role with working as an emergency doctor on the Covid front line. Even papers normally favourable to the Conservatives sympathised with her. *The Sun* published its

---

[19] The quotes from Davey can be found in Jon Stone (2020), 'Hancock is "misleading the public" over testing figures', *The Independent*, 2 May, www.independent.co.uk/news/uk/politics/coronavirus-testing-figures-uk-target-criticism-hancock-a9495621.html.

[20] Stewart and Campbell (2020), *Guardian*, 2 May.

[21] Aaron Sharp (2020), 'Matt Hancock shamelessly fiddled figures to reach coronavirus tests target', *Daily Mirror*, 2 May, www.mirror.co.uk/news/politics/matt-hancock-shamelessly-fiddled-figures-21964848.

[22] For details, Hansard: https://hansard.parliament.uk/commons/2020-05-05/debates/22A7FFC5–7540-4F1F-8685-8BB2BA355DE9/Covid-19TestTrackAndTrace.

[23] See: David Judge (2022), '"Would I Lie to You?": Boris Johnson and lying in the House of Commons', *Political Quarterly*, 93(1), 77–86.

[24] The Labour leader questioned Johnson about the figures at prime minister's questions and Johnson typically conceded nothing. See Hansard, https://hansard.parliament.uk/Commons/2020-05-06/debates/4D4A836F-EBB7–4255-B84C-1537BDE1DCC4/Engagements.

report with the headline: 'Tone deaf Matt Hancock slammed for telling shadow minister & frontline A&E doctor to "watch her tone"'.[25] The Johnson-friendly *Telegraph* referred to Hancock's 'huffy and condescending reply'.[26] Not the ideal breakfast time reading for a beleaguered minister.

The UKSA and Hancock's Numbers: The Background

Two days after Hancock had been questioned in Parliament, the inevitable happened. An opposition member of Parliament – Daisy Cooper, deputy leader of the Liberal Democrats – wrote to Ed Humpherson, the director general for regulation, requesting him to investigate whether 'the Government's claim to have hit "100,000 coronavirus tests a day" by the end of April is a misrepresentation of the statistics'.[27] Humpherson passed the letter on to Norgrove, chair of the UKSA. The Authority was now officially involved.

In an earlier chapter, we mentioned that shortly being appointed as chair in 2017, Norgrove gave an interesting interview to the *Civil Service Review*.[28] He talked about his own background and how he saw his new job. Norgrove said that he was not a trained statistician but having studied economics he was familiar with using numbers. He had joined the civil service, first working as an economist in the Treasury, and then rising to become Margaret Thatcher's private secretary during her time as prime minister. He talked about being interviewed for the post of the UKSA's chair. The interviewers had let him know that the role demanded standing up to authority. He told them that he had experience of working with 'a huge range of very difficult people', including Thatcher.[29] He thought this had helped him get the job.

[25] Sascha O'Sullivan (2020), 'Tone deaf Matt Hancock slammed for telling shadow minister & frontline A&E doctor to "watch her tone"', *Sun*, May 5.

[26] Michael Deacon (2020), 'Matt Hancock is facing the test of his life ... and in the Commons he finally snapped', *Telegraph*, 6 May, www.telegraph.co.uk/politics/2020/05/05/matt-hancock-facing-test-life-today-commons-snapped/.

[27] Office of Statistical Regulation (2020), 'Daisy Cooper MP to Ed Humpherson: coronavirus testing programme', 7 May, https://osr.statisticsauthority.gov.uk/correspondence/daisy-cooper-mp-to-ed-humpherson-coronavirus-testing-programme/.

[28] Jim Dunton (2017), 'Sir David Norgrove interview: new chair of UK Statistics Authority on elections, the misuse of numbers and working for Margaret Thatcher', *Civil Service World*, 8 June, www.civilserviceworld.com/in-depth/article/sir-david-norgrove-interview-new-chair-of-uk-statistics-authority-on-elections-the-misuse-of-numbers-and-working-for-margaret-thatcher.

[29] Ibid.

Norgrove also spoke about the inherent weakness of the UKSA. Parliament had not granted the Authority the power to prevent public bodies, including government bodies, from using numbers wrongly. He said: 'You can't stop people misusing data: all you can do is point it out and hope that either they respond or that the public pressure forces them to respond'. Behind-the-scenes persuasion was his preferred way of operating. If the UKSA suspected that a public body was misusing official data, the Authority's chief statistician would contact the head statistician of the public body and together they would try to sort out the problem. Should they succeed in doing so, then there would be no need to involve the UKSA's chair or even to make a public announcement.

There would, however, be occasions when matters could not be settled this way. Then the Authority might need to go public, principally by writing public letters which are a means of exerting what Norgrove called 'public pressure'. As he said in the interview, Ed Humpherson, the head of the Office of Regulation, wrote most of the public letters to officials of public bodies. However, Norgrove felt that it was his duty to write the public letters if the abuse of data was 'particularly bad' or if it was 'a very senior person or a minister who's misused data'. A letter from him was, he said, 'the last resort'.

In line with this procedure, Humpherson had passed the letter from the deputy Liberal leader on to Norgrove. When Norgrove then wrote to Hancock it was the beginning of a very public correspondence and also a last resort.

The Diplomatic First Letter

Norgrove's first letter to Hancock was a model of diplomatic language: he did not challenge the minister's figures directly. As we discussed in the previous chapter, the senior figures in the UKAS, like good British civil servants, prefer to use roundabout, polite language to keep the channels of communication intact.[30] This means that they tend not make outright accusations, but they are skilled in dropping hints. We cannot go into full details of Norgrove's diplomatically expressed accusations here. Anyone particularly interested can consult our technical writings on this

---

[30] For a comparison of the working language which British senior civil servants use and that which civil servants in other countries use, see: Dennis Grube (2013), *Prime Ministers and Rhetorical Governance*, London: Palgrave Macmillan.

incident.[31]Nevertheless we cannot avoid all technical matters, especially if we want to understand exactly what Norgrove was saying and, indeed, what he was doing. Biljana Scott, a linguist who has studied diplomatic language, uses the linguistic distinction between 'paratactic language' and 'hypotactic language' to describe the nature of diplomatic language.[32] In hypotactic language, statements are connected together to form an outwardly expressed and recognisable argument: one statement serves another as a speaker or writer makes a point and arrives at a conclusion. In paratactic language, by contrast, a series of grammatically unconnected statements is made. There is no 'therefore', 'thus' or other point-making connections between assertions.[33]

Diplomats, however, will use the latter type of language to make their points. They will rely on the recipients of their apparently unconnected statements to fill in the links, and thereby understand the argumentative points that are being made without being openly expressed. It is as if both parties are using a shared code which might not be understood by outsiders who are accustomed to using and hearing plainer language and direct point-making. In Chapter 6, we quoted Lenin, who prided himself on his plain speaking, quoting Bismarck that when diplomats say they accept something in principle, their fellow diplomats will know they are rejecting it in practice.[34]

Norgrove's letter has a distinctly paratactic or diplomatic tone, as if he seeks to communicate criticism of Hancock's use of statistics without actually criticising the minister. Following the formal address 'Dear Secretary of State', Norgrove's opening paragraph was a strange one. Normally, business letters start with a paragraph in which the writer explains why they are writing the letter. For instance, 'I am writing to you to complain about the poor service I received. . .'; or 'I wish to apply for the post of. . .' And then the letter will seek to justify the purpose of the

---

[31] See fn. 14.

[32] See, for example: Biljana Scott (2011), 'Skills of the public diplomat: language, narrative, and allegiance', in Ali Fisher and Scott Lucas (eds.), *Trials of Engagement*, Leiden: Martinus Nijhoff, pp. 231–50; Biljana Scott (2018), 'Poetry and diplomacy: telling it slant', *Training Language and Culture*, 2, 51–66.

[33] For more on the distinctions between paratactic and hypotactic language, see: Mikhail Dymarsky (2014), 'Towards the history of two oppositions: parataxis vs. hypotaxis and coordination vs. subordination', *Language and Language Behaviour*, 14, 69–77; Richard Lanham (2003), *Analysing Prose*, New York: Continuum; Jeanne Fahnestock (2011), *Rhetorical Style*, Oxford: Oxford University Press. For an important use of the distinction, introducing it to modern rhetoricians as an indicator of argumentation, see: Chaim Perelman and Lucie Olbrechts-Tyteca (1958/1969), *The New Rhetoric*, Notre Dame: University of Notre Dame Press, especially pp. 157–8.

[34] See above, p. 136.

letter, and lead to a conclusion: 'for all these reasons, please would you recognise that I deserve recompense, employment etc.'.[35]

Daisy Cooper, in her letter to Humpherson, had used this conventional form. She begins by explaining why she is writing: 'I am concerned that the Government's claim to have hit "100,000 coronavirus tests a day" by the end of April is a misrepresentation of the statistics and as a result will decrease the public's trust in Official Statistics'.[36] There follows her justification for feeling concerned – namely that there are problems with the numbers being cited by the government, and she lists some of the problems. These are some of the problems raised by Full Fact and cited in Parliament by opposition parties. Her conclusion is to urge the UKSA to investigate these problems. It is a very hypotactic document with a clear argument, and each part of the letter serves the other parts to make the argument.

By contrast, Norgrove's opening paragraph is odd for a business letter. He gives no reason why he is writing. He does not use either the first person or second person singular at the start: there is no 'I am writing to you because...' The opening paragraph comprises three statements of fact, all of which Hancock, the letter's recipient, could be presumed to know already:

> On 2 April the Government announced its goal to carry out 100,000 COVID-19 tests a day by the end of April and on 6 May announced its ambition for 200,000 tests a day by the end of May.[1] There has been widespread media coverage of the Government's progress.[37]

This opening paragraph tells Hancock nothing new, nor contains anything that openly explains why Norgrove was writing to him. The three statements are not argumentatively connected, and, in this respect, it appears to be a piece of paratactic writing.

The usefulness of parataxis in diplomatic writing is illustrated by the third statement: 'There has been widespread media coverage of the Government's progress'. What is omitted is as significant as what is

---

[35] Instruction guides for writing business letters tend to recommend this format. See for example: BBC Bitesize. KS3, 'How to write a formal letter', www.bbc.co.uk/bitesize/topics/zv7fqp3/articles/zkq8hbk.

[36] Office for Statistical Regulation (2020), 7 May.

[37] UK Statistical Authority (2020), 'Sir David Norgrove letter to Matt Hancock regarding Covid-19 testing', 11 May, https://uksa.statisticsauthority.gov.uk/correspondence/sir-david-norgrove-letter-to-matt-hancock-regarding-covid-19-testing/. The superscript in the quotation was in the original letter. It referred to a note at the end of the letter, citing the parliamentary report of prime minister's question time for 6 May 2020, when Johnson announced his ambition for 200,000 tests a month.

written. Norgrove uses the neutral phrase 'widespread media coverage'. He does not say that much of this coverage was critical, repeating claims about Hancock manipulating the numbers or being huffy and tone deaf. At no point in the letter does Norgrove mention these criticisms. And what could be more diplomatic than describing that the media was covering the government's *progress*? It is a nice, positive word with which to end the diplomatically neutral opening paragraph.

There is, however, one matter that the opening paragraph does achieve. It signals, without openly stating, that the topic of the letter is the measurement of total testing figures. By phrasing the opening in this way, Norgrove leaves Hancock to assume that, as the UKSA's chair, he would not be writing an official letter unless something was possibly amiss with those figures.

Norgrove continues his diplomatic tone into his second paragraph, which starts in a friendly manner: 'I know you are a strong supporter of the proper use of statistics and data'. And as a strong supporter of statistics, the minister would know that 'it is important that the target and its context should be set out'. He means the target number of Covid tests that the government is aiming to achieve. But surely, Norgrove himself set out the government's numerical targets in his first paragraph. What does he mean by the 'context' of the target? Like a bird of prey flying in decreasing circles above its target on the ground, Norgrove is rhetorically circling around his own target, which of course is the topic of testing targets. Still he does not swoop down to attack the target.

Norgrove, however, is tightening his rhetorical circle. He lists some different testing targets, such as testing capacity (i.e. the number of tests available at a given time), the number of tests that have been administered and the number of completed tests that have been received for analysis. He continues: for sake of clarity, it is helpful to set out which type of target the testing numbers are 'intended to reflect'. Who could possibly disagree? Norgrove is expressing a statistical truism; no one could say 'Oh, no, it's better to have all the different targets jumbled together, so no one can know quite what the numbers refer to'.

It is the same with Norgrove's next claim that 'sole focus on the total national number of tests could mask helpful operational detail' – i.e. that it might be helpful to break down the results to show whether the rates of testing vary in different areas, whether there are differences between numbers of people tested in health centres or at home, whether the rates for testing vary in different parts of the country, and so on. Again he is making a point by declaring a statistical truism. In theory, no one could say that they would prefer not to have this kind of information.

In practice, a governing politician might want less information to be distributed to the public. They might prefer that only favourable information about testing and targets is in the public domain. But a politician cannot voice this thought except behind a firmly closed door. At most, a politician, following the practice of Bismarck, could say publicly in response to the sort of demands that Norgrove is presenting: 'In theory I agree with you', while meaning 'in practice I would prefer the public to remain in ignorance if we fail to meet our targets'. That last thought must be strictly kept away from public ears.

About two-thirds the way through Norgrove's letter, he makes a criticism of the way that the data on tests are being presented: 'There is limited detail about the nature and types of testing and it is hard to navigate to the best source of information'. The criticism is phrased purely as if the writer is being helpful. Norgrove is not saying that data is being hidden, fudged or massaged. He wants Hancock to cooperate in clearly presenting the very data that might confirm whether he has been manipulating the numbers. But Norgrove cannot utter this directly, at least not at this stage of his correspondence.

So, Norgrove completes his first letter, urging the government to 'show more clearly how targets are being defined, measured and reported'. Then he signs off and, as it were, flies off circling high into the diplomatic sky.

The Effects of Norgrove's First Letter

Norgrove was using his diplomatic tone for a purpose. He wanted to suggest in a coded way that he could put pressure on the minister but that he would prefer that Hancock agreed to cooperate and ensure that the testing statistics were more open. The pressure, like its purpose, was being indirectly expressed. The UKSA's chair was hoping that Hancock would take the hint and realise that Norgrove could write the sort of letter that would attract the sort of eye-catching press headlines that we discussed in the previous chapter.

If Norgrove's initial aim was to avoid provoking this sort of press coverage, then his first step was successful. Only two of Britain's national newspapers reported his letter – the *Guardian* and the *Independent*. Both are left of centre, and both are what used to be called 'broadsheets', although their pages these days are not as physically broad as they once were. Both newspapers lack the mass circulations of the tabloid press, which along with the right-wing broadsheets ignored Norgrove's letter. Hancock would not worry about bad press in the left-wing broadsheets for they were never going to be his supporters. But he would not wish the right-wing press to publish the sort of 'national watchdog slams government' headline to follow up their coverage of the huffy, tone deaf minister reacting to criticism in Parliament.

The way the *Guardian* and *Independent* covered the story gives a clue why the rest of the press did not consider it a story for them. Both papers reported that the chair of the UKSA was criticising the minister's statistics, but that he was not doing it overtly. According to the *Independent*, Norgrove's letter was 'framed in diplomatic language but represents a serious challenge'.[38] *The Guardian* reported that the distinguished statistician Sir David Spiegelhalter 'described Norgrove's letter as a "diplomatically-worded but strong public rebuke"'.[39] Significantly both reports add something that Norgrove had not mentioned in his letter: that Hancock had met his target by adding in tests that had not been carried out.

The two broadsheets used the same 'diplomatic language but...' format. Small words like 'but' can play an important role in political language. According to one notable analyst of political language, when two phrases or statements are connected by 'but', the second one typically serves to counter the expectations that the first one sets up.[40] In the present example, a reader hearing that Norgrove wrote a diplomatically phrased letter might correctly assume that he used polite language. However, they would be wrong if they also assumed that, as a polite diplomat, he avoided using any threat. Instead he was using a code that the recipient could interpret as a challenge or rebuke, although none was overtly uttered. He might have been diplomatic, but he was rebuking in a diplomatic way.

Accordingly, Norgrove had not provided the newspapers with a clear story to report. Journalists who quoted from Norgrove's letter would need to interpret its meaning. Tabloid newspapers prefer dramatically screaming headlines. A story matching the headline 'Statistical watchdog uses diplomatic language to criticise minister' would be a bit too dreary for their

---

[38] Andrew Woodcock (2020), 'Coronavirus: Matt Hancock urged to improve "trustworthiness" of daily testing figures by UK statistics watchdog', *Independent*, 12 May, www.independent.co.uk/news/uk/politics/coronavirus-uk-tests-matt-hancock-figures-statistics-a9510206.html.

[39] Matthew Weaver (2020), 'UK statistics chief calls for clarity over daily Covid-19 test count', *Guardian*, 12 May, www.theguardian.com/world/2020/may/12/uk-statistics-chief-calls-for-clarity-over-daily-covid-19-test-count.

[40] John Wilson (2015), *Talking with the President*, Oxford: Oxford University Press.

tastes. The left-wing tabloid *Daily Mirror* shows this. Earlier, even before the parliamentary debate, it had published its Hancock shamelessly fiddling figures story. The paper might be all for publishing stories directly accusing the minister of manipulating his metrics, but after Norgrove's letter – nothing.[41]

So, Hancock seemed to have escaped. Norgrove had not mobilised the press to exert political pressure on the minister. There were no equivalents of the 'Watchdog slams Boris' stories which even the *Telegraph* published about Johnson's misuse of statistics.[42] Hancock must have thought that he had escaped lightly. Perhaps for a brief moment he felt untouchable.

Hancock in reply reacted by treating Norgrove's polite but complex diplomatic language as if it were pure and simple friendliness. He thanked Norgrove for his letter 'setting out the importance of clear, open and transparent reporting of statistics on COVID-19 tests' and he declared that 'I strongly support this'.[43] He reacted as if Norgrove's diplomatic praise were literal praise: 'I welcome your positive comments about the information we publish about testing each day'. There is nothing indirect about Hancock's language, as he describes his own performance: 'As you know I have authorised publication of the most full and complete data about our COVID-19 response'.

We see here the weakness of diplomatic language when its recipient is intent on ignoring the code and taking polite expressions as statements of fact. The diplomat might say 'I agree with you in theory' and the determinedly non-diplomatic recipient replies 'I am so pleased that you agree with me'. To say that Hancock used direct language in his reply does not mean that he wrote honestly; nor does it mean that the indirect language of politeness is dishonest. In Norgrove's case, he would have hoped that the minister and his advisors would have picked up the hints about the testing figures being inflated.

There is something curious about Hancock's reply. He waited seventeen days before replying. Of course, being minister of health during a pandemic is a time-demanding job. It would be understandable if replying to the chair of the UKSA were not Hancock's number one priority. Yet, the timing of Hancock's reply seems so fortuitous as to be beyond chance. In the letter, Hancock takes up Norgrove's point that what counts as

[41] For details of the press coverage of Norgrove's letter, see Marinho and Billig (2024).
[42] See Chapter 9.
[43] UK Statistics Authority (2020), 'Response from Matt Hancock to Sir David Norgrove – COVID-19 testing', 28 May, https://uksa.statisticsauthority.gov.uk/correspondence/response-from-matt-hancock-to-sir-david-norgrove-covid-19-testing/.

testing should be clearly stated. He states: 'We are today publishing a clear definition of how our target of capacity to perform 200,000 tests a day by the end of May will be measured and reported'.

Hancock seems to be telling Norgrove to wait for the clear definition that his original letter requested. How long should Norgrove have to wait? He need not wait more than an hour or two, because the information will be published later that very day. If Hancock felt that he could not publicly let Norgrove know the definition before it was published, then he himself could have waited a couple of hours before sending his reply to the UKSA's chair. After all, Hancock had already waited seventeen days to reply. Hancock's letter seems oddly timed, unless he had timed his letter to perfection. He is able to avoid informing Norgrove what the clear defin-ition of the target was, while at the same time he is assuring Norgrove that a definition was so imminent that it had already been formulated.

Hancock was acting like someone who has something to hide. Earlier, we said that a politician can manipulate statistics by manipulating the time when the data is collected. It is the same when trying to persuade critics that their data has not been manipulated. Sometimes a politician might think it advantageous to manipulate the moment when they justify them-selves and their data. But this sort of manipulation sometimes only provides fragile protection.

Norgrove Turning Undiplomatic

Norgrove's second letter, unlike his first, has a conventional first para-graph: 'Thank you for your letter of 27 May, in which you described some welcome, though limited, additions to the official data on COVID-19 tests, including a proposed note on methods (not yet published at the time of writing)'.[44] This opening sentence shows a change from the diplomatic phrasing of Norgrove's first letter. He refers to the additions that have been made as 'welcome', but the praise is then qualified, for, as he puts it, these additions are 'limited'.

The opening sentence contains an implied reproach. Norgrove draws attention to the fact that the methodological note which Hancock said would be published the same day as he had sent his first letter still had not

---

[44] UK Statistics Authority (2020), 'Sir David Norgrove response to Matt Hancock regarding the government's Covid-19 testing data', 2 June, https://uksa.statisticsauthority.gov.uk/correspondence/sir-david-norgrove-response-to-matt-hancock-regarding-the-governments-covid-19-testing-data/.

been published. If Norgrove suspected that Hancock had been playing fast and loose with the simple truth, then mentioning the non-appearing methodological note right at the start should alert Hancock that he is not going to find things quite so easy this time around.

In the opening paragraph, Norgrove sets out why he is replying. The second and final sentence of the paragraph reads: 'I am afraid though that the figures are still far from complete and comprehensible.' His language is far less diplomatic but, as we shall see, he is writing strategically and will be working on behalf of manipulated numbers. Hence, he does not labour his point about the methodological note. It is an oblique reference, placed within brackets. Outsiders might miss its significance, but Hancock, and certainly his advisors, are likely to recognise the tone of irritated reproach.

The rest of the letter is not as diplomatic as his previous letter to Hancock. There are a number of clearly critical comments. Regarding the analysis and presentation of the testing data, 'the aim seems to be to show the largest possible number of tests, even at the expense of understanding'. Coming straight to the point, Norgrove writes:

> the headline total of tests adds together tests *carried out* with tests *posted out*. This distinction is too often elided during the presentation at the daily press conference, where the relevant figure may misleadingly be described simply as the number of tests carried out' [emphases in the original]

Nevertheless, there is still a vestige of diplomacy. Norgrove is raising the serious statistical accusation that Full Fact levelled against Hancock's testing figures right at the start of the incident and that we discussed earlier in this chapter. Full Fact had said that the figure for the overall total tests carried out had been illegitimately boosted. The figure had included tests which private companies had sent to potential patients. There had been no check whether the tests had been returned and analysed – or even if they had been used at all. Norgrove in his letter does not refer to Full Fact, nor explicate exactly what he means when he writes 'the headline total of tests adds together tests *carried out* with tests *posted out*'. He certainly does not say: 'you have manipulated your statistical methodology to increase the number of tests said to have been carried out by adding in tests that were only posted out and never carried out'. Nor does he say that this error is too complicated and too contrary to common sense to just have been an accident.[45]

---

[45] For details, see: Marinho and Billig (2024).

If you look closely at Norgrove's use of language, you can see that he does not directly implicate Hancock in producing and presenting the misleading statistics. He writes abstractly about 'the aim', not 'your aim'. He uses abstract, impersonal language when he writes about the calculation of the total number of tests said to be 'carried out'. He does not say 'you' or 'your statistician' added in tests that were only posted, not actually administered or analysed. Who did the wrongful adding up? It would appear that the numbers did it themselves: it is 'the headline total' that adds 'together tests *carried out* with tests *posted out*'. But of course, the headline total cannot do this: it is produced by the person or persons doing the adding. Norgrove writes that this distinction between tests carried out and those only posted out 'is elided in the daily press conference' and the total may misleadingly be described as the number carried out. Norgrove does not claim 'you elide it in your daily press conference' and 'you describe the figures misleadingly'. It is as if these statistical claims create themselves without ministerial intervention, even seemingly without human intervention: it is the 'headline total' that adds the numbers together. Norgrove knows that numbers are not so talented that they can add themselves up, but he is still being diplomatic.[46]

Norgrove's aim is to persuade Hancock to change the figures for the tests and the way they are presented. Norgrove is aware that Hancock would prefer to stick to the numbers that make him look good. If he is to shift Hancock then he must put pressure on the minister. For that, Norgrove must convince the press that there is an unmissable story.

This he managed to do successfully, for practically every national newspaper – whether left or right, broadsheet or tabloid – carried the story of his second public letter.[47] Norgrove's critical language, unlike his diplomatic language, had caught the press's attention. In their turn, the journalists filled in the major missing detail in the second letter – namely, the absent object of Norgrove's criticism. Hancock's name was in every story and appeared in many of the headlines: the numbers were no longer adding themselves. Moreover, Norgrove had provided key words, phrases and even sentences for the stories. Practically every report in the following

---

[46] In English there are a number of grammatical ways to describe an action being performed without specifying who might have performed it. A speaker/writer might name the action and use it as the subject of a sentence, as if the action itself were the actor; or the speaker/writer might use the passive voice to say that information *was* presented or *was* elided, thereby avoiding having to specify who presented and elided the information. See: Michael Billig (2008), 'The language of critical discourse analysis: the case of nominalization', *Discourse & Society*, 19, 783–800.

[47] For details, see: Marinho and Billig (2024).

day's national newspapers contained quotations from Norgrove's letter. The most quoted statement was: 'the aim seems to be to show the largest possible number of tests, even at the expense of understanding'.

On the other hand, the newspapers provided their own words to describe what it was that Norgrove had delivered to the minister: a 'rebuke' (*Independent*), 'an unusually stern reprimand' (*Financial Times*), a 'damning verdict' (*Mirror*). The *Telegraph* headlined its report 'Matt Hancock under fire over incomprehensible testing targets'. Hancock was the clear loser of that morning's battle for ethos.

The newspapers did not need to decode the meaning of Norgrove's second letter, but they needed to explain who Norgrove was. Some called him 'the statistics watchdog', while others inaccurately but respectfully described him as the nation's 'top statistician'. None questioned his right to make statistical pronouncements. This unfamiliar figure from the back-rooms was the day's hero; Hancock was the familiar villain.

Hancock's Brief and Friendly Reply

Norgrove's second letter and its coverage in the press had an immediate effect. Hancock's second letter to Norgrove was all sweetness and light. It seems the very day that he received Norgrove's letter, Hancock had phoned him to discuss how they could work together.[48] The minister wrote as if the two of them were already on friendly, first-name terms: 'Dear David' and 'Yours ever, Matt'.[49] The tone of Matt's short letter to David was cooperative. He was 'keen for us to work closely with your team on developing the presentation on the range of information we publish'. He continued: 'I've asked my officials to continue to work with you on improving the presentation of these [the testing numbers]'.

At first sight, this looks like a victory for Norgrove and his strategic thinking. His shift from diplomatic to direct language had paid dividends. This became particularly apparent two months later when the government website issued a long, somewhat technical announcement about changes to its methodology for counting Covid tests. The changes included an 'all tests processed' measure that specifically excluded tests that had only been

---

[48] UK Statistics Authority (2020), 'Matt Hancock's reply to Sir David Norgrove', 11 June, https://uksa.statisticsauthority.gov.uk/correspondence/matt-hancock-response-to-sir-david-norgrove/.
[49] For details, see Billig and Marinho (2023).

sent out.[50] This, of course, was a major demand not just of Norgrove but also of Hancock's parliamentary critics and, before them, Full Fact.

As well as introducing the new measure, and thereby contracting the category of 'tests carried out', the announcement said that 'an adjustment' had been made to existing calculations of Covid testing. It would seem that Norgrove had successfully stood up to the power of the minister, who was now backing down. But politicians do not switch off their politics easily. The announcement of the new measurement and the statistical 'adjustment' was very low key. Nothing was mentioned at the daily press conference. The information came in the middle of a longer technical website posting. The word 'reduction' was not used. It was merely: 'An adjustment of -1,308,071 has been made to the historic data'.

Imagine if the minister had discovered that there had been a miscalculation and that statisticians had underestimated, not overestimated, the testing figures by the same number. It is hard to believe that the government would have hidden away the new number, nor that the recalculation would be neutrally called an 'adjustment', nor that it would be merely a 'historic' number. The rhetoric of 'increase', 'success' and 'more than a million' would have been to the fore, and the press would have been alerted. Instead, what we see is a textbook example of how to bury an inconvenient number.[51]

With the total number of Covid tests being substantially reduced, Hancock's great testing achievement would be under threat. It should have been so simple to inspect the relevant figures. One might think that it would not be technically difficult to reduce an overall total for each day. But now it had become impossible. But now it had become impossible because there were unlabelled data columns with different numbers but the same labels. As investigators, both of us authors looked independently at the data, and neither of us could interpret it. Nor could we find or even calculate a figure for the day which Hancock had previously declared as his great testing triumph.

Hancock, in his second letter, might have written that he would be consulting the UKSA to improve the presentation of the Covid testing data. However, the presentation of the data for Hancock's pivotal day conveniently worsened. And he did not request assistance to make it

---

[50] For details and analysis of the announcement, see Billig (2021). The announcement was made on the government website on 14 August 2020, www.gov.uk/government/publications/coronavirus-covid-19-testing-data-methodology/covid-19-testing-data-methodology-note. This page is no longer available.

[51] For more details of the way that the revised figures were buried, see Billig (2021).

clearer. Hancock's publicly expressed wish for statistical transparency had self-interested limits.

Manipulating Numbers, Concepts and the Past

Hancock had every reason to feel politically insecure. Just over a year after his seemingly conciliatory letter to Norgrove, he was forced to resign his post in disgrace and Johnson did little to save him.[52] Hancock had broken the Covid regulations that were in force at that time. These were to limit socialising to within one's own family. At work Hancock had met someone who was not part of his own household, and he was photographically caught socialising with her in an intimate manner. The public were reacting fiercely against politicians who were not keeping to the strict rules that they were imposing on the rest of the country. In Hancock's case, there was added scandal: it was his mistress whom he was meeting intimately in his office. There was scant sympathy for Hancock as his marriage and political career imploded simultaneously.[53]

The example of Hancock shows that statistical manipulation is not necessarily something that stands on its own, but someone who engages in one form of manipulation is likely to engage in other forms. The hunger of politicians for recognition or the hunger to be right all the time can lead them to manipulate people, facts and facts about people. More than this, when a manipulator like Hancock seeks to justify manipulation, they can find themselves manipulating the past and other matters besides.

Norgrove believed that Hancock deliberately distorted his testing figures. Normally chairs of the UKSA, whatever their private beliefs, do not make public their views on the dishonesty of politicians. Norgrove,

---

[52] For Hancock's resignation letter, written on 26 June 2021, see: https://assets.publishing.service.gov .uk/government/uploads/system/uploads/attachment_data/file/997053/Letter_from_Matt_ Hancock.pdf.

[53] During the Covid crisis Stephen Reicher, a noted social psychologist, sat on the committee that advised the British government about the relevant evidence from the behavioural sciences. Reicher has written about the discrepancy between the evidence that the public generally kept to the rules, often at considerable personal cost to themselves, and the government's continuing failure to trust the public on this matter. This discrepancy could well be a factor in both the government's willingness to break its own rules and the public's outrage when this was revealed to have occurred. For Reicher's insights on the government's misunderstanding of the public, see: Stephen Reicher (2023), 'Amid the drama of the Covid inquiry, Chris Whitty quietly pointed to an important truth. Will anyone listen?', *Guardian*, 24 November, www.theguardian.com/ commentisfree/2023/nov/24/covid-inquiry-chris-whitty-ignorance-psychology; Stephen Reicher (2022), 'In pretending that Covid is over, the UK government is playing a dangerous game', *Guardian*, 5 July, www.theguardian.com/commentisfree/2022/jul/05/pretending-covid-over-uk- government-virus-risk-public-health-measures.

however, spoke about his experiences with Hancock in a lecture that he gave in October 2021 at University College London. The topic was 'Covid and the use and abuse of statistics'. Norgrove's tenure as chair of the UKSA had less than six months to run and perhaps he felt that the constraints of his position were easing.

In the lecture, he talked about the minister of health's method of counting Covid tests by including tests which had merely been sent out. Norgrove described this as 'poor practice, to say the least'. He complained that, following his letter to the minister, it took so long for the figures to be corrected. Leaving behind any coded words of diplomacy, Norgrove went on to say that this was the one case that he could think of during the Covid crisis when 'the data were deliberately distorted'.[54]

Nevertheless, it is not just Norgrove's views on Hancock that illustrate how different forms of manipulating can become interconnected. Hancock's views on Norgrove reveal this too, perhaps even more starkly. After he was forced out of office, Hancock was determined to present his views on the pandemic, for he believed he had things of great importance to say and that these should be made into a book. This became *Pandemic Diaries*, which he produced with the right-wing journalist Isabel Oakeshott. The book was published in late 2022 and received almost uniformly bad reviews.[55] Hancock was much mocked for grandiosely claiming to have foreseen practically everything of significance about the pandemic.

The reviewer in the *Guardian* noted something very odd about the book. Hancock was calling his book a diary but it lacked the distinguishing characteristics of a diary. Political diaries tend to be written by political protagonists who record their thoughts and feelings when the events are actually unfolding. Diaries are not written after the events have happened – those are memoirs or histories. Nor are diaries written by hired ghost-writers. As the *Guardian's* reviewer noted, 'assembled after the fact, these "diaries" strain the usual definition'.[56] Some habits are hard to break. No longer possessing the political power to stretch concepts such as 'new

---

[54] UK Statistics Authority (2021), 'Sir David Norgrove speaks at University College London: Covid and the use and abuse of statistics', 28 October, https://uksa.statisticsauthority.gov.uk/news/sir-david-norgrove-speaks-at-university-college-london-covid-and-the-use-and-abuse-of-statistics/.

[55] Matt Hancock with Isabel Oakeshott (2022), *Pandemic Diaries: the Inside Story of Britain's Battle Against Covid*, London: Biteback.

[56] Gaby Hinsliff (2022), '"Pandemic Diaries" by Matt Hancock review – rewriting history', *Guardian*, 13 December, www.theguardian.com/books/2022/dec/13/pandemic-diaries-by-matt-hancock-review-rewriting-history.

hospitals' or 'Covid tests carried out', Hancock was now stretching the concept of 'a diary'.

In his *Diaries* Hancock presents himself as someone who is deeply concerned with the accuracy of statistics. In the entry given for 24 December 2020 he complains about Boris Johnson yet again giving out inaccurate statistics, this time inflating figures for the number of vaccinations administered. Hancock fears that he will be blamed for the exaggeration. He does not specifically talk about his public correspondence with the UKSA's chair, but he does mention that 'the statistics regulator' Sir David Norgrove 'frequently' rebuked him. This was so unfair, he writes, 'because I've fought hard to maintain the accuracy of statistics'.

If Hancock believed that his statistics were basically accurate, then there must be some other reason why Norgrove would have 'frequently' criticised him. Hancock has a theory. Norgrove 'seems to hate Boris', and had not forgiven the prime minister for his 'notorious "£350 million more for the NHS" claim'. Therefore, Norgrove was only getting at Hancock as a way of getting at Johnson: 'I really resent being caught in the crossfire'.[57]

Hancock's self-serving explanation is implausible because it omits key elements of the story. For example, he does not mention that Norgrove initially wrote to him diplomatically, seeking to work cooperatively with Hancock in order to resolve specific statistical problems that had already been aired in Parliament. Nor does Hancock mention that he ignored this diplomatic approach. There is a further omission: Hancock does not say why, after the second letter, he was more than willing to work with Norgrove and why he agreed in the end to reduce substantially the total number of tests carried out.

Hancock's account fits a wider pattern – members of a government blaming statistical regulators or other trained statisticians for finding faults with governmental statistics. In broad outlines, it resembles Trump complaining about fake media which, so he claims, creates the statistics that he doesn't like and which criticises the statistics that he does like. According to Hancock, it's because Norgrove hates Johnson that he criticises blameless Hancock. Norgrove must be a phoney regulator: surely no properly independent statistician could have anything but praise for Hancock's continual striving to be statistically accurate. There is, however, a key difference between the political culture that surrounds Trump and that surrounding Hancock. Trump and his opponents have no independent statistical authority to which all can appeal and whose competence is

---

[57] Hancock with Oakeshott (2022), p. 251.

basically trusted by almost all. For Trump, any producer, regulator or analyst of statistics can, if the occasion demands it, be called a phoney.

Hancock, in his self-justification, omitted to mention something politically, personally and statistically significant. When the newspapers reported Norgrove's rebuke, almost without exception every paper cast its story as the respected watchdog admonishing the politician's dubious numbers. Hancock does not say why even much of the right-wing press failed to take his side. It cannot all be blamed on Norgrove's supposed hatred of Johnson. It is more plausible to suppose that the regulator and the press questioned Hancock's claims not because they all hated his political boss but, quite simply, because neither he nor his numbers could be trusted.

CHAPTER 11

Final Comments

Underlying this book there have been two questions, both of which are contained in its overall title: how do politicians manipulate statistics and how can they be stopped from doing so? It would be good if we could now announce that, after all the earlier chapters, we have arrived at a point where we can give clear, definitive answers to both questions; and that, in consequence, we are standing close to solving the serious, worldwide problem of politicians manipulating statistics. Sadly, if a simple, guaranteed solution does exist, then we must confess that our skills as investigators fall well short of discovering it.

So, in this final chapter we are not going to make big claims. We have not discovered an infallible method for determining exactly when politicians have been manipulating statistics and when they have not been. Sometimes, it is easier to spot cases of political manipulation, and sometimes more difficult. Throughout the book we have tried to work with examples where the manipulation is clear – but often the manipulation only becomes clear after the details have been closely examined. Since most actual acts of statistical manipulation occur out of public sight, in many instances the details can only be guessed at. So, there might be many more cases, especially of attempted but unsuccessful manipulation, that never come to light.

Nor have we been able to propose a strategy that would be guaranteed to prevent the sort of cases that we have been examining. We cannot say what the Russian people could have done to prevent Stalin from manipulating his census and murdering his statisticians; nor can we say with any certainty what would have stopped the democratically elected Greek government from falsifying its debt figures and from prosecuting the chief statistician who wanted to produce as accurate numbers as he could. And what strategy could we possibly recommend that would persuade Donald Trump to cease claiming that honest numbers, such as the Bureau of Labor Statistics unemployment figures, were phoney and that his own numbers, especially those relating to his presidential defeat, were honest? Trump remains far too convinced of the rightness of his own views to be persuaded by mere statistical calculations or technical matters of methodology.

In this final chapter, we hope to draw together some of our preceding themes, in order to say something about the statistical heroes and villains of today. Two of the themes refer to the nature of statistics. First, as we have said again and again, despite its mathematical nature statistics is not a precise science. The measurement of large-scale social phenomena, such as the cost of living, the rate of unemployment, the number of crimes committed and so on, is never absolutely correct. Complex phenomena are changing all the time, and as they change so they need to be measured in changing ways.[1] Statisticians are always running to keep up with the present, and they should not be overconfident that they know how to measure the future. The problem is that unscrupulous politicians will try to exploit the uncertainties of statistics for their own benefit.

The second theme relates to the consequences of statistics being imprecise. Even if perfection is not possible on this side of statistical heaven, this does not mean that all measures are equally inaccurate. It is still possible to identify some measures as being worse than others and others as better. Where two or more measures are available, we cannot trust our politicians always to cite the most accurate ones. What they should not do, but which too many do, is to flit between measures, citing whichever measure happens to produce the most politically advantageous data at that moment.

In these closing pages we will say some brief words about why the manipulation of statistics may be a special danger nowadays. This will take us back to the very start of this book. Our opening chapter began with the problem that more and more people seem to be distrusting politicians. If they distrust politicians, then they will distrust the numbers that they spout to support their politics. The distrust of politics creates conditions that the statistical manipulators can exploit, but it also creates opportunities for new heroes to oppose and expose them.

Knowledge and Power

We have assumed that very few government ministers have the time, knowledge or energy to design and conduct their own data-gathering

---

[1] For a good discussion of this problem see: Georgina Sturge (2022), *Bad Data*, London: Bridge Street Press, chapter 4.

exercises. They rely on the services of their professional statisticians to do this for them. In an ideal world, the statisticians would refuse to conduct surveys or use measures that compromise the integrity of the data. But the world of politics is far from ideal. Ministers tend to be endowed, even overendowed, with interpersonal and persuasive skills, but not with numerical ones. In consequence, they might try to manipulate their statisticians to manipulate the statistics for them. We have offered examples of this happening, showing that usually the process involves complex and interrelated series of actions.

The manipulation of statisticians will not generally be visibly performed in front of the public. However, what happens behind closed doors does not always stay behind closed doors. The manipulative behaviour of ministers can become public knowledge, especially if the statisticians object to the way they are being treated. We presented the stories of senior Greek and Argentinian statisticians. They told the public how manipulative government ministers were threatening them with serious consequences if they did not covertly manipulate the country's statistics.

Not all the manipulation of statisticians is as extreme as the Greek and Argentinian situations. Sometimes, the manipulation is inbuilt into the culture where the official statisticians are working. We have discussed the situation of statisticians in British government ministries – doing the minister's bidding can be a good career move. We retold some of René Padieu's indiscrete anecdotes about senior ministers and statisticians in France. Padieu, an academic philosopher of statistics, spoke about ministers putting pressure on statisticians to change the way they were collecting data. As in the Greek and Argentinian cases, French ministers would appeal to the statisticians' patriotism: you would be acting in the best interests of our country, they would say, equating their own political interests with those of their nation.

Padieu's anecdotes are much more than *amuse-bouches* in the dry texts of statistical philosophy. They give substance to a very serious point: namely that the corruption of statistics is not confined to autocracies, but is also an ever-present danger in democracies. Wherever there is political power, governments will try to exert it to produce the numbers that suit their political interests. There is, according to Padieu, the continual possibility of conflict between power and knowledge – between *le pouvoir* and *la connaissance*. In his view, statistics most definitely is the sort of knowledge that routinely clashes with power. We have taken up Padieu's basic point, not least because it suggests what might be done to curb the power of governments that manipulate their statisticians into manipulating statistics.

Even if most politicians lack numerical skills, they do not lack verbal ones. This is important because statistics never comprises just numbers. Numbers need to be labelled and some labels carry political and moral implications. There are inevitably gaps between numbers and words; and politicians can seek to exploit these gaps. We have given examples of the various ways that politicians have manipulated statistics by manipulating the labels to affix to the numbers. For example, we saw how the French minister of the interior, Gérald Darmanin misused numbers to justify repeating claims most commonly associated with the extreme right.

In Britain, Boris Johnson and members of his government also manipulated numbers by manipulating language. When claiming to be meeting their target for building new hospitals, they counted as 'a new hospital' a new building which was built on an existing hospital site, or even a refurbishment of an old building. The prime minister claimed to have reduced crime, but that was only true if computer and other white-collar crimes were not counted as crimes. And so on.

The lesson is simple: politicians who have cavalier attitudes towards truthful telling are not suddenly transformed into being fussily fair and acutely accurate when it comes to describing numbers – unless, of course, it happens to be in their interest. There is a further implication: there are infinite ways of manipulating language. For that reason, there would have been little point in trying to compile a complete list of the ways statistics can be manipulated, because it would always be incomplete. Rather than having a falsely complete list, it is better to be ready to react to a new twist of a political manipulator's creative imagination.

Authority and Strategy

In the second part of the book, we looked at one way to discourage democratically elected governments from acting as if they owned their country's official statistics. This is to establish independent agencies to regulate the quality of official statistics. Our models have been the United Kingdom Statistics Authority (UKSA) and the French Authority for Public Statistics (ASP). Both authorities were legally established by politicians to make it more difficult for fellow politicians to freely manipulate official statistics.

These statistical authorities possess no legal powers to prosecute those who manipulate statistics, and no powers to forbid governments from publishing statistics that fail to meet due statistical standards. They can only operate by persuasion and that means persuading politicians and the public. In order to be persuasive, the authorities and their representatives must appear to be completely independent and above the political fray. Any recommendations or criticisms that they issue must not only be based on statistical considerations, they must also be seen to be based on the numbers.

Nevertheless, the statistical authorities have to operate in contexts that are intensely political. This has led them to be strategic in the ways they express their judgements. They will tend to speak and write using diplomatic language. We have commented upon a linguistic curiosity. Although the French and British authorities seek to expose statistical manipulation, they do this without officially using the word 'manipulation'. The coincidence between the French and British authorities is too striking to be chance, and we have sought to explain why avoiding the m-word brings them strategic benefits.

The big issue is not the use or non-use of one particular word, but it is something much more basic. It relates to Padieu's idea of a confrontation between power and knowledge: how can regulators ensure that their knowledge prevails over power? It seems that the odds are stacked in power's favour. However, as we have seen, knowledge can prevail within a political culture that distrusts politicians and respects regulators. For statistical knowledge to prevail regularly, the role of the press and other media is crucial.

This has emerged in what we have called our 'biographical chapters', especially in the chapters that looked at two statistical offenders: Darmanin and Johnson. Both tried to ignore regulators and to devalue statistics. Johnson, in particular, has a long history of ignoring, resisting and even insulting the UKSA and its chairs. More generally his government sought to undermine the power of Britain's regulatory bodies.[2] Britain has numerous regulatory bodies, which operate nationally to preserve standards in a wide variety of cultural, economic and professional areas. It is hard to say quite how many regulatory bodies there are in Britain. Even the National Audit Office, the regulatory body with the task of scrutinising

---

[2] Andrew Blick and Peter Hennessy have argued strongly that the Johnson government posed a threat to the British constitution: Andrew Blick and Peter Hennessy (2019), *Good Chaps No More? Safeguarding the Constitution in Stressful Times*, Report of Constitution Society, pp. 15f, https://consoc.org.uk/wp-content/uploads/2019/11/FINAL-Blick-Hennessy-Good-Chaps-No-More.pdf. See also their specific discussion of the Johnson government's threat to the independence of British regulatory bodies: Andrew Blick and Peter Hennessy (2022), *The Bonfire of the Decencies*, London: Haus Publishing, pp. 44ff.

public spending, was imprecise about the number of such bodies in its published *Guide to Regulation*.[3]

Basically, politicians like Darmanin and Johnson rarely prevail over regulatory bodies. In a conflict between a politician and a regulator, the default option for members of the public in Britain and France is to trust the regulator and distrust the politician. When reporting such clashes, newspapers will tend to publish default option stories. In Britain, the regulator, regardless of what is being regulated, will be portrayed as the 'watchdog' which is protecting, or doggedly watching over, the nation. So, when Johnson clashed with the chair of the UKSA, he was met with a barrage of 'watchdog slams/reprimands/rebukes Boris' stories. Even newspapers that generally supported Johnson were unable to resist the attractions of such headlines. In the French press, the equivalent story is about national statisticians criticising/correcting ministers for their misuse of national statistics.

To use Padieu's sort of terminology, knowledge tends to defeat power in this battle for ethos. This is a battle that can be decided in the morning's headlines. We can be sure that politicians do not enjoy such defeats, especially in newspapers that they consider to be their friends. In the previous chapter, we saw a government minister backing down after facing fierce 'watchdog rebukes minister' stories in the papers. The stories followed a public letter from the UKSA's chair. Knowledge was again defeating power.

If the statistical regulators take the plumes of victory in this battle for ethos, then this is not because of their personal reputations or because newspapers editors have carefully assessed the statistical strengths and weaknesses of the particular issue. It is because of the strategic thinking of regulators. To successfully oppose power with knowledge, regulators must know more than their specialist expertise. They must also know, metaphorically speaking, how to bark like a watchdog.

Making an Exception of America

There were no equivalents of the UKSA and the ASP in either Greece or Argentina when the senior statisticians were being threatened. There was no legally established, independent regulator to whom the statisticians could appeal for protection and justice. And there certainly was none in

---

[3] National Audit Office (2017), 'A short guide to regulation', www.nao.org.uk/wp-content/uploads/2017/09/A-Short-Guide-to-Regulation.pdf.

Stalin's Russia, just as there is none in today's China. The supposedly independent body for Chinese statistics regularly proclaims its allegiance to the leader and the Party.

Most disturbingly, the United States has no equivalent statistical body, which might be trusted to adjudicate disputes about counting voting figures or calculating employment statistics. Instead everyone claims an equal right to have and express their opinion even on technical issues that they know little or nothing about. And that includes the president. In short, the country has no established culture of national regulators. There may be some national bodies that are generally respected, and also some local ones, but there is little widespread call for more national regulation. Perhaps the country is too large for such a culture, and too committed historically to the rights of individual states. Certainly at present it is too divided. There has been a historic distrust of central, Washington-based government. If there are to be regulators, then individual states might prefer to have their own, rather than rely on a central body. Then, there would be a multiplicity of statistical authorities, each voicing its own judgement. We cannot tell what might happen in the future, but the present signs are not auspicious.

We have had occasion to refer to Hannah Arendt and her argument, which she formulated while living in the States, that democracy requires shared facts. If everything becomes an opinion then democracy is weakened and liable to implode.[4] It is as if Arendt were foreseeing a president who would turn the counting of presidential votes into a matter of opinion. If something as straightforward, and as crucial for democracy, as counting votes is an opinion, then there is little hope for sharing more nuanced statistics about social trends and social policies. Numerical battles will be fought in the so-called culture wars.

In these disputes it is just your word against mine, and mine, because it is mine, is right. When the battling opinions become soaked in the rhetoric of nationalism, the danger is doubled. It is your word against mine; and for the sake of our great country, everyone should recognise my word as the voice of patriotism and yours as the voice of betrayal. Such a cultural climate is not a happy ground for breeding statistical watchdogs. Everyone will want their own watchdog; and my hound will bark like a true patriot and yours will squeal like a traitor.

---

[4] Hannah Arendt (1967/1977), 'Truth and Politics', in Hannah Arendt, *Between Past and Future*, Harmondsworth: Penguin, pp. 223–59.

Heroes and Villains

This book has thrown up its own heroes and villains. By writing biographical chapters and chapters investigating named individuals involved in specific incidents, we have encouraged the emergence of heroes and villains from around the world. The villains are politicians who manipulate, lie and bully; the heroes are statisticians and public officials who resist them. We have not based our later chapters on social trends that might themselves be examined numerically. Instead, we have directly examined incidents and people's motives; and, in this respect at least, the book has strong psychological themes.

The biographical chapters are based around predictable villains – Trump, Johnson and Darmanin. Almost inevitably, those who oppose the efforts of villains to manipulate official statistics will appear by contrast as heroes. These include the senior officers responsible for running elections in the state of Georgia; the heads of the statistical authorities in Britain and France; and the persecuted senior statisticians Andreas Georgiou and Gabriela Bevacqua, working respectively in Greece and Argentina. These heroes tend not to fit the heroic mould. Essentially, they are backroom figures, spending their time working in their offices, attending meetings and writing reports.

The earlier historical chapters also threw up some heroes, most notably Adolphe Quetelet, William Farr and Florence Nightingale. They would seem to be appropriate heroic figures. Today, as social scientists, we prefer our heroes to have endured great sufferings and deprivations, or to have written bold, enduring works, especially books expressing radical philosophies. William Farr, emerging from humble origins but banging his head on a concrete ceiling, fits the first type; and Quetelet, the prodigy with great works of astronomy, statistics and sociology to his credit, fits the second.

As for Nightingale, she was an acknowledged hero in her own times, but for her nursing work rather than for her campaigning statistics. As a woman her achievements as a statistician were more unlikely in the nineteenth century than her heroism as a nurse. Nightingale's fame as a nurse has persisted to this day, at least in Britain. And so has her anonymity as a statistician. How many students of the behavioural sciences, taking an introductory course in statistics, will hear mention of her name? As the importance of computer-assisted statistics has grown, so also the fame of Quetelet and Farr has faded.

Our new heroic figures are the statisticians and statistical officials who stand up to power. This includes Brad Raffensperger, Georgia's secretary of state who resisted the demands and threats of the US president and refused to find him the extra presidential votes that he demanded. In today's political climate, the backroom officials often have to operate against the mega-personalities of elected leaders – against the Trumps and Johnsons of this world, who use their charisma to bully and manipulate. These politicians are populists who are so supremely confident of their personal abilities that they will magic up their own numbers to suit their own purposes. Would-be populists like Darmanin will not let statistics and its professional authorities stand in the way of the upward-rising graph that represents their success story.

It is sometimes said that we are living in a 'post-truth' era, in which truth and shared facts are secondary to personality and emotional appeal. This is the political climate that Arendt feared because it encourages the growth of political authoritarianism.[5] The notion of 'post-truth' is more than a purely academic concept because it has gained wider traction. In 2016, the year of Trump's presidential victory and the year of Brexit, it was the Oxford Dictionary's word of the year. The Dictionary said that although the word had been in existence for the previous decade, it was 2016 when its usage showed 'a spike in frequency'.[6]

In an era that seems to be made for those politicians with stage-strutting mega-personalities, the public servants who seek to maintain honest statistics and accurate vote counting are the sort of unheroic bureaucrats who do their work out of public sight. We have written about the actions of the chairs of the UKSA and the presidents of the ASP. We will happily admit our ignorance: we know nothing about their personalities. We only know of them through official documents. If any of them were to sit opposite us on a train, we would not recognise them and we would miss the opportunity to ask them about their professional lives.

These public servants are not public celebrities, but they would not be able to act so effectively against personality-driven manipulators if they were known as the big egos of the statistical world. They are backroom types, acting in the public world to ensure the integrity of public statistics. Typically, the top figure in the British statistical authority is appointed not

[5] See, for example, Lee McIntyre (2017), *Post-Truth*, Cambridge, MA: MIT Press; Lee McIntyre (2021), 'The hidden dangers of fake news in post-truth politics', *Revue internationale de philosophie*, 297, 113–24.

[6] Oxford Languages (2016), 'Word of the year 2016', https://languages.oup.com/word-of-the-year/2016/; see also: Alison Flood (2016), '"Post-truth" named word of the year by Oxford Dictionaries', *Guardian*, 15 November, www.theguardian.com/books/2016/nov/15/post-truth-named-word-of-the-year-by-oxford-dictionaries.

just for their familiarity with numbers but also for their experience as a senior civil servant in liaising with other senior civil servants and, most importantly, for their experience in dealing with difficult politicians. When the newspapers in Britain have lined up behind the 'nation's statistical watchdog' in the various conflicts with Johnson and his ministers, the reporters always had to explain who David Norgrove and Andrew Dilnot were. The editors and their writers were aware that those names would mean nothing to the overwhelming majority of their readers. The tabloids had no readily recognisable nicknames to use in their headlines: no 'Numbers Norgrove', no 'Big Data Dilnot' who was rebuking 'Boris' once again.

It is hard to imagine public figures with greyer personae. Not since Florence Nightingale have statistical heroes had heart-stopping back stories. Our heroes tend to be mostly, but certainly not exclusively, male members of the professional upper-middle class. Like the senior election administrators in the US, they are generally well paid. The present and past chairs of the UKSA have all been knighted; the non-executive members of the board hold a glittering collection of honours, awards and professorships.[7]

The presidents of the ASP in France tend to be similar although they may have more academic publications than the chairs of the UKSA. But the number of these post-holders is small – at the time of writing there have only been four chairs of the UKSA and three presidents of the ASP. The current president of the ASP is Mireille Elbaum. She had a notable academic career which includes a substantial book about political economy.[8] In terms of celebrity, none of the eight even make the D list. They can travel on trains without other passengers asking them to pose for selfies.

All this talk about the statistical agencies being led by heroes may give the wrong impression. It is as if the only heroes are the leaders. However, these new heroes are heads of teams and their teams should be considered just as heroic, and sometimes they can be even more heroic than their leaders. In the old days, the census data could not have been collected, analysed and presented without large numbers of employees, whose names never appeared in any of the reports. It is the same for the modern regulatory agencies, although their bureaucracies tend to be far smaller. The Erlbaums, Norgroves, Humphersons and so on could not perform

---

[7] Professor Sir David Spiegelhalter, probably Britain's most distinguished statistician, is a non-executive member. For a full list of the UKSA's executive and non-executive board members, see: UK Statistics Authority, https://uksa.statisticsauthority.gov.uk/the-authority-board/.

[8] Mireille Elbaum (2011), *Économie politique de la protection sociale*, Paris: Presses Universitaires de France. For Elbaum's academic publications, see: www.cairn.info/publications-de-Mireille-Elbaum–21530.htm; www.lesbiographies.com/Biographie/ELBAUM-Mireille,10415.

their heroic acts of resistance without the efforts and support of those unnamed statisticians and modern clerks who continuously check, calculate and corroborate the figures. These employees, unnamed in official reports and letters, will assist in preparing the numbers and statistical interpretations that their named seniors will publicly use. The whole success of statistical regulation depends on heroic sub-heroes who are never likely to receive honours, awards or great remuneration.

On some decisive occasions, it is the sub-heroes who have shown the way and provided the leaders with the examples to follow. We have described two such incidents in the history of the French statistical authority, when the resolve to oppose a senior politician came from the ordinary statisticians rather than from the top. This first happened when the minister of the interior was misusing statistics in order to claim that the children of immigrant parents were failing disastrously at school. The directors of INSEE and the ASP were hanging back, reluctant to enter the fierce public controversy. But the ordinary statisticians, supported by their trade unions, rebelled and made a public stance. They were giving their workplace superiors a lesson in how to resist power. Ten years later, it happened again. Top-level statisticians were hesitating, this time when facing Darmanin. Once again the ordinary statisticians turned to their unions, and they gave their leaders a revision lesson.

The executive directors of the French and British statistical authorities, together with their statistical teams, may be the ideal figures to combat the dangers of 'post-truth' politicians. The statisticians do not propose alternative truths to counteract the semi-truths and simplified slogans of populist leaders. The statisticians are well aware that absolute statistical perfection is not possible and that measures of complex social phenomena will have their imperfections. On the other hand, this does not mean that all statistical claims are equally valid. Many of the regulators' statistical judgements against politicians are based on pointing out the limitations of statistical claims. Statisticians will know that some claims are more plausible than others and some measures have more obvious imperfections than other measures. No absolute number might be attainable – even when doing something as straightforward as counting votes. However, admitting a plausible error in the region of under a hundred votes is very different from claiming that a whole election has been deliberately rigged and that millions of votes have simply disappeared.

We should distrust the boastful claims of politicians who have a reputation for making misleading statements. Now is a time when we need awkwardly stubborn non-heroes. Statistical regulators can and often do point out that there are different ways of measuring crime rates, but politicians should not just select one measure, especially if that measure produces the numbers that they like. As we mentioned earlier, measures relying on police recordings of crime measure rates of crime less accurately than measures based on well-conducted surveys, although neither measure is, or could be, perfect. However good a measure is, there is always room for improvement.

By their training and professional practice, statistical regulators are certainly not post-error. They are rather like practical Popperians in their professional procedures. Karl Popper was a committed believer in scientific progress but he distrusted the idea that science was based on finding and accumulating absolute truths. He claimed that science progresses through refutation and showing that some claims are less accurate than others.[9] Similarly, the statistical regulators are committed believers in statistics and they believe that statistical progress needs to be based on discovering the weaknesses of overconfident claims especially overconfident dismissals of statistics in general.

When times change, then societies and international organisations may need different types of heroes who are suitable for the moment. In the modern era, politicians with ever-expandable egos should be seen to constitute the danger, not the hope. Certainly, we cannot trust the numbers that politicians are constantly tossing our way, especially those politicians who are trading on possessing authentic, anti-political mega-personalities. They present themselves as politicians who can be trusted because they are not like the ordinary politicians who cannot be. But, in terms of statistics and other matters they can be especially untrustworthy.

Now is a time when we need awkwardly stubborn heroes who will resist the power of personality with calm arguments. It is also an appropriate moment to admire the example of those politicians who gave away political power in order to establish the statistical agencies. In present times the old values of public service can seem hopelessly low key, politically unambitious and well out of date. Yet, in times of uncertainty there is all the more reason to cling to the notion of demonstrable error, rather than provable truth.

In that light, we should be thanking non-heroic heroes for honest efforts to expose statistical untruth. They are, indeed, modern watchdogs who fulfil a vital function. They do not guard absolute truths, as if they are prowling the perimeters of sacred temples. Instead, they offer a limited but invaluable protection against political leaders who seek to charm the public with dazzling words and manipulated numbers.

---

[9] Karl Popper (1972), *Conjectures and Refutations*, London: Routledge and Kegan Paul.

Index

Als, Georges, chief Luxembourg statistician, 129
Arendt, Hannah, 42, 59, 67, 88, 90, 102, 247
Argentina, 109–15
  American Statistical Association (ASA),
    support for Bevacqua, 113
  Bevacqua, Graciela, 109–13
  Carriquiry, Alicia, writing about Bevacqua,
    110
  Cavallo, Alberta, Billion Prices Project, 113
  consumer price index, 110–12
  Instituto Nacional de Estadística y Censos
    (INDEC), 94, 109, 111
  Kirchner, Nestor, 110
  Moreno, Guillermo, minister for domestic
    trade, 110–15

Best, Joel, 2, 6, 24, 63
Blair, Tony, UK prime minister, 126
Brexit Bonus Survey, 43–5
Brown, Gordon, UK chancellor and prime
  minister, 127, 132

Cairo, Alberto, *How Charts Lie*, 46
Campbell's law, 23–5, 58, 63, 105, 222
China, People's Republic of, 104–9
  China Daily, 106–8
  National Bureau of Statistics (NBS), 93,
    104–9
  political targets, assessment of, 107–9
  statistical fabrication, 106–7
Chote, Sir Robert, fourth chair of the UKSA, 215
cohabitation, ministers and statisticians, 129,
  134, 153, 156
conspiracy theories of statistics
  Binney, Bill, 78–9
  Jones, Alex, 65–6
  Kirk, Charlie, 79
crime rates, 177–9, 197–200, 209–11

D'Éstaing, Giscard, French president, 151
Danziger, Roni, studies of political flattery, 67

Darmanin, Gérald, 169–88
  ASP, reaction to Darmanin, 184
  ASP, relations with, 171–2
  crime rates and victimation, 177–9, 186
  critical, attitude towards, 183
  ensauvagement, use of word, 174–9, 183
  immigration, views on, 174–7
  L'Express interview, 179–84
  minister of the interior, appointment, 172
  political background, 172
  presidential ambitions, 173
  sexual offences, accused of, 186–8
  statistics, critical attitude towards, 174, 185
  Tourcoing and its butchers, 181–6
deception, active and passive, 60
Diamond, Sir Ian, UK national statistician, 48–9
Dilnot, Sir Andrew, second chair of the UKSA,
  202–3
diplomatic language, function of, 135–8,
  226–30, 233–4, 245
diplomatic language, linguistic features, 225–9

elections, manipulation of, 42
Erlbaum, Mireille, president of ASP, 250
ethos, battle for, 170, 191, 201–3

fact checkers
  Factcheck, 86
  Full Fact, 143–4, 212–14, 221
  PolitiFact, 72, 75–6
  Washington Post, fact-check team, 63, 71, 79,
    138
Farr, William, 19–27, 248
  early life, 19
  Nightingale, Florence, collaboration, 25–7
  statistical nosology, 20–3
  vital statistics, 19
flattery, political, 67–8
France, Authority for Public Statistics (ASP),
  145–68
  ASP foundation, 146–9

France, Authority for Public Statistics (ASP) (cont.)
ASP, *Ten Years in Service*, 148, 156, 158
ASP's Avis, 155
Bureau, Dominique, president of ASP, 148, 161–2
Cuneo, Philippe, 148–9
educational achievement and immigration, 163–7
European Code of Practice, 147–8
independence, importance of, 147, 155–6
manipulation, avoidance of word, 157–9
manipulation, use of word, 159–62
Ministerial Statistical Services (SSM), inspections of, 153–9
public controversies, mode of operation, 162–6
Statistical Independence Seminar, 2008, 149
France, National Institute for Statistics and Economic Studies (INSEE), 146, 150, 160, 163–7, 177, 179, 185
fraud, scientific, 58
French Statistical Society, 149–50

Galton, Sir Francis, racist statistics, 33–5
Gilbert, Laura, director of data science, 208–9, 212
Great Britain, development of public statistics census, 30
General Register Office, 16
registrar general, 16, 20, 22, 27, 30
Registration Act 1836, 16–17
Greece, 115–21
EU and Eurozone applications, 116–18
EU checking Greek statistics, 116–18
Georgiou, Andreas, chief statistician, 115, 118–20
government manipulation of statistics, 115–21
government prosecution of Georgiou, 118–19
Hellenic Statistical Authority (ELSTAT), 118–20
International Statistical Institute and Georgiou, 120
National Statistical Service (NSSG), 116
Guéant, Claude, French minister, 163–7

Hacking, Ian, 11, 15, 217
Hancock, Matt, UK minister of health, 216–40
Covid testing targets, 220–2
Hancock reactions to the UKSA, 231–2
Hancock, *Pandemic Diaries*, 238–9
Hancock, views on the UKSA chair, 239–40
Hancock's political fall, 237
Norgrove views on Hancock's manipulation, 237

press coverage of Hancock's claims, 223–4, 229–31, 234–5
press criticism, effect on Hancock, 235–7
statistical correction hidden, 236
Harford, Tim, 6, 22
health statistics, 19–31, 216–40
Huff, Daryl, *How to Lie with Statistics*, 2
Humpherson, Ed, UK Statistics Regulation, 143–4, 208–9, 211–12, 224

International Statistical Congresses, 31–3
national versus international interests, 32
Quetelet, influence of, 31
Randeraad, Nico, history of Congress, 31–3

Johnson, Boris, UK prime minister, 189–215, 219
Brexit, £350 million gains, 203–7
crime on London's transport, 191–7
dishonesty, habitual, 190
Johnson's journalism, 189, 197, 199, 204
populism, 189
reoffending rates, Johnson's claims, 197–200
the UKSA and its chairs, Johnson's arguments with, 191–7, 200–2

Kimmel, Alan, 60

Lagarde, Christine, 146
Lavrov, Sergei, Russian foreign minister, 69
Lawson, Brendan, *Life of a Number*, 6, 204
Le Pen, Marine, French politician, 173–4
Lenin, Vladimir, 136, 226

Macron, Emmanuel, president of France, 172, 186
Malthouse, Kit, UK politician, 197, 209–10
manipulation, definitions, 40–2
manipulation, negative concept, 39, 53–6
Fromm, Erich, example, 53
manipulating people and manipulating information, 54–6
Thomas Carlyle, early use of negative sense, 53
manipulation, positive concept, 49–53
Faraday, Sir Michael, *Chemical Manipulation*, 50–1
manipulating variables positively, 52
therapeutic sense, 50
manipulation, statistical
concept, first use, 51–2
manipulating numbers by manipulating language, 36, 217–19, 221–2, 243–4
preconditions for, 35–8
schematic guide, 92, 97
science and statistical manipulation, 59

stages of manipulation, 95–8, 152
surveys, biased, 43–5
visual misrepresentation of numbers, 45–8
maxim of relevance, 182
metonymic error, 210, 213
MeToo Movement and effect on sexual crime
    rates, 177–8, 181
Mink, Reimund, 6, 116–17, 136
Moy, Will, Full Fact, 143, 212

national agencies for statistics, 92–4
Netherlands
    Statistics Netherlands, 94
Nightingale, Florence, 25–31, 248
    Farr, William, collaboration, 25–7
    political contacts, 27–8
    Quetelet, contact with, 32
    statistical diagrams, 29–30, 47
    statistical manipulation, criticisms of, 48
Norgrove, Sir David, third chair of the UKSA,
    140, 144, 205–6, 210–13, 224–39
Norman, Jesse, UK member of parliament, 202–3

Oxford English Dictionary, 39, 49, 53

Padieu, René, statistics philosopher, 149–53,
    160, 162, 243, 245–6
Pali-Lehohla, statistician-general of South Africa, 91
p-hacking, 57
Popper, Sir Karl, 252
post-truth, 249, 251
poverty figures, 207–9
probability theory, 11
prostitution rates, nineteenth-century London,
    36–7
psychological research, use of deception, 59–61

Quetelet, Adolphe, 12, 17, 31–4, 52, 121, 248

Rayner doctrine, 125–6
Rees-Mogg, Jacob, UK minister, 43–5
regulatory bodies, ethos of, 213–15, 245–8
Reicher, Stephen, 237
reoffending rates, 197–200
Ritchie, Stuart, *Scientific Fictions*, 58
Runciman, David, *Hypocrisy*, 41

Sarkozy, Nicolas, president of France, 146,
    172–3
Scholar, Sir Michael, first chair of the UKSA,
    132, 136–7, 192–5, 197–9
Scotland
    General Register Office of Scotland, 18
    Sinclair, Sir John, *Statistical Account of
        Scotland*, 13–15

Scott, Biljana, 226
self-regulation, 62
Soviet Russia (USSR), 98–104
    Central Statistical Office, 99, 102
    Kraval, Ivan, chief statistician, 99–102
    Merrivale, Catherine, historian, 98, 100
    population decline, 99–102
    Stalin's missing census, 98–104
    Starovsky, Vladimir, chief statistician, 103–4
    Tolts, Mark, statistical analyst, 99, 104
Spicer, Sean, Trump's spokesperson, 76
Spiegelhalter, Sir David, 4, 6, 41, 57, 230
statistics, concept of
    history of concept, 10–38
    numberless statistics, 13–15
    numerical statistics, development of, 15–19
    statistics, pure and applied, 11–13
statistics, public
    coverage in media, 3–4
    imprecise nature of, 6, 242
    metric society, 23
    rhetorical use of numbers, 3–6, 204–5
Sturge, Georgina, *Bad Data*, 6, 204
Sunak, Rishi, UK prime minister,
    215
symbolic numbers, 204–5

Thatcher Margaret, statistical policy, 125
trade unions, statisticians', 164, 184, 251
Trump, Donald J., 45–8, 63–90
    Dominion voting machines, Trump's claims,
        80–1, 87
    election results manipulated, Trump's claims,
        64–6, 77–88
    Georgia inquiry, 2020 election, 81–6
    Georgia, election officials, 85–7, 249
    Giuliani, Rudy, Trump's lawyer, 83–4
    master manipulator, so-called, 46, 63
    Pick, Jacki, lawyer Georgia inquiry,
        82–6
    Raffensberger, Brad, phone-call, 86–8
    self-deception, 67–70
    self-flattery, 68–70
    statistical analysis 2020 election, Eggers et al.,
        78, 80–1
    statistical claims from extreme sources, 65
    unemployment figures, Trump's views on,
        70–7
    untruths, record of, 63
    visual misrepresentation of numbers, 45–8,
        81–6
Trump, Donald J. Junr., 70–7
trust/distrust of politicians, 1, 242
trust/distrust of statisticians, 1, 160
trust/distrust of US elections, 88–90

unemployment rates, 70–7, 211–12
United Kingdom Statistics Authority, *See also*
    chairs of the UKSA – Scholar, Sir Michael;
    Dilnot, Sir Andrew; Norgrove, Sir David;
    Chote, Sir Robert; *see also* Humpherson,
    Ed, UK Statistics Regulation
    Code of Practice, 132–5
    diplomatic language, use of, 142, 226–30,
        233–4, 245
    establishment of the UKSA, 122–32
    fact checkers, relations with, 144
    manipulation, avoidance of word, 48, 137
    mode of operation, reactive, 140
    neutrality, importance of, 124, 137

public letters, function of, 140
    Statistics and Registration Services Act, 130–2
    trust in statistics, UKSA surveys, 138–40
    UK statistics, poor reputation, 127–9
    the UKSA and its past, 123–5
USA, politics and statistics, 63–90, *See* Trump,
    Donald J.
    Bureau of Labor Statistics, 70–7
    census and politics, 33

Walkowitz, Judith, *Prostitution and Victorian
    Society*, 36

zombie numbers, 204

For EU product safety concerns, contact us at Calle de José Abascal, 56–1°, 28003 Madrid, Spain or eugpsr@cambridge.org.